Murder During the Hundred Years' War

Murder During the Hundred Years' War

The Curious Case of Sir William Cantilupe

Melissa Julian-Jones

First published in Great Britain in 2020 by
Pen & Sword History
An imprint of
Pen & Sword Books Ltd
Yorkshire – Philadelphia

Copyright © Melissa Julian-Jones 2020

ISBN 978 1 52675 079 2

The right of Melissa Julian-Jones to be identified as Author of this work has been asserted by her in accordance with the Copyright, Designs and Patents Act 1988.

A CIP catalogue record for this book is available from the British Library.

All rights reserved. No part of this book may be reproduced or transmitted in any form or by any means, electronic or mechanical including photocopying, recording or by any information storage and retrieval system, without permission from the Publisher in writing.

Typeset by Mac Style
Printed and bound in the UK by TJ Books Ltd,
Padstow, Cornwall.

Pen & Sword Books Limited incorporates the imprints of Atlas, Archaeology, Aviation, Discovery, Family History, Fiction, History, Maritime, Military, Military Classics, Politics, Select, Transport, True Crime, Air World, Frontline Publishing, Leo Cooper, Remember When, Seaforth Publishing, The Praetorian Press, Wharncliffe Local History, Wharncliffe Transport, Wharncliffe True Crime and White Owl.

For a complete list of Pen & Sword titles please contact

PEN & SWORD BOOKS LIMITED
47 Church Street, Barnsley, South Yorkshire, S70 2AS, England
E-mail: enquiries@pen-and-sword.co.uk
Website: www.pen-and-sword.co.uk

Or

PEN AND SWORD BOOKS
1950 Lawrence Rd, Havertown, PA 19083, USA
E-mail: Uspen-and-sword@casematepublishers.com
Website: www.penandswordbooks.com

Contents

Who's Who		vii
Chapter 1	The Discovery of a Body	1
Chapter 2	Sir William de Cantilupe the Younger	23
Chapter 3	The Indicted Suspects	63
Chapter 4	Motives for Murder: Material Gain/Loss	112
Chapter 5	Motives for Murder: Affairs of the Heart	121
Chapter 6	Motives for Murder: Communal Revenge or Communal Vengeance?	133
Chapter 7	Justice, Law Enforcement and Cross-County Networks	142
Chapter 8	The Trial's Outcome and Aftermath	161
Appendix		169
Notes		189

AS I was walking all alane	*As I was walking all alone*
I heard twa corbies making a mane:	*I heard two ravens lamenting:*
The tane unto the tither did say,	*The one unto the other did say,*
'Whar sall we gang and dine the day?'	*'Where shall we go and dine today?'*
'—In behint yon auld fail dyke 5	*"In behind the old fail dyke*
I wot there lies a new-slain knight;	*I know there lies a new-slain knight*
And naebody kens that he lies there	*And nobody knows that he lies there*
But his hawk, his hound, and his lady fair.	*But his hawk, his hound, and his lady fair.*
'His hound is to the hunting gane,	*His hound is to the hunting gone*
His hawk to fetch the wild-fowl hame, 10	*His hawk to fetch the wild-fowl home,*
His lady's ta'en anither mate,	*His lady's taken another lover,*
So we may mak our dinner sweet.	*So we may make our dinner sweet.*
'Ye'll sit on his white hause-bane,	*You'll sit on his white breast-bone*
And I'll pike out his bonny blue e'en:	*And I'll peck out his bonny blue eyes*
Wi' ae lock o' his gowden hair 15	*With many a lock of his golden hair*
We'll theek our nest when it grows bare.	*We'll feather our nest when it grows bare*
'Mony a one for him maks mane,	*Many people mourn for him*
But nane sall ken whar he is gane:	*But none shall know where he is gone*
O'er his white banes, when they are bare,	*Over his white bones, when they are bare,*
The wind sall blaw for evermair.' 20	*The wind shall blow for evermore.*

Twa Corbies, (Scottish Version collected in the seventeenth century), Traditional.[1] Arthur Quiller-Couch, ed. 1919. *The Oxford Book of English Verse: 1250–1900*, No. 380.

---

1. For more on the ballad, see: William Montgomerie, 'The Twa Corbies', *The Review of English Studies*, 6:23 (Jul., 1955), 227–232.

Who's Who

Nobility: The Cantilupes

*The immediate family of **Sir William VII de Cantilupe**, or **Sir William the younger**, murdered in 1375*

Sir Nicholas II/the elder	Sir William's grandfather (d. 1355)
Sir William VI/the elder	Sir William's father (cut out of succession by apparent family agreement in favour of his sons; gained the lands and title anyway when they both died without children of their own)
Sir Nicholas III/the younger	William's older brother, died of natural causes (?) but of whom Sir William was accused of murdering (d. 1370/71)
Lady Maud Neville	Sir William's wife (d. by 1386) [Indicted for murder, conspiracy to murder and aiding/abetting the murder: **acquitted on all counts** as no-one testified against her]

Nobility: The Neighbours

Sir Thomas de Kydale	Sheriff of Lincolnshire, second husband of Lady Maud (d. 1381)
Sir Ralph Paynell	Previously a sheriff of Yorkshire, father-in-law of Sir Nicholas the younger [Indicted for aiding and abetting the murder, **acquitted**]
Lady Katherine Paynell (the younger)	Daughter of Sir Ralph and Lady Katherine Paynell (the elder), annulled her marriage to Nicholas the younger

Household Servants Indicted for Murder

[Grouped by Outcome, Listed Alphabetical by Surname]

Robert of Cletham	Household Steward [indicted for aiding and abetting but **acquitted**]

John Barneby of Beckingham	Chamberlain [failed to turn up to court, **outlawed, pardoned by King Richard II in 1387 at the petition of Queen Anne**]
John Taillour of Barneby	*[John Barneby of Beckingham's alias in 1387]*
Robert Cook of Scotton	Boteler (Butler) [convicted of petty treason, **drawn to place of execution and hanged**]
Agatha Frere/*Lovell*	Lady Maud's maid [convicted of aiding and abetting, but **escaped from Lincoln gaol** and **waived** (*waived: female equivalent of outlawed*)]
Robert Gyse	Sir William's armour-bearer [convicted of petty treason, **drawn to place of execution and hanged**]
John Astyn	Servant [failed to turn up to court, **outlawed**]
William/Walter Chamberlainman	Servant, but not the chamberlain [failed to turn up to court, **outlawed**]
Augustine Forester	Servant, possibly the forester [failed to turn up to court, **outlawed**]
John Henxteman	Servant, possibly the stable groom [failed to turn up to court, **outlawed**]
William de Hayle/Hole	Servant [failed to turn up to court, **outlawed**]
Augustine Morpath of Scotton	Servant [failed to turn up to court, **outlawed**]
Henry Tasker	Servant, possibly a piece-worker [failed to turn up to court, **outlawed**]
Augustine Warner	Servant, possibly a [rabbit] warrener as the name suggests, that is, a gamekeeper of rabbit warrens, since the keeping of rabbits required a special licence [failed to turn up to court, **outlawed**]

The Cantilupe Genealogy (Abridged)

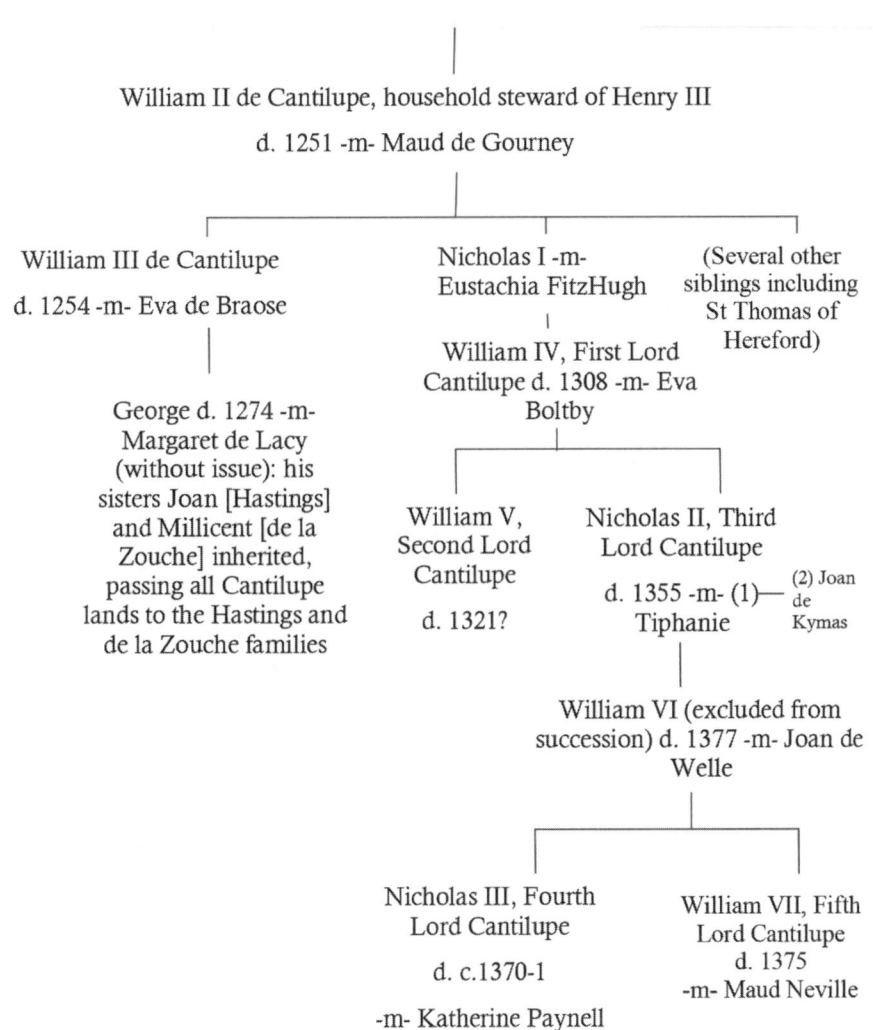

Chapter 1

The Discovery of a Body

'*Murder is unique in that it abolishes the party it injures, so that society has to take the place of the victim and on his behalf demand atonement or grant forgiveness; it is the one crime in which society has a direct interest*'

W. H. Auden

The main focus of this book, the murder of Sir William de Cantilupe in 1375, is an intriguing tale, and the telling of it covers a lot of ground. We know how he was killed, who were accused and who was convicted, but apart from this we know very little. We do not have the witness testimony, any record of private correspondence, or even a suggested motive, since these elements were not recorded in the court rolls. Discovering the reasons for William's murder involves understanding the context of Lincolnshire and Nottinghamshire society, the fissures and feuds in his social network, and digging into fourteenth-century life. Comparing other murder cases is also useful; murder rates were exceptionally high at this time, so there are no shortage of examples.

In exploring Sir William's context, this book necessarily touches upon a variety of issues that some readers may find distressing or difficult, including domestic violence and sexual assault, and, where Sir William's brother Nicholas is concerned, a traumatic experience of having, in this case, atypical genitalia, in the Middle Ages. This latter issue is both pivotal to understand the circumstances of Nicholas's death and Sir William's own arrest for his older brother's murder, but also to understand the reasons why certain nobles were embroiled in the case, such as the family of Nicholas's ex-wife. However, readers should be warned that the ways in which medieval thought equated androgyny and 'hermaphroditism' with monsters and mythical creatures, not to mention the events themselves which caused a crisis within the Cantilupe family, do not make easy reading.

2 *Murder During the Hundred Years' War*

These subjects are necessary to fully understand the circumstances of Sir William's murder, and form the backbone of the debates around why he died, since motive, typically for the time, is not recorded in the trial records. Similarly, investigating other examples of murders, from the killing of husbands by their wives, knights by their squires and armour-bearers, and masters by their servants, needs to be considered if we are to fully explore the myriad possibilities. The jurors convicted two people for the murder, but whether they were truly guilty or not will never be known – they never changed their 'not guilty' plea, but neither did anyone else indicted for the murder. As the story progresses, it is left to the reader to make up their own mind about the most likely scenario and the most likely culprits, and whether the verdict was correct or fair.

While Sir William's life and times will be discussed at length, it seems most fitting to begin where the fourteenth-century investigation itself began: with the coroner, the sheriff, and the discovery of the body.

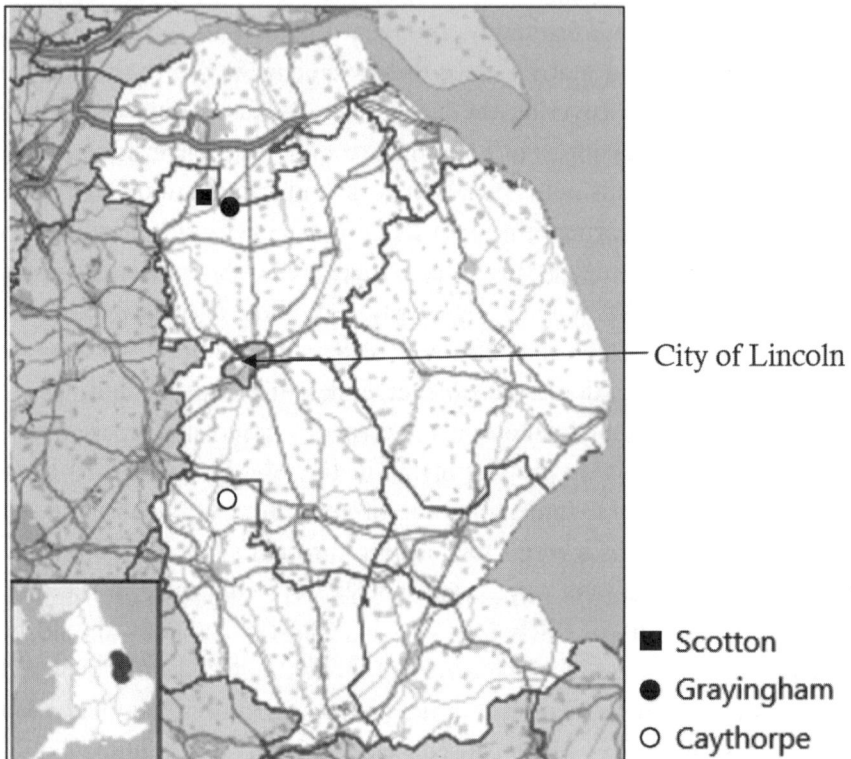

Late May in rural Lincolnshire was at the heart of the agricultural seasons that governed the lives of its inhabitants. A fair few tenants of the local manors were doubtless praying for a good harvest that year, but for the villagers of Grayingham, the fields were about to reveal a rather gruesome surprise.

The body of a man around 30 years of age had been lying undiscovered for several months, presumably in a ditch that prevented it being spotted sooner. He was dressed in riding clothes, a belt around his waist and spurs at his heels. The first finder raised the hue to alert the sheriff and the coroner, who would be responsible for the ensuing investigation.[1] Finding a body was a serious matter. The village was now collectively responsible for it, and could face a steep fine if it could be proved that they had hidden it or covered it up for any reason.

The body should not be moved from its position, no matter how inconvenient it was, until the coroner arrived to begin his inquest. In London or other urban centres, anyone found dead in the street or in the middle of a busy thoroughfare was generally moved into a house and laid out there for the examination to take place, but in more rural areas the bodies were preserved in situ for as long as possible. If the coroner were delayed, the finders had to preserve the scene and corpse as best they could until his arrival. In an age without instant communication, the inquest might begin several days after the discovery. A message had to be sent to wherever the coroner was known or thought to be, which might be in the city of Lincoln some miles away, and if he was away on other business (the role of coroner was, after all, unpaid), then the delay might be longer. In one instance, a Devonshire coroner was forced to delay an inquest by eight days, during which time the locals had to construct a hedge around the body to protect it from the elements as best they could and post guards to prevent any human or animal interference.[2]

In this case, the coroner for the riding of West Lindsey was a man named William de Kirkton or Kirton, of whom personally little is known. He was a wealthy merchant based in London in his late forties or fifties, but was himself a Lincolnshire man whose family were originally from the village of Kirton, as his name suggests. Also involved in the investigation was the sheriff of Lincolnshire, Sir Thomas de Kydale. Younger than William de Kirton, Sir Thomas was a widower in his late thirties or early forties, and the father to a young son of around 10 years of age who was also named Thomas.

William de Kirton viewed the body where it was found and determined that the man had been dead for some months, the remains affected by exposure and animal activity, but on stripping the body and turning it over, carefully looking for wounds and contusions and feeling for broken bones, the cause of death was obvious. Beneath the shirt the coroner discovered 'diverse mortal wounds' caused by a blade. William de Kirton's job was to measure the stab wounds where possible and make notes on their depth, breadth and shape. The quality of the man's clothes, the details of the belt and spurs, all pointed to the fact that this was a member of the knightly class, very likely a member of the local elite community. He was quickly identified as Sir William de Cantilupe the younger, of whom nothing had been seen since at least Easter that year, and that meant two possibilities. Either it was a case of murder by highwaymen or robbers on the road, or they were looking at a far more serious charge, that of petty treason. Murder was bad enough, but petty treason, the slaying of a man either by his wife or by his servant, represented a subversion of the social order.

The coroner's conclusions and the sheriff's investigation led to a major trial in Lincoln at the court of the King's Bench. In all, fifteen people were indicted for the crime, including members of the local elite, and eventually, despite consistent not guilty pleas by every single one of the accused, two individuals were finally convicted and hanged on the (uncorroborated) eyewitness testimony of another chief suspect.

The trial and its background, with the many twists and turns leading up to Sir William's death, have long been of interest to legal scholars and more recently to scholars concerned with medieval marriage and constructions of gender identity. A traditional interpretation of events, filling in the unfortunate gaps in the evidence with some assumption and conjecture, has been presented and accepted largely uncritically by all who have considered the case.

This book is not an attempt to 'uncover the truth'. That is not possible to do with the surviving evidence, which does not include witness testimonies or private, unrecorded conversations, or even a great deal of information about the individuals concerned. Historical detective work of this type can be frustrating, especially when there is so much 'reading between the lines' to do, and it is tempting to construct narratives that fit the surviving evidence. For this reason, context is crucial – in order to consider the most likely scenarios, it is important to know as much about the background as possible, and try to understand human behaviour under various circumstances. Using this case as a window, the world of fourteenth-century England will be explored and a number of possibilities set out for the reader to consider. The 'traditional' interpretation of the case, first proposed by Rosamund Sillem in the 1930s, framed it as a conspiracy masterminded by Lady Maud, Sir William's widow.

Considering various motives for murder and alternative interpretations of the events of 1375, the following chapters will explore who Sir William was, his family context and what it meant to be a man of his social standing, and look at who benefitted from his death. Each motive – money, sex, revenge, jealousy – offers ways to consider the society in which he lived, with examples of comparable crimes. These will be considered in their own chapters, allowing for a much fuller consideration of the evidence than has been applied to the material to date, and a consideration of the trial and its aftermath for the people concerned.

Medieval Murder in Context

Detective stories have captured the imagination for centuries. The questions of who killed another person and why have occupied the thoughts of more than just law enforcement officials, as the 'peculiarly English genre' of the amateur detective can attest.[3] However, this is far from being the preserve of nineteenth- and twentieth-century popular crime fiction. The twelfth-century *Life and Passion of St William the Martyr of Norwich*, completed 1172/73 by Thomas of Monmouth, is one such example, as confidence in St William's sanctity rested on who had killed him and how they had killed him. Thomas of Monmouth set himself up as the amateur detective to piece together the evidence and construct William as a holy martyr, and his case for William's martyrdom is outlined in the first two books of his seven-volume work.[4]

Medieval fascination with this kind of crime did not begin and end with the saints. If the murdered person was a significant individual in terms of socio-economic status, people were just as interested by the circumstances and details of their death as at other times in history, even though murder rates were comparatively high.

The diatribe of Burchard of Worms, an early eleventh-century bishop, encapsulates the common perceptions of the prolific nature of medieval violence:

> Homicides take place almost daily among the family of St. Peter, as if they were wild beasts. The members of the family rage against each other as if they were insane and kill each other for nothing ... In the course of one year thirty-five serfs of St. Peter belonging to the church of Worms have been murdered without provocation.[5]

Yet Burchard's complaint is somewhat disingenuous – when people did kill one another, it usually wasn't 'for nothing'.[6] To borrow a phrase from James Buchanan Given, whose research focused on medieval homicide and inquisition, murder is a social act.[7] The interactions between two or more people resulting in acts of murder can horrify and fascinate, particularly in cases where the killing itself seems, on the surface, senseless or irrational. Yet beneath this are complex layers of psychological and sociological processes, and, like every other form of human behaviour, even murders that appear motiveless are not without social meaning.[8] This was as true at any point in human history as it is today. Violence of the kind condemned by Bishop Burchard was often intrinsically part of family feuds and acts of vengeance for slights (even perceived slights) which could turn bloody and brutal.[9] While the officials of fourteenth-century England might have liked to think they were more sophisticated than their forebears, violence and feuding were impossible to prevent, and additionally, homicidal acts were not only committed in this context, but also out of the usual oldest human motives: love/lust, revenge, jealousy, and material gain.

Whatever the reasons, it is an undisputed fact that interpersonal violence (whether it led to death or not) was a recurring fact of life in the Late Middle Ages at all levels of society. Some studies have estimated that the murder rates in thirteenth-century England were about twice as high as they were in the sixteenth and seventeenth centuries, which were themselves five to ten times higher than the 1980s.[10]

Coroners' rolls for this period reveal regional patterns to violent crime, which help in understanding how 'typical' this murder case of 1375 was, and what the coroner may have expected based on his experience and the experiences of his fellow officials.

Firstly, based on recorded eyewitness testimony and estimated times of death found recorded in the fourteenth- and fifteenth-century coroners' rolls for Northamptonshire and the cities of Oxford and London, a murder victim was most likely to be killed in the evening or at night, and at a time of year when the population were most active.[11] While in Oxford the majority of violent deaths occurred in the academic term, in rural Northamptonshire the number of deaths was greatest between March and August, following the shift of agricultural seasons.[12] This pattern followed the changes in social activities through the year, food shortages and competition for resources and jobs, and the fact that the longer daylight hours meant more social interaction.[13] March–August was also when the majority of deaths by misadventure occurred, especially in the fields.

By contrast, in Oxford, the summer had the lowest rates of violent death due to the absence of the clerks from the university in the summer vacation. In London, an urban centre whose population worked and socialised together all year round, the murder rates showed very little seasonal variation at all.[14]

In rural Lincolnshire, a similar pattern to the Northamptonshire rolls would be expected. A body found in a field in May fits the pattern quite well, and the coroner would, so far, be unsurprised. From experience, he would also be expecting a man to have committed the crime: assuming that the pattern held across the shires, in rural Northamptonshire, 99 per cent of murders or manslaughters were committed by men. In clerk-dominated Oxford the rate was 100 per cent, and even in a more diversely populated urban centre like London, the figure was 93 per cent, and even among the 7 per cent of murders committed by women, there was often a male accomplice.[15]

Given these statistics, a coroner like William de Kirton, faced with evidence of a violent crime, would be forgiven for assuming that he was looking for a man or a group of men. After all, of the other murders and violent crimes committed in Lincolnshire and heard at the Sessions of the Peace from 1373–75, the vast majority had been committed by men.

William de Kirton's examination of the body, as decomposed as it was by then, revealed 'diverse mortal wounds'. Sir William de Cantilupe the younger had been stabbed multiple times, and the coroner was satisfied that these wounds were the cause of death. If it were more likely that Sir William had been murdered by a man or more than one man, then who could have done it and why?

First Impressions: the Highwayman Ruse

The most obvious solution, given that Sir William was dressed in his riding clothes, was that he had been accosted on the road and killed by highwaymen. But how likely was this? Why did Kirton and Thomas de Kydale discount this idea and pursue the young knight's household and his wife if a gang of ruffians was the most obvious conclusion to draw?

First, given the number of stab wounds Kirton had found during his examination, he would have expected the shirt to have corresponding rips and blood stains, but reading between the lines of the later testimony, that was apparently not the case. If the shirt had been ruined by decomposition and animal activity this would have been more difficult to see at first, but Kirton was not fooled. It was apparent that despite the attention to detail – the belt and spurs Sir William was wearing – these were not the clothes he had been killed in. This logically meant that the change of clothes was a ruse intended to throw suspicion on strangers, and therefore away from people Sir William probably knew. As to whom these people might be, their identities came to light when the investigation into the late knight's household began, led by Lincolnshire sheriff Sir Thomas de Kydale.

The ruse may have worked better if Sir William's killers had paid closer attention to detail, as law enforcement officials would have been familiar enough with criminal bands roaming the countryside: they were a real threat to merchants, and bands of men occupied in daylight robbery and extortion rackets operated across the country.

'Highway robbery' has become synonymous with romantic eighteenth-century figures like the English Dick Turpin or the sixteenth-century Welsh 'Robin Hood', Twm Sion Catti, but it was in fact a much older crime that was very common in medieval England. The sheriff may well have suspected such a criminal band, but this did not narrow down his search for the perpetrators even to a section of society. The existence of such a gang would not have ruled out any of the local gentry or even clergy; this was the standard pattern for such bands from the previous century, too, and could have involved people from all levels of society including the royal court.

In 1248, for example, a daring robbery of foreign merchants who were ambushed at Alton, Hampshire, directly involved members of King Henry III's own household. A large gang waylaid the merchants in a forest and got away with thousands of pounds' worth of cash and goods, which they split between them. King Henry was understandably embarrassed, and made a furious, impassioned speech on the subject denouncing the perpetrators, but the householders in question alleged (to the king's further embarrassment) that they had been driven to robbery because of the lateness of their pay.[16] In the fourteenth century, more organised criminal gangs whose activities formed a way of life rather than a one-off event, like the infamous Folvilles and their counterparts, the Coterels, were the landed gentry of their localities. Both gangs moved around frequently and operated in more than one shire, looking for new opportunities to pillage and steal, but also to evade capture.[17]

The first record of the Coterels' criminal activities is dated 2 August 1328, but the story began a little further back. Master Robert Bernard, king's clerk and a teacher at the University of Oxford, had been instituted as vicar of Bakewell church, Derbyshire, in 1327, but on Christmas Day of that same year certain of his parishioners attacked him during the service, stripped him of his Eucharistic vestments and ejected him from the church.[18] This was quite a statement, and not the kind of thing that Master Bertrand, whose extracurricular activities included embezzlement and failure to pay stipulated charitable sums to the poor, took lying down. In 1328 he instigated the Coterel brothers – James, John and Nicholas – along with their (aptly named) associate Roger le Sauvage and their followers – to attack Walter Can, his replacement at Bakewell. The Coterels, le Sauvage and their company 'threw down' Walter Can and stole 10 shillings from the offerings.[19] After this act of vengeance, the Coterels and their associates continued to perpetrate acts of violence for profit, taking full advantage of the political upheaval at the start of Edward III's reign. Master Bertrand continued to collaborate closely with James Coterel, and was, for reasons of corruption, intimidation or simple bad judgement, supported by the Cathedral Chapter of Lichfield even when this, and other crimes, became known.[20]

Contemporaries of the Coterels, the Folvilles had also operated a little earlier, during the reign of Edward II, and during this time were engaged in a feud with King Edward's favourite, Hugh Despenser. They were outlawed in Leicestershire after murdering one of Despenser's associates, but after his execution and King Edward III's accession in 1327, they were pardoned and returned to act with impunity under the protection of Roger Mortimer, Earl of the March and a sworn enemy of the Despensers.[21] Like the Coterels, the Folvilles also pillaged and stole their way around the counties in which they operated, holding large illegal assemblies of their followers and engaging in various nefarious deeds. The two gangs collaborated on several occasions, most memorably in the kidnapping of the royal justice, Richard Willoughby, sent to Derbyshire to bring the Coterels to justice. After this outrage, with the gang extorting a huge sum from Willoughby in return for his freedom, the young Edward III clamped down on these gentry gangs and 'robber barons', but when war broke out with Scotland the Coterels all received royal pardons in return for their military service.

It is worth remembering that at the time Edward III was still a teenager and needed all the support he could get: he came to the throne aged 14, with his mother Isabella and her lover, Roger Mortimer, as de facto ruler of England until he came of age. In 1330, 17-year-old Edward mounted a successful coup, executed Mortimer, exiled his mother and began his personal rule. War with Scotland gave him the opportunity to prove himself further, but also required the cooperation of his unruly knightly subjects, as did his aggressive foreign policies. Ten years later he declared himself the rightful king of France, intensifying territorial disputes on the continent and beginning the Hundred Years' War. It is against this backdrop that our murder victim Sir William de Cantilupe grew up, of which more will be said later.

As Edward III's reign progressed and legislature was tightened in some areas while more military demands were made of the gentry in light of Edward's expansionist aspirations, it became more difficult for gangs like this to operate even with the protection of greater magnates who benefitted from their crimes, as Edward III wielded power more firmly than his father. A lucrative business, the targets of such gangs were predominantly merchants and members of the elite, from whom both money and goods could be taken. Since the king also needed the goodwill of the mercantile classes for the purposes of loans and taxation, several attempts were made later in his reign, particularly through 1346–50, to classify highway robbery as a form of treason and impose the penalties for that crime.[22] The balancing act of keeping the nobility loyal but in check and the merchants happy was a difficult one, and should also be borne in mind in the context of this particular murder case, especially regarding the members of the nobility who were brought to trial in connection with the killing.

If William de Kirton and Sir Thomas de Kydale had been taken in and decided that they were looking for highway robbers in the Cantilupe case, they could well be looking at a much wider network than a local gang of ruffians prowling the Lincolnshire countryside. All of these earlier examples had cross-county connections, involved political factions within the royal court, and revealed corruption within certain parts of the church. If Kirton's inquest decided that Sir William had been murdered by such a group, then they might be looking at anyone in the locality or further afield. If the perpetrators were protected by other members of the elite or even by elements within the church, it would be harder to bring them to justice. It was already likely that they were looking at what has been brilliantly termed by Barbara Hanawalt as a 'fur collar' crime.[23]

There were a few bands of ruffians in West Lindsey, several of whom appeared in the local courts repeatedly on charges such as theft and assault. However, these groups were not as organised as the Coterels and Folvilles, revolving instead around one or two individuals and focusing their actions on other individuals or families in ongoing feuds. In two instances, these feuds ended in murder, but in both cases the killer was well-known to the victim. These two other killings stand out as contemporary comparisons to the Cantilupe case: firstly, the murder of Robert Gascal and his servant John, and secondly the murder of an especially wayward monk of Humberstone called Robert Neweland or Neuland.

Robert Gascal was a clerk of Wold Newton, and he had made many enemies over the years due to his own criminal activity. In 1373 and

1374 he was indicted before the Lindsey justices for seizing and robbing the chaplain of Ulceby one night in 1369; stealing a cow from a certain Nicholas Twyte in 1371, and breaking the close of the prior of Sixhills and cutting down and carrying away the said prior's trees in 1374.[24]

Gascal eventually got his comeuppance: in 1374, the year before Sir William's murder, a special commission was issued to hear his complaints that his own close had been broken, his goods taken, and a band of armed men, led by the parson of West Keal, had assaulted and threatened him.[25] In May 1375, around the time Sir William's body was discovered, an inquisition was held to investigate Gascal's petition 'that many evil-doers lay in wait for him at [Wold Newton], chased him to the church there and besieged him therein and afterwards took and imprisoned him.'[26] The complaints did him no good: on 21 June 1375, he and his servant John (known as both John de Thorgamby and elsewhere as John Shepherd, the former indicating the place he was from and the latter either his or his family's profession), met a violent end at the hands of six of their neighbours, namely Richard Spenser and Alice his wife, William and Thomas Wariner, Thomas Pynder, and William Gentil. The Spensers were eventually acquitted in 1377, although some juries claimed they were the primary perpetrators, but the others failed to appear at their court dates (as in the Cantilupe case with the majority of the indicted servants) and were outlawed.[27]

It may seem incongruous to find juries making claims about defendants in this manner, but it was not the role of medieval jurors to be impartial and have no prior knowledge of a case. Quite the opposite. A jury was instead made up of twelve knights of the shire (or, if not enough knights could be found to make up the twelve, freemen could also serve, but their inclusions were sometimes challenged by one or other of the parties). These men often knew the plaintiffs and defendants at least moderately well, had a lot of contextual knowledge of the crime and the individuals concerned, and could bring their own evidence into the deliberations. If, for example, it was a case where there was little to no material evidence to support a claim or accusation, then the jurors would rely on their own knowledge of the individuals, character witnesses, and hearsay or common gossip that corroborated or undermined the claims brought before the court.

In this local example, the murders of Gascal and his servant took place after several years of violent crime, theft and trespass on both sides, and seemed to have revenge or robbery as a motive. Was the same true for Sir William? Could there be hidden factors in his death – feuds with other gentry, for example, who might have procured a band of men to waylay him on the road and kill him? Or did the multiple wounds indicate that the 'robbers on the road' were people he knew?

The traditional interpretation of the evidence put forward by scholars since the 1930s frames the Cantilupe and Paynell feud of 1367–69 (of which much more will be said in the next chapter) and the remarriage of Lady Maud to the sheriff, Sir Thomas de Kydale, as highly suspicious and therefore obvious motivations for the murder.

However, the other case mentioned as a comparative – that of Robert Neuland, a monk of Humberstone Abbey – stands as a warning against making such assumptions. Humberstone Abbey was a Benedictine house that could only support around twelve monks at a time, and by the time of the Reformation only had four. In the mid-fourteenth century it was visited several times by bishops of Lincoln and more than once was found to be in an unsatisfactory condition. In 1358, a new commission was issued to correct the house on account of the 'crimes, excesses and other insolences' committed there on a daily basis.[28]

Robert Neuland was indicted at different sessions of the peace in Lindsey in 1374 and 1375 for numerous offences, including a series of violent attacks on John Harmer, a resident of the village of Humberston, John's wife Matilda and John's father Henry Harmer, in 1371, 1373 and 1374. This seems to have been part of an ongoing feud between Neuland and Harmer, during which Harmer, on one occasion, fled from an enraged Neuland and Neuland's unnamed associates, escaping them by hiding in a ditch up to his shoulders in ditch-water, 'in fear for his life'.[29] On another occasion, he was assaulted in the cemetery of Humberstone 'even to the shedding of blood … whereby the said cemetery is still polluted'.[30]

Presumably in retaliation for these incidents, Harmer was indicted for conspiring with Robert and William de Thirnsco 'to destroy Robert Neuland' in 1373, by accusing him of assaulting Matilda Harmer, John's wife (it seems this was physical rather than sexual assault). On this count,

14 Murder During the Hundred Years' War

Harmer was arrested and imprisoned for conspiracy to murder and bringing false testimony until the keepers of the peace acquitted him at Kirton Lindsey, on 26 January 1374.[31]

The following year, Robert Neuland was indicted for the theft of sheep from Wellow Abbey in 1375 and for waylaying, assaulting and wounding Robert Accwra, a 'fellow monk' of Humberstone, also in 1375.[32] Neuland, together with a man named William West, who may or may not have been a monk as well, assaulted Accwra 'with swords and sticks', so that he lay that night 'in danger of death'.[33] The chief constables of Bradley and constables of Humberstone went to seven men of Humberstone and charged them to help bring Neuland and West in should Accwra die. The seven men 'thoroughly refused' (*penitus recusarunt*) to go with the said constables or lend them support, 'in contempt of the king'.[34] Accwra apparently survived, as no more is said about this case in these records.

Given the track record of Neuland so far, if one were to make an educated guess as to the identity of his killer, it would surely be the Harmers, or perhaps a recovered and vengeful Robert Accwra, or a friend or kinsman of either the above. In fact, Neuland's end was far less narratively satisfying, a reminder that real life is less sensational and less well-plotted than a detective novel. Ironically, it was neither the wronged monk nor the Harmers who finally ended Neuland's career of crime, but William West, who went from being Neuland's accomplice to being his killer. In a somewhat prosaic and anticlimactic end to Neuland's colourful life, apparently motivated by greed, West killed him and robbed him of 40 shillings and a 'pouche' and dagger, on 1 August 1378.[35]

This twist in the tale should stand as a warning against making assumptions based on the 'most likely' scenarios. We are also not privy to all the context, but only to those incidents brought before the court and then only in brief slivers of information, filtered through the scribes themselves and what they thought was pertinent to record and in what manner.

Bearing this in mind as the Cantilupe case unfolds, the next section will look at what the coroner's inquest decided, an appraisal of the real scene of the crime, and provide an overview of scholarly opinion on the case, which has been largely consistent since the 1930s. In the following chapters the traditional interpretation of the evidence will be considered alongside alternative views, taking into account a fuller context of Sir William's life and times, the suspects themselves as far as we can reconstruct information about them, and various possible motives for the murder.

Looking Closer to Home

After discounting the highwaymen theory, the sheriff looked closer to home to establish what had happened to the young noble. Sir William's primary seat was at Greasley, Nottinghamshire, but over the period of Lent and Holy Week he and his wife had been staying at Lady Maud's manor of Scotton, a few miles away from Grayingham where the body had been discovered.

Scotton manor had been closed up and the household dispersed, but Lady Maud had not returned to Greasley castle. Sir William held multiple manors across Nottinghamshire, Lincolnshire and Buckinghamshire, but after making inquiries as to her whereabouts, Kirton and Kydale discovered his wife in Caythorpe, a manor belonging to Sir Ralph Paynell, some 40 miles from Scotton.

Sir Ralph Paynell was a well-known lord and no stranger to exercising cross-county power, who had himself served a term as sheriff of Yorkshire. He was married to Katherine, and they had a daughter, also called Katherine after her mother. The younger Katherine had at one time been Maud's sister-in-law (the wife of Sir William's late brother, Sir Nicholas), but was now married to John Auncell. Maud had apparently kept up good relations with the Paynells, as it was discovered that she had been living with Sir Ralph since Sir William's disappearance, and with her was her chambermaid Agatha Frere and Sir William's squire, Richard Gyse.

Witnesses claimed that one night, Maud had closed up Scotton manor and left with these two companions, making the 40-mile ride across Lincolnshire to Caythorpe without explanation.

Kydale placed Lady Maud, Agatha Frere and Richard Gyse under arrest for murder and arrested Sir Ralph Paynell as an accessory for sheltering suspected murderers after the fact.

This gave rise to another issue: if Sir William had not been killed on the road but had, in fact, been killed elsewhere – at the manor itself, for example, which was starting to look more likely – then because of the layout of the manor house and the number of servants living there, it was impossible (or highly improbable at best) that such a murder could have taken place without everyone in the manor knowing about it. Warrants for the arrest of the whole household were issued, and the entire group of servants were named and indicted for the murder of their master. The first three to be appealed were Augustine de Morpath, [Augustine] Warner and Richard Gyse 'of Scotton'.[36] Augustine de Morpath was named multiple times as the primary suspect, but it is notable that Lady Maud never named him nor Augustine Warner in her testimony, and instead threw the blame onto Richard Gyse and the butler, Robert Cook.

Scotton Manor: the Real Scene of the Crime

The arrests provided some fruitful evidence. It turned out that Sir William had indeed been murdered at Scotton manor, as Lady Maud seems to have confessed privately to Sir Thomas de Kydale, and that the deed had been committed in the bedchamber itself, while Sir William lay in bed. This would account for the apparent change of clothes, but her testimony raised further problems: due to the size and layout of the manor house, and the way the murder had been covered up after the fact, there was no way for the murder to have been committed in the bedchamber without the whole household knowing it was happening.

The jurors listed a core of seven servants whom they suspected of committing the deed, adding other names to the list in some cases. All the servants including the steward, the squire and the chambermaid – the only other woman in the house apart from Lady Maud – were indicted, but all pleaded not guilty. Initially, the servant who appears first in the list of names is a man named Augustine Morpath, and since the lists are not alphabetical this might be because he held a prominent position in the household or because it was felt he was the ringleader of the plot. His position in the household is not stated, but it was likely one that afforded him the means (i.e., gave him access to knives), so perhaps he was the cook or the pantler (the keeper of the pantry).

To understand the predicament of the sheriff and the judiciary, faced with a conspiracy and wall of silence, we need to look more closely at the manor house itself and how it was organised.

Firstly, it should be noted that the present manor house in Scotton is situated on the southern edge of the village and is known as the Old Manor House, dating from the sixteenth century with nineteenth- and twentieth-century remodelling and extensions. Despite levelling and landscaping, traces of a moat remain, and some medieval pottery was discovered in adjacent plough-soil.[37] While contemporary with our murder case, this is a second manor, built on an ancient manorial site mentioned in Domesday, but *not* the manor house with which we are concerned, of which sadly nothing physical remains.

A map of 1682 marked the main site at Scotton near the parish church, referred to as the 'The Manor House' with a 'Hall Close' and 'Malthouse', which served the needs of the village's brewers. By the time of the Tithe Award Map of 1839 it had fallen into disuse and was known simply as the 'Hall Close'.[38] This manor was subinfeudated[39] to the Nevilles by Peterborough Abbey, and it stood on the south side of the church, in which several Nevilles are entombed. Maud's father gave the manor to her upon her marriage, but it did not belong to her husband as a result – the terms of the agreement with Peterborough Abbey were with her family, not his, and so if she died before her husband, it would revert back to the Nevilles of Scotton, or their next heirs, rather than automatically pass to Sir William de Cantilupe.

This site, nearer the church, was at the heart of the village. Scotton Manor had to be large enough to house all the listed servants in the indictment, plus the lord and lady, and somewhere for noble guests to stay, so while a modest size in comparison to larger manorial houses it could accommodate a good number of people in the hall, and some servants would sleep in the manor itself while others lived out, either in the village of Scotton or slightly further afield, as in the case of the steward, Robert de Cletham. It also had a stable block and a spring or well in the courtyard to draw water, which proved significant for the murder plot.

A medieval manor house was generally based on the Saxon hall, a simple rectangular building with various functions. It became more elaborate through the centuries, until by the fourteenth, the country house began to reflect a growing desire for private spaces and different needs. By 1375, a typical English manor house was functional and not excessively large. If fortified, it would have a small gatehouse or large porch that led into the courtyard, while the house itself comprised of two levels within the outer walls. Like a small castle, it would have had kitchens connected to a food store, a buttery and pantry, and the main hall where most of the daily business was conducted, the meals served, and the family and guests entertained. The separation of the buttery, where the butts of wine were stored, from the pantry, wherein was kept all the items for setting the table, including cutlery and knives, reflected the growing importance of the Eucharist and the sacred duality of bread and wine that permeated secular thinking.[40] The pantler and butler were separate jobs and in theory had separate access rights within the domestic domain. This may account for Robert Cook the boteler (butler) being further down the list of indicted suspects and might mean that Augustine Morpeth was listed first because he held a position in the household such as cook or pantler with access to the knives.

On the second floor was usually a guest room or a withdrawing room that afforded the family some privacy, and a bedchamber that was the private sleeping quarters of the lord and lady. The bedchamber was typically the smaller of the two rooms on the upper floor with access to the garderobe.[41] These rooms often had separate entrances, meaning the bedchamber door was the only way in or out.

It is notable that Lady Maud, initially accused of murder, then of planning and orchestrating the murder, then finally just of aiding and abetting the crime, was present in the bedchamber at the time of the deadly assault.[42] Maud was at the very least an eye-witness to the crime, which was why her testimony was vital in a case where no-one pleaded guilty. The finger-pointing and indictments of all the other servants in the manor indicates the complexity of the case, and that if this was a household conspiracy then the plan couldn't have been carried out without the involvement and knowledge of everyone else, even if they had private reservations about the deed.

The densely populated structure of the medieval village, with thin walls and a communal expectation to know one another's intimate business, meant that neighbours and friends were often called upon as 'witnesses' of sexual and other misdemeanours even if they only heard things through the walls.[43] If people knew such intimate details about each other's lives in this context, how much more so would the servants who lived in the manor know about what went on in every room?

It was becoming apparent that Sir William's murder was more complicated that it had first appeared, and that he had been killed with the full knowledge and complicity of his entire household, which included his own wife. The question of 'why' was not considered important enough to record, since it was the 'who' that posed the bigger question. The charge was no longer murder but petty treason, and if Lady Maud or Agatha the chambermaid were convicted then they would be burned, while the male servants would be drawn to the place of their execution and hanged.

For decades the trial has intrigued historians working on medieval law. Statutes of the realm, beginning with Edward III's statute of 1352, constructed the murder of a husband by his wife, a (male) master by his servant, or a prelate by a lay or religious person, as an act against the hierarchical and patriarchal social order, and therefore of treason. An assault on such figures was then considered analogous to an attack on the sovereign and their government.[44] It is worth noting again here that the concept of 'high' treason, that is, an act of treason against one's sovereign or country, evolved from the more local or domestic concept of treason against one's lord, not the other way around.[45] Given how heinous a crime this was, it is rare to find cases of petty treason in fourteenth-century sessions of the peace, especially ones this clearly delineated under the statute.[46] The Lindsey peace roll records only the bare facts about the case: the gruesome and gory details were supplied by the juries who made their presentments at the *Coram Rege* – the court of the King's Bench: these are supplied in the appendix.[47]

With such gaps in the records, it is not possible to have as full a picture of this event as modern historians have the luxury of with their source material. This is partly what makes the case so tantalising, but also so frustrating to piece together. Nevertheless, scholars have drawn their own conclusions from the evidence and most seem to agree on a 'traditional' interpretation of the facts, set forward by Rosamund Sillem in the 1930s. The reasons why the case is so interesting, and the reasoning behind the traditional interpretation of the evidence, will now be discussed.

Scholarly Opinion

Since the 1930s, the gentry in the case have been centred in the interpretations of the trial over the servants, who were the convicted perpetrators. Scholars have chosen to assume that these were the pawns and patsies in a tale of intrigue, where Lady Maud was the mastermind and other nobles played supporting roles in full knowledge of her crime. Her motive was simple: by 1379 she had married the sheriff, Sir Thomas de Kydale, and that was enough to convince Sillem that this was a crime of passion, perpetrated to remove an unwanted husband to make room for the lover.

In his 1939 review of Rosamund Sillem's work on the Peace Rolls, H.M. Cam remarks on this 'melodramatic' incident as a worthy feature of her study, remarking, '[t]he modern amateur of detection would have no hesitation in recognizing where motive and opportunity lay, and one would doubt whether a modern jury would have acquitted Maud de Cantilupe'.[48]

The 1920s and 30s are considered the Golden Age of detective fiction, but despite the similarities that can be drawn between historians and the great literary detectives, historians are not permitted their fictional counterparts' degree of certainty surrounding the conclusions of a case.[49] Historians are often caught by the sense of seeing the dead 'through the dust of a document', as Shannon McSheffrey eloquently put it, but this vision is, all too often, 'a mirage'.[50] There are gaps in the surviving evidence, testimonies and conversations that went entirely unrecorded, gossip that we cannot be privy to, archival red herrings and simple human error in secondary transcriptions and translations, sometimes based on scribal errors in the original documents themselves. A modern jury would at least have heard the witness testimonies, which, although heard in the Cantilupe trial, were not recorded. All that was required for the purposes of record-keeping were the basic details of the crime, the names of those involved and whether or not the defendants turned up to their court dates, the charge itself, and the outcome. The rest is lost to history and remains conjecture. Nevertheless, the version that Sillem offers as an interpretation is a good one and should be given full consideration. It has been accepted largely uncritically by almost everyone else who has come after her as the most obvious and satisfying of conclusions and will therefore be known as 'the traditional' view or interpretation.

The traditional view, first posited by Sillem and expanded upon later, centres Sir William as the cuckolded victim. His positioning as a tragic figure is implied by the sensationalised and sexualised focus on Lady Maud and Sir Thomas de Kydale, and the more recent discovery of a bitter grudge borne by Sir Ralph Paynell against Sir William's late brother, Sir Nicholas, to whom Sir Ralph's daughter, the younger Lady Katherine Paynell, was married for a short time.

It is largely accepted that Maud wanted William out of the way so that she and the already-widowed sheriff would be free to marry, which they had done by 1379. This reading of the evidence paints a picture worthy of *The Canterbury Tales* or the bawdier *Decameron*. In this version of events, Maud either seduced or bribed the young Richard Gyse and persuaded him to murder her husband, roping in a number of other servants into the plot with further bribes and/or coercive threats. Carole Rawcliffe took this uncritically in her brief biography-sketch of Maud's third husband, John Bussey, stating that the 'notorious' Maud Neville committed the murder with her 'young lover', presumably meaning Richard Gyse.[51] In Simon Payling's study of murders among the fifteenth-century gentry, the case is referred to in brief as an example from the previous century, where again Sillem's suggestion that Maud escaped sentencing due to the corrupt influence of the sheriff is cited uncritically.[52]

The wicked sheriff stereotype is easy to accept, particularly as those knights who held the office of sheriff tended to play to type. Local gentry and aristocratic communities were largely self-regulating, and as the Crown was dependent upon them for law enforcement, a degree of criminality and corruption amongst them was tolerated.[53] In terms of corruption among the gentry communities as a whole from which the sheriff was elected, Simon Payling has argued that the Crown's failure to punish the landed classes for violent crimes resulted in a culture where such violence was both legitimised and normalised.[54]

Of all the possible interpretations of the evidence – many of which will be thoroughly explored in the following chapters on motives – why did Sillem choose this one?

The obvious reason presents itself as soon as we consider the historiographical trends of the 1930s: most of the early work on peasants was a top-down view, looking at peasant life through the lens of lordship and medieval law.[55] It was natural to centre the elite when they were a main focus of historians at the time, and female sexuality was at the forefront of contemporary debates in the interwar period.[56] Maud's sexuality and its apparent expressions in her two successive marriages was therefore of great interest in the case, and neither Sillem nor her successors have had much trouble believing the worst of Maud's morals and character. After all, the stereotypes of Lady Macbeth/sexualised villainess and her counterpart, the scheming/lascivious sheriff, have permeated popular culture as points of reference, due largely to the ongoing popular fascination with the Robin Hood myths and Shakespeare's perennially popular Scottish play, and even if they have basis in fact, their existence creates an invisible bias that encourages acceptance of this interpretation over others that also fit the same facts. Love triangles, betrayal and a background of family drama are all elements that add to the emotional impact of this version for even a modern historian. Sir Thomas de Kydale could, of course, pack the jury with Neville and Paynell supporters and bribe or coerce them to make things go their way. With Ralph Paynell's support and the fact that seven other knights were willing to mainprise [bail] her, closing ranks around one of their own, Maud was protected from the worst punishments possible for the crime, and found not guilty.

With all the elements of a Christie novel and the themes of eroticism and high-level corruption worthy of a gothic horror potboiler, it is, in short, a *good* story.

Now that the interpretation has been set out and contextualised, it is time to turn to the victim himself and the gentry involved in his death. Who were they? What did their careers look like? What scraps of information can be found in the surviving records that can give us a picture of who they were, and illuminate the world in which they lived?

Chapter 2

Sir William de Cantilupe the Younger

'Man is an animal, suspended in webs of significance he himself has spun'
Clifford Geertz

Whether we assume William was the innocent victim of his wife's machinations or not, we should look into his family history and career to understand him and his family context. A shadowy figure, he left nothing behind for us to understand him. The best we can do is to consider the personalities of his family as revealed to us in patches through the lens of documents that had particular agendas, get a feel for family traits and the ways the older generations raised the younger ones and with what levels of success. By the time we reach Sir William (who will be called Sir William the younger or Sir William VII to differentiate him from his father, Sir William the elder, and the other five Williams in his family line), we may have a picture of the family context that can assist in forming rough estimates of his natural and/or nurtured traits.

William Cantilupe and his older brother Nicholas each received a share of their grandfather's estate, despite them being underage at the time of his death and the fact that their father (Sir William the elder) was still very much alive. Their father was excluded from the succession of the lordship in favour of the two young boys, presumably to make them more attractive marriage prospects since William the elder was already married and had lands and manors of his own, but it is worth exploring who their grandfather Nicholas (d. 1355) was, to understand the status of the Cantilupes within the county.

The Cantilupes: An Abridged Family History

The Cantilupes had risen to power largely by accident. Walter Cantilupe, the twelfth-century patriarch of this particular line, was a man of the earl of Lincoln, William de Roumare.[1] We know next to nothing about him as a person, but copies of his seal still exist, visual evidence of how he chose to present himself. These are not seals that seal a document closed and are broken when the document is read, but the equivalent of medieval 'signatures' or authentication stamps, affixed to documents at the bottom via tags of parchment. The metal alloy seal matrix, which makes the impression in the wax, was itself sometimes given to emissaries or messengers as proof the document came from the person the messenger claimed had sent it.[2]

Walter's personal seal is not sophisticated like the earl's; no equestrian symbols were used, since he was not of the same level of society as the exalted mounted knights he served. Instead, his large seal bore the more visceral image of a wolf biting the neck of a sheep.[3] Since this was his chosen image to communicate his identity to readers of his letters and legal documents, we should wonder whether this was a persona he projected, or whether it reflected a true portion of his personality in some way. The family's locative surname came from a Norman town in La Manche, Chantiloup, roughly translated as 'singing wolves', so this was also a reference to his Norman origins and identity.

As Walter's sons rose in prominence through their administration skills rather than their military prowess, this early iconography was dropped in favour of variants on the simpler, far less original (but more presentable in royal courtly circles) fleur-des-lys design which also made its way onto the Cantilupe coats of arms.[4] Walter's son William (whom we shall call William I, possibly named after the earl, but more likely after Walter's brother or father), ended up in the household of John Lackland, the runt of the Angevin litter, who eventually – and unforeseeably, at the time – became king of England after the deaths of all his older brothers including Richard I, who died without issue.

William I, John's household steward during his less influential years, found himself the royal steward when John took the throne in 1199. He was handsomely rewarded with lands and official judicial positions. William I rode out the baronial discontent which engendered Magna Carta, outlived his king and supported John's son, the young King Henry III, who was only 9 years old when he came to the throne.

As the royal steward, William I exerted a great deal of influence over the young king and remained in this exalted office throughout his life, being granted and gifted many lands in the Midlands where he made Aston Cantlow in Warwickshire his *caput* or chief seat, and making an excellent marriage to Maud or Mazilia de Bracy, which brought him further lands in Kent. He died in 1239, and was succeeded in his role of royal household steward by his son, William II, who died in 1251.[5] William II continued to expand and consolidate the Cantilupe manors and reputation. By the time of his death, the family had landed possessions in almost every county of England, and he had secured the wardship and marriage rights to Eva de Braose, whom he married off to his own son William III.[6]

Through Eva, whose mother was a Marshal co-heiress, the Cantilupes inherited a part-share of the earldom of Pembroke, lands in Wales, and lands in Ireland.[7] However, their legacy was to be cut short. William III, the oldest of several children, contracted some kind of fever and had to leave the king's service in France where he was serving on campaign. He died in his Wiltshire manor of Calne, a gift from King Henry, in 1254.[8] His brother Nicholas (whom we shall call Nicholas I) also died around the same time, both brothers leaving widows and under-age sons. William III's wife Eva died when their son George was only 3, and is entombed in Abergavenny Priory. George was betrothed and quickly married to Margaret de Lacy of the Herefordshire branch of the de Lacys, great magnates of the realm, whose kin were earls of Lincoln.[9] George died aged 21 of unrecorded causes, with no children. His two married sisters, Joan Hastings and Millicent de la Zouche, inherited everything between them, passing the lands in Wales and Ireland to the Hastings family (including the earldom of Pembroke) with the rest going to the la Zouches.[10] The rest of the family were left with the manors given to them by association with their greater relatives and through advantageous marriages.

With the deaths of William III and the next oldest Cantilupe brother, Nicholas I, Bishop Thomas of Hereford became the head of the family. He saw to it that his widowed sister-in-law Eustachia FitzHugh was provided for fairly when, after his brother Nicholas's death, Eustachia was left without any horses under the terms of the will. The impact it had on Eustachia was enough to prompt her brother-in-law Bishop Thomas de Cantilupe to give her horses from his own stables at Hereford to use until she was able to buy her own.[11] He also took Nicholas's son William IV to the king's court himself, introducing him to the right people.

William IV (Sir William the younger's great-grandfather) was left to make the best he could from his father's own lands and make a good marriage that would rebuild his family's fortunes and influence. This was achieved through the patronage of his uncle Bishop Thomas, who was liked and respected by both Henry III and his son prince Edward, who became King Edward I.[12]

Bishop Thomas seemed genuinely fond of his nephew, who accompanied him to the second Council of Lyons in 1274.[13] Prior to William IV's education in Paris, Thomas had apparently also schooled him at his own expense at Oxford, where Thomas had been the chancellor of the university.[14] Yet Thomas's virtues of prudence and chastity apparently did not rub off on the young man as well as the bishop might have hoped. During his last journey to Rome it was asked why his nephew was not accompanying him on this occasion, and Thomas evasively replied that this was because young men were more immodest and less bashful than in his day, when he would have pulled his hat over his eyes to avoid the gaze of a handsome woman – the implication being that William would not![15] Nevertheless, moral conduct aside, Bishop Thomas continued to support his nephew's education and left provision for him in his will in the form of 30 marks.[16]

William IV had two sons with his wife Eva Boltby, naming the oldest after himself (whom we will call William V) and the youngest after his father (whom we will call Nicholas II). William V mysteriously enfeoffed[17] his younger brother of his lordship and then disappears from the records in 1321, and so the lands and title passed to Nicholas II, confusingly titled the third lord Cantilupe.[18] It could be that William V had a long-term illness which prevented him from carrying out his duties as lord, as he seems to have died not long after the enfeoffment.

It is this Nicholas, the grandfather of the murdered William VII, to whom the family owed its improved status in the fourteenth century following the loss of young George and the vast bulk of the family lands with him. Understanding the background of Nicholas II gives us a clearer picture of the pressure placed on the youngest members of his family, and goes some way to explain his own drive and ambition.

Nicholas II married twice, once to Tiphanie, about whom little is known, with whom he had a son William VI, and after her death to Joan Kymas, herself a widow, with whom he had no children.

Nicholas was a retainer of the Black Prince (Prince Edward, heir to the throne and so-called because of the armour he wore), with an illustrious reputation. He no doubt hoped his family would be incorporated into the royal household once the Black Prince took the throne, but this was not to be: King Edward III was a long-lived monarch, dying in 1377, and Prince Edward died the year before his father, in 1376. Neither of Nicholas II's grandsons lived to see either royal funeral.

Nicholas II was not only a military leader but also a pious man, founding Beauvale Priory in Nottinghamshire near his primary seat at Greasley, and a chapel in Lincoln Cathedral itself, where he was entombed.[19] The year before his brother died, Bishop Thomas, his great-uncle, was canonised to become St Thomas of Hereford, his shrine the site of several miracles.[20] Nicholas made sure to visually connect his own tomb to his now saintly kinsman. He wanted it to reflect his family's status, and connect them in public thought with not only St Thomas of Hereford but also the great magnates that their family counted as relations and allies. How he chose to present himself after death gives us an insight into his priorities, and the socio-political trajectory he intended his grandchildren to pursue.

The Cantilupe shields – now very worn – decorate the south side of Nicholas's tomb chest, facing the Cantilupe chapel, while the side facing the centre aisle of the choir remains plain.[21] Contrary to modern popular understandings of 'family crests', in this period the design was chosen by the individual and was meant to represent them personally rather than their family as a whole, while the iconography chosen would very often be used by multiple members of the same family to create visual connections with their kin. This meant that while several elements and colours remained the same, and some knights might adopt the arms of their grandparents without further embellishment, most of the time individual knights would put their own twist on the design by adding or subtracting something. Earlier on, knights of lower status did not have their own shields but bore those of the greater lords they served – the great William Marshal, for example, at the start of his career, bore the arms of his Tankerville lord.[22] By the fourteenth century, any knight could have a coat of arms of their own, and it was so common that they retrospectively invented coats of arms to decorate the tombs of their long-dead kinsmen who had never borne any in life, but this new norm had not been achieved without criticism from various quarters who wished to uphold the hierarchy within the elite stratum of society.

Nicholas II de Cantilupe, although not an earl or holding a high royal office like his forebears, had served his king well, and his status and respect in the county and beyond certainly put him as a 'great man' of the Midlands, a knight of whom great things were expected, and great deeds should be remembered. The choice of Lincoln Cathedral as the location for his chantry and monument served as a physical, visual reminder to the locality, pilgrims and visitors to the cathedral, and the Cathedral Chapter, that Nicholas de Cantilupe was possessed of power and affluence, that his thirteenth-century kinsmen had been royal stewards, and that his recent ancestors had cultivated close personal relationships with both kings and greater magnates. It was a reminder that his family had, in the previous century, produced two bishops and that the Cantilupes were still a significant family despite the vast majority of their lands being carved up after the main branch failed in the male line. Additional to a deliberate reminder of status, the display of arms and borrowing of iconography in use by other family members also demonstrated that the bearer had taken on the moral and physical qualities of their ancestors.[23]

To this end, Fig. x. demonstrates how Nicholas and his father chose to develop their armorial bearings, based on the arms of their ancestors. It is worth noting here that 'family' was an extensive and fluid concept for people of Nicholas's status, and that this was an inherited understanding. David Crouch has noted that in the case of twelfth-century studies, the 'Anglo-French' groups he took into consideration 'could hold together different models of the family in [their] consciousness'.[24] This was seemingly a matter of pragmatism and convenience. When beneficial to emphasise a matriarchal link, the choice of arms would transmit this, emphasising links of blood descent or horizontal links with the conjugal family as it pleased them, dependent upon the attitudes and aims of the kin group. Crouch goes on to cite a thirteenth-century legal example of flexible land inheritance, in order to show that notions of the family and family succession retained this variformed tractability well into the middle of that century and, indeed, beyond.[25]

Family and lordship did not have to be as straight-forward as father to (oldest) son succession, although this was the norm. In the Cantilupe case, passing over the son to the grandson as Nicholas II did is not an indication that the 'left out' William was in disgrace. It simply meant that it was agreed within the family that while a marriage had been contracted and lands given out, the two young grandsons would be better marriage prospects themselves if a greater inheritance were coming directly to them.

Nicholas II died in 1355. His son, William VI, was aged around 30, and while he did not inherit the lordship, he did inherit those lands that Nicholas had gained through his second marriage to Joan Kymas, even though Joan still lived. These manors were worth a handsome total of 800 marks per year. A mark was worth 13s 6d, or two-thirds of £1, which had the equivalent buying power of around £331 in 2017. This would mean that the equivalent buying power of 800 marks was roughly the same as £265,000 in 2017's rates.[26] This was hardly a case of William VI being passed over or slighted, but seems to be a case where the passing of the bulk of the inheritance to his young boys had been discussed and agreed among the members of the family. Joan, his stepmother, held other lands as her dower, which gave her an independent income of her own.

William VI, designated 'the elder' in the legal and fiscal records of the time, was also named as the heir of his father's Nottinghamshire and Derby lands, although Nicholas had demised these onto other knights in his lifetime, and there were no lands to inherit there until those knights died. Similarly, he is named as the heir of the Buckinghamshire lands, although again, it was found that Nicholas II had demised these lands to the same three knights, Thomas de Newmarche, Hugh de Cressy, and John Bussey the elder.[27] John Bussey was a kinsman of the Paynells, and Sir Nicholas II must have known Sir Ralph and his father (another Sir Ralph) fairly well from military service and time spent in the counties.

Everything else, including the title of Lord Cantilupe, went directly to William VI's oldest son, Nicholas III, who was 13 years old at the time of his grandfather's death, and Nicholas's little brother William VII or William the younger, the William with whom we are most concerned, then aged 11.

Sir William's Childhood

Sir William the younger was born *c*. 1344, the second surviving child of Sir William the elder and Lady Joan de Welle. His parents were not long out of their teens by the time William came along, and a great deal was riding on both boys making a name for themselves in the household of some great magnate the way their grandfather had done.[28] We do not know what William's childhood was like – nothing survives that might give us this information. We can, however, consider medieval childhood more broadly and extrapolate from the 'typical' conditions, factoring in the major events of the time and the impressions we have of his family's circumstances and careers.

Childhood in the Middle Ages has been the subject of its own study for many decades, and some scholars like Philippe Ariès have argued that children did not lead separate lives from adults, making the controversial claim that 'in medieval society, the idea of childhood did not exist.'[29] Others, like Shulamith Shahar, have taken the opposite view through more thorough examinations of the evidence. In her influential study of childhood,[30] Shahar pointed out that there were differences in the lives of men and women, masters and servants: why weren't there also differences in the lives of adults and children?

Children of this period certainly played with toys, for a start. We know from the records of the king's household expenses that Edward I's 5-year-old son Henry had a toy cart that cost 7*d*. when new and 2*d*. to mend when it broke.[31]

As a privileged child growing up in the luxury afforded by his family background and his grandfather's illustrious career, William very likely had his own toys like the ones found in various archaeological digs in London and elsewhere. The medieval toys discovered in these digs include toy soldiers in the form of mounted knights on horseback around 55mm high, small metal alloy models that were evidently created in moulds and mass-produced in this way (although 'mass production' was on a different scale to today's version of this concept, such toys could be produced in large numbers and sold at markets and fairs across the country). Such toys had been around for years: Bishop Thomas of Hereford (d.1282), that sainted kinsman of this Cantilupe branch, had some toy knights that he used to play with as a boy when his ambition was to become a knight like his father and older brothers. His uncle, Bishop Walter of Worcester, had prophecied over him that he would instead become 'a knight of Christ', and so Thomas entered the church and the service of God rather than tournaments and military service.

In fact, by 1300, craftsmen were making and selling toy versions of objects from adult life, in much the same way as doll-house furniture and accessories were popular in later centuries, and in England these, like the toy knights, were made from the same kind of metal alloy as pilgrim badges and brooches. This suggests that they were made by the same craftsmen and sold at shops, markets and fairs.[32] Not all toys were military in nature: other examples included simple mechanical ones, like a small bird 27mm in height dating from Edward I's reign, originally mounted on a pivot so that when tipped its tongue stuck out.[33]

But the life of a noble child in this period could not be all fun and games. As well as ball games and the usual rough-and-tumble sports complained about by their elders, children as young as 5 from all social ranks practiced/played at fighting with weapons, from sticks to weaving grasses and sedges into 'swords', encouraged by the adults.[34] The chronicler Fortescue, writing in the later fifteenth century during the Wars of the Roses, described the adolescent delight a young Prince Edward took in 'attacking and assaulting the young companions attending him, sometimes with a lance, sometimes with a sword, and sometimes with other weapons, in a warlike way and according to the rules of military discipline.'[35]

As they grew older, noble children who were expected to be mounted in combat and be proficient at hunting, were given their own horses; this, too, was part of a long cultural tradition within this section of society. Edward I's second son, Henry, was given his first horse, a white palfrey, when he was 7 years old.[36] They were taught swordsmanship, and both girls and boys were taught to hunt and shoot a bow.[37]

For boys, medieval educational theory and discourse concurred that military training and strenuous physical exercise should begin aged 14, but although in these works the educationists had little to say on the subject of girls and physical exercise, in practice, girls also took part in these kinds of activities. Boys of the same social rank often learned these skills together, making it likely that the affinities (and, indeed, the hostile factions) that can be seen in adulthood between members of the knightly class were formed in their boyhood.

Childhood interests often bore fruit in adulthood, and so a military ethos was inculcated in children at an early age. Nevertheless, childhood games could grow into adolescent pressures as William and his older brother were also being trained to follow in the footsteps of Sir Nicholas II.

Growing up with the shadow of their active grandfather hanging over them could not have been an easy feat. There was a lot to live up to – the Cantilupe reputation and family history demanded excellence in at least one area of knighthood, whether administrative, acquisitions of territory and rents, or military prowess. The previous generations had been some combination of shrewd, prudent, and personable: kings had enjoyed their company, and even when the more principled among them had turned against their royal lord and sided with the rebellious barons, the Cantilupes had returned to royal favour with very little sanction. They had been able to negotiate for good marital alliances with other barons, had pushed themselves and their kin forwards in the right circles, and steadily gained wealth and lands as a result. They were appropriately pious, and several of those who went into the church excelled in their careers. Sir William the younger and his older brother, Sir Nicholas III ('the younger'), doubtless had the successes and models of their forebears drummed into them from an early age, especially given the energetic, impressive career of their grandfather.

However, the two young boys were growing up in a time of turmoil and dramatic social change, the effects of which resonated far beyond their short lives and would still be felt for many years to come. When William was about 4 years old and Nicholas his brother was 6, the Black Death came to England.

Over the past year there had been rumours and tales of a great plague sweeping through China, but China was so far away it didn't seem to make much difference to the daily lives of Europeans. The trade routes brought the stories, as well as the goods from the Far East – and in 1347, they brought the plague itself.

As with many diseases and bacterial infections, the stronger and better nourished a person, the better their immune system, and the higher the chances of survival and recovery. When the Black Death came to England, it encountered a population whose living standards had been gradually decreasing for decades. Between 1315 and 1322, the Great Famine, brought about by unusually prolonged rainfall and cold spells, had killed around 10–15 per cent of the population.[38] Reports of cannibalism had filtered down from Northumbria, straining the social fabric with panic and anger as people sold their possessions to afford the bare necessities. The cost of food and livestock increased, but as livestock were slaughtered for meat, including breeding stock and animals raised for dairy, their numbers steeply declined and would take time to recover. The cost of meat and dairy also rose, and this had a further, longer lasting impact on diet and nutrition. By the 1340s, while both rents and income had gone up, the effects of this prolonged poor and limited diet were still present in the population. Yet this wasn't the only culprit: the economic growth of the previous century had resulted in a population expansion, forcing farmers to plough poorer soil in order to keep up with the demands of feeding the increasing population, resulting in lower and lower returns even before the Great Famine.[39]

Historians have long debated the living standards of the fourteenth century and the origins of the economic and agrarian crisis in its early decades, but one thing became clear: when the Black Death epidemic came through, it swept away the weakest first, the majority of these being among the lower-born, poverty-stricken masses whose nutrition and subsistence levels had been sub-par for at least two generations if not three.

That year, William the elder and Joan must have counted themselves fortunate to have escaped with their lives and the lives of their children, while across the country harvests continued to fail, and people died too fast and in too great numbers at once for the living to bury them in anything but mass graves. That particular epidemic died out in 1349 (it would return to Britain multiple times) but the psychological impact on the survivors cannot ever be fully understood. A more recent study of psychosocial effects of the Ebola outbreak 2013–16 has some striking parallels with contemporary fourteenth-century reports of the Black Death's effect on communities: the isolating, scapegoating and ostracising of individuals and groups, breakdown in trust between communities and outsiders, shifting roles and restructuring as leaders and necessary lynchpins in the community died and left their roles vacant.[40] The study also found on an individual level that survivors, carers and loved ones of patients could be left with long-term psychological effects such as depression, anxiety and Post Traumatic Stress Disorder [PTSD]. Assuming that human reactions to such conditions remain similar no matter how distant in time the experiences are, then the chances are reasonably high that as William and Nicholas grew up they would have encountered these kinds of mental health problems in people they knew, whether in their own family members or servants, or in their peers and their households.

Things were not all bleak, however. Edward III's foreign ambitions were not dampened by a hellish year of disease and death. With Sir Nicholas the elder's illustrious career, the material results would have been evident to his young co-heirs. The successes of the English campaigns in the first phase of the Hundred Years' War from 1337–60 brought with it 'an abundance of rewards' in the form of French wall-hangings, cloth, silk, gold- and silver-plate and jewellery.[41] The involvement of the Cantilupes in the earlier phase of the war, and the main branch's increasing prominence, not to mention the involvement of the wider local Lincolnshire elite, meant that their manors would have seen the benefits of plundering Caen and Calais in material terms.

Sir William VII's mother, Joan de Welle, was likely the granddaughter of an active member of the local gentry, Adam de Welle (d. 1311).[42] Adam's son Robert inherited the de Welle lands in Northamptonshire and Lincolnshire, the latter county being where the majority of Adam's lands were held, making Robert's daughter Joan a good match for Sir Nicholas II's son.[43] With Sir Nicholas II choosing to be entombed at Lincoln Cathedral, this is another indication that while the family's seat was still in Nottingham they were spending more time and energy in consolidating and expanding their holdings in the neighbouring county. The two young boys would therefore have spent their childhood divided between the two counties, but more likely spending time in Lincolnshire visiting their mother's relatives and their grandfather's manors. With the decision to bypass Sir William the elder, the boys could look forward to claiming an impressive inheritance. This was not an unusual arrangement: another member of the neighbouring elite, Sampson de Strelley, also inherited directly from his grandfather, and by 1368 was married to

Elizabeth Hercy, referred to as a 'kinswoman' of the two young Cantilupe heirs and therefore must have been a relative on their mother's side.[44]

From this point onwards, William and Nicholas were excellent catches for the other local elite and their daughters. Sir Ralph and Lady Katherine Paynell had a daughter a few years younger than Nicholas, and Joan Kymas set about negotiations to secure Katherine for her step-grandson. William, a co-heir with his brother, was not to be left out: the local branch of the Nevilles also had a daughter about the right age, and it is likely that negotiations for Maud and William's match took place about the same time, although all we know about their marriage is that it had taken place by $c.1370$.

Lady Joan de Kymas's prominence in the negotiations comes in part from the fact that she was in control of Greasley castle and the manor of Ilkeston after her husband's death. It was found that Sir Nicholas the elder had enfeoffed Sir Thomas Newmarche, John Bussey (the elder) and Hugh Cressy manors in Buckinghamshire as well as Greasley castle, the manor and advowson of the church at Ilkeston, a parcel of land at Kinmarley, and 13d of rent in Hemsull, Nottinghamshire, before he died. After his death, the Derbyshire and Nottinghamshire manors and castle were granted to his widow by these three feoffees for life, with successive remainders to Sir William the elder, his son.[45] Upon Joan's death, this reverted to Sir Nicholas III, and from him to his ill-fated brother, Sir William VII.

The boys grew up being trained by their parents and step-grandmother to take over the running of the estates and lands left to them with Lady Joan de Kymas in control of the family's Nottinghamshire seat. They also grew up knowing that their careers were mapped out for them, but *success* in those careers rested firmly on their shoulders. Their grandfather had set that bar high. From at least the age of 14 they were trained to be knights, already knowing who they were going to marry.

The Cantilupes in Crisis

In 1371, our Sir William, now 26 years old, returned to England from France, under arrest for murder. A surprising event in his otherwise unrecorded life, it ended his military career and is the last time he appears in the records until he was discovered in a Lincolnshire field in 1375.

He had been on campaign since 1368, and at the time of his arrest was in Aquitaine on the king's business. Escorted back across the Channel, Sir William was imprisoned in the Tower of London until his name was cleared, but that cut his military career short. The man he was accused of murdering – by poison – was his own brother, Sir Nicholas III, who had joined him in Aquitaine not on the king's business but to seek an audience with the pope and challenge the ecclesiastical court's decision to annul his marriage to Lady Katherine Paynell. Lady Katherine had been pursuing an annulment since 1367, and testimony of her allegedly impotent husband's cruelty had resulted in the court granting a separation for her own protection.

How did this happen? Was William the kind of man to poison his own brother, and how did they get to this crisis point? To answer this we must turn to Nicholas's life, which, from the time of his marriage, was falling apart.

William VII became a knight like his brother, and had been knighted by 21, probably around the time of his brother's marriage but no more than a year later. He inherited his share of their grandfather's lands but was now not expected to be a lord unless he married well: the expectation was that Nicholas and Katherine would have their own children. At least, this was the assumption of those who did not know the younger Nicholas de Cantilupe well.

Relations soured between the Cantilupes and the Paynells, coming to a violent head not long after Sir William the younger left for Calais. Frederick Pedersen has described this crisis as 'pivotal' to understanding the reasons for Sir William's murder,[46] but this is only insofar as the traditional interpretation is correct. The details of this family drama will be considered here in their proper chronological place, and also in the section of the following chapter that deals with Sir Ralph Paynell as an individual suspect.

This crisis point for the family came after a great deal of effort had been undertaken to make Sir Nicholas an attractive marriage prospect for Sir Ralph's daughter. Sir William the elder had been removed from the succession in favour of his sons, and their step-grandmother, Joan Kymas, had negotiated for Katherine Paynell's hand in marriage, and the marriage was contracted when they were both underage with a view to formalising it when they were older. One of Sir Ralph's own kin-by-marriage, Sir John Bussey the elder, was one of three feoffees holding the Cantilupe seat of Greasley and other important manors in Nottinghamshire, Derbyshire and Buckinghamshire, and was instructed to hold it for the widowed Joan and then on her death to parcel it out amongst the two young grandsons. Giving the Paynells more direct access to the Cantilupe lands via Sir John Bussey senior's connections with the family was a clever move. However, when it came to it, Katherine was deeply unhappy with the match and a key part of the annulment proceedings was that she had been underage when the marriage was brokered.

The typical way of contracting such marriages can be seen in other cases, and not all of them went as well as the matchmakers hoped. Recognised 'marital affection', a vague term which implied sexual relations but could just as easily refer to the non-sexual relationship between the couple, was an important element of a medieval marriage, even though many were contracted/arranged rather than love-matches at all levels of society. We have limited knowledge of Nicholas and Katherine's earlier circumstances, but they were far from unusual as other contemporary examples illustrate.

The lack of affection between them seemed to be mutual, given the deterioration of the relationship, and looking at other comparable cases brought before the ecclesiastical courts can provide more context regarding how this kind of situation was viewed by the church and by those pressured into unsuitable matrimonial unions.

One case that illustrates the difficult aspects of medieval marriage is that of Aungier vs Malcake, brought before the archbishop's court at York in the spring of 1357. William Aungier was a 14-year-old seeking to annul his marriage to Johanna Malcake, a 16-year-old.[47] This may seem incongruous to modern readers who might consider teenagers under the age of 18 to be children, but the age of consent was 12 for girls and 14 for boys in line with the medieval canon law understanding of the average age of puberty, and by 14 William Aungier would already have started his career and been inducted into the responsibilities of his community, while Johanna was certainly designated a woman aged 16, which is the current age of consent in the United Kingdom today.

38   *Murder During the Hundred Years' War*

The two had never consummated their union, as they had been married in the church at Fenwick while they were underage – William had been 8 and Johanna 10 – and afterwards had been put in the marriage bed together as a formality [as in, to sleep in the same bed that night with no expectation that the marriage would be consummated so early].[48] The marriage had to be ratified formally when William Aungier, the youngest of the two, came of age. This was the situation that Nicholas Cantilupe and Katherine Paynell had been in – the marriage had been contracted under similar circumstances, but in their case it was Katherine who was the youngest of the couple.

William Aungier saw very little of his 'wife' after this sleepover, except for the usual controlled meetings arranged by the families to see if they could get along together. However, when he turned 14, he heard some disturbing news: Johanna Malcake was pregnant and admitted to having sex with several 'men' whose names she claimed not to know. It is not stated whether these 'men' were her age, younger, or older; 14-year-old William Aungier was himself designated a 'man' in the records, and not a 'boy'. She was at the time living with her uncle, and he also claimed not to know the names of the 'men' Johanna had been involved with, which could simply be true, or could have been said to protect his niece and the men/boys involved from retribution (especially if they were married or betrothed themselves), or could paint a more sinister picture of what was going on under his roof.

The families were keen to cement the marriage regardless, and William was immediately packed off to her house and spent a week there, steadfastly refusing to consummate their marriage. Towards the end of the week he was persuaded by the Malcakes' neighbours to spend one night in bed with her, but he was unhappy about this and again refused to have sex with her, discussing the situation with his own young friends. His witness, William Raynald, testified that William Aungier had told him:

> It displeased me [William Aungier] that I knew her once for she does not prize an affection that is upheld. And therefore, for sure, I intend never to consent to her that she be my wife, nor to cohabit with her.[49]

(The formal phrasing of this declaration is not to be taken literally as an exact account of what either Raynald or Aungier said: witness testimonies were not transcribed word-for-word and cannot be taken as straightforwardly as this in this period, especially given the translation from the language spoken at the trial into Latin.)[50]

Their marriage was annulled.

Marital affection, therefore, was a recognised ingredient that should be present in a union, and effort was put into its development between spouses. If witnesses could be produced to testify that 'marital affection' was present between two people, this was part of the evidence considered in these kinds of courts. While it was expected to have a sexual component, this wasn't necessarily the case. If this was not present in Katherine and Nicholas's marriage, even after two years, the chances of being granted an annulment were higher. Katherine's situation was similar to William Aungier's in that while they had both been underage when the marriage was contracted, she had shared the marriage bed with her husband when she came of age, which meant that things were more complicated.

Sillem struggled to account for Sir Ralph Paynell's involvement in William VII's murder and his willingness to shelter Lady Maud and her two servants. However, when she examined the Calendar of Patent Rolls, she found Sir Ralph being accused of attacking Nicholas III's castle at Greasley and 'ravishing' Katherine his wife, carrying her away along with goods and chattals, but could not find any other information that year relating to the event.[51] The Patent Rolls misdate the event to 1366, the cause of Sillem's confusion: the attack actually took place in 1368, and the terminology is in itself misleading. In his complaint Nicholas painted his father-in-law as a marauder at the head of a criminal band, but in fact Katherine's father was responding to his daughter's allegations of spousal abuse and mounting an armed rescue.

Nicholas III married in 1366 × 67, although as his bride was underage at the time the marriage was contracted, they had to wait until she came of age (18) for the marriage to be formalised with her consent. Katherine Paynell, daughter of Sir Ralph and Lady Katherine Paynell of Caythorpe, Lincolnshire, seemed happy with her family's choice of husband at first, although she had not spent much time with him. The wedding took place, and Nicholas took his title of Lord Cantilupe.

There was already a rumour that Nicholas was impotent, which the Paynells, to their credit, ignored. However, this rumour was not just the idle salacious gossip of tenants and servants, but came from within Nicholas's own family. With all the Cantilupe, de Welle and Paynell relations gathered for the occasion, Katherine was approached by one of her new in-laws, Elizabeth de Strelley, not long before her wedding day. 'My lady', Elizabeth teased the young bride, 'I will give you a penny if you ever have joy of your husband.'[52] Katherine didn't know what to make of this and apparently brushed it off at the time, as the wedding took place and the couple went to live with her father at Caythorpe in Lincolnshire for a year.

Things fell apart between the couple almost immediately, with an unsuccessful wedding night and Katherine's discovery that the rumour had basis in fact.

When her tall, deep-voiced, 22-year-old husband showed very little interest in her, 18-year-old Katherine waited until he fell asleep and then (without his consent) attempted to arouse him by putting her hand between his legs. She tried several times to identify what she expected to be typical male genitalia, but could not, testifying that it was 'as flat as the back of a man's hand'.[53] Nicholas strenuously, and at times violently, denied this was the case, but he did not attempt to have intercourse with her and repeatedly refused physical examinations that would prove her story false.

Three days after they had solemnized their vows, Katherine's closest friend, Margaret de Halton of Holland (the Holland of South-East Lincolnshire, that is), found herself consoling the weeping young bride. Margaret is described as Katherine's *socio in lecto*, literally 'companion in bed', a friend or attendant with whom a bed or at least the bedchamber was shared. As a result of sharing a room and a bed with Katherine for several years growing up, Margaret was privy to most if not all of Katherine's secrets. Bedfellows were common at all levels of elite society for the next few centuries: Anna Whitelock's study of Queen Elizabeth I's bedfellows describes their role as taking care of the queen's body, checking for illnesses, dressing and preparing her for her public duties, and protecting the queen from assassination attempts by poison or violence.[54] Taking on a scaled-down version of this role as a member of a gentry or baronial household, Margaret de Halton's relationship with Katherine was as attendant, confidante, friend and staunch supporter.

Katherine finally revealed to Margaret that the reason she was so upset was because Nicholas could not have intercourse with her, as he did not have 'sufficient natural members because his testicles were missing'.[55] Elizabeth's taunt now made more sense, and gave Katherine's story credence.[56]

Elizabeth was the wife of Sampson de Strelley, a neighbouring lord in Nottinghamshire who was at least 21 years old in December 1355,[57] the year of Sir Nicholas senior's death, when Nicholas the younger was 13 and William was 11. This supports the idea that Elizabeth was an older cousin related to Nicholas the younger via his mother Joan de Welle, and that these female relationships were close enough for her to know details of Joan's son's intimate physical appearance, most likely because she had known him as a baby and/or a young boy. In turn, this would account for another piece of Katherine's testimony: she could prove that it was 'the rumour of the county' that her husband was impotent, and this 'common knowledge' must have come from within the family household itself. This implies that at least one if not several of Nicholas's close family were aware that he could not procreate or have sexual intercourse, but perhaps hoped that this would not matter to Katherine, or rather cynically trusted that as a young and naïve woman her allegations, should she make any, would not be believed. As far as they were concerned, there was always Sir William the younger to produce heirs who would inherit the lands and title instead.

Unfortunately, as far as Katherine was concerned, it *did* matter, and she did not wish to be tricked into a marriage with a man she didn't know particularly well, owed nothing to, and could not provide her with what she wanted. As far as Nicholas was concerned, Katherine's revelations were a massive violation of his privacy, not to mention a blow to his reputation, and must have affected him on a deeply personal level. At a time when people were immersed in a culture of heteronormative binaries, being born intersex or with medical conditions resulting in atypical genitalia, such as Congenital Adrenal Hypoplasia (posited by Pedersen as a possible retrospective diagnosis in this instance),[58] was not something widely discussed let alone understood. That Nicholas was not open with his bride beforehand is hardly surprising, and it is very likely that he was under pressure from his own family to keep silent about it until after the marriage had taken place.

Moreover, much of these attitudes can be attributed to the harmful labelling of intersex people as 'monstrous' in medieval thought, where androgynous people were included in bestiaries like the twelfth-century *De Monstris* (*Of* or *Concerning Monsters*).[59] The marginalisation and othering of people born with 'atypical' bodies at this time was a serious matter, and one that few people had a framework for outside of this harmful monstrosity concept. In public discourse and medical, philosophical and ecclesiastical works, debate and theory abounded regarding the reasons for intersex characteristics, with such (usually male) commentators including both 'effeminate'-behaving/presenting men and 'masculine'-behaving/presenting women in these discussions.

Albert the Great (*c.* 1200–80) included 'hermaphrodites' in his study *De Animalibus* (*Concerning Creatures*), written 1258–62, dehumanising those with intersex characteristics. In this treatise he defined the existence of two sets of genitals as 'a case of superfluity caused by a superabundance of matter', using the analogy of the engendering of twins.[60] While medical theories were applied, other attitudes to atypical sexual characteristics were not sympathetic. The French poet Eustache Deschamps (*c.* 1340–1406) wrote his scathing *Ballade Contra les Hermaphrodites* in which he described them as corrupt in body and mind, framing female-presenting intersex people as moral as well as physical aberrations.[61]

Facing this level of public hostility, misunderstanding and stereotyping, it was incredibly difficult for someone of any rank who didn't fit the binary mould, but by virtue of his Sir Nicholas was, at least, more privileged than most. He had access to education and knew his way around the law, he could pay attorneys, and he was part of the governing elite of his locality. He was also male-presenting, and this was a successful shield for a while, given his father-in-law's initial refusal to believe his daughter's revelation.

Sir Ralph Paynell put Katherine's marital troubles down to her age and inexperience – implying that her confusion was down to her looking in the wrong place or covering for her own deficiencies in pleasing her husband, telling her that it was because 'she was foolish and didn't know what she should do' (*quod fuit fatua et quod non intellexit quid fecit*).[62]

Katherine's testimony could, in some interpretations, create an impression of a young girl given to emphatic hyperbole: at one point she swore she would be burnt at the stake if anyone could prove her story false. This, however, could just as easily be read as a young woman standing up within a male-dominated court and knowing that she would not be believed unless she gave extreme assurances of her truthfulness in this case, and expressing that she clearly understood the seriousness of what she was saying. It is also not a case of Katherine choosing an extreme punishment at random: this was the female punishment for petty treason. While perjury and defamation were not in themselves components of petty treason, the connection is an interesting one for Katherine to draw. She would not have been burned at the stake for perjury, but by equating her reputation-destroying allegations to the murder of her husband, she expressed how seriously she took the case.

After her father's initial dismissal of her story she appealed to Lady Katherine her mother, supported by Margaret de Halton, and her story was given more credence. Her mother arranged for her to see Master Thomas Waws, who was well acquainted with canon law and best placed to advise her. Waws was persuaded that Katherine was not a liar, and in his turn arranged for her to speak to John Buckingham, then bishop of Lincoln, on several occasions, to discuss the possibility of annulment and separation. Each time she had her mother and Margaret with her for support. She was advised to return to her husband and attempt to consummate the marriage again, and if after the customary period (of two years) nothing had happened between them, she could return home and the marriage could be annulled.

The couple lived at Caythorpe for a year, and the following year went to Greasley castle, the Cantilupe seat. Margaret was one of those close friends and advisors who persuaded Katherine to live with Nicholas for a time. Katherine went to Greasley with Margaret and two churchmen, her ally Master Thomas Waws and another cleric, Master Robert Bekeby, but her relationship with Nicholas did not grow into anything approaching mutual affection, as her counsellors and friends had hoped.[63]

In August 1367, Katherine's two years were finally up and she was told in confession by her priest that she could now go home to her family and start the annulment proceedings with a clear conscience.[64] She wasted no time and went back to her father's manor of Caythorpe.

At this point, Nicholas panicked. After two years of cohabitation he had failed to convince his wife to stay married to him. If she went through with the annulment, Nicholas's reputation would be destroyed in court and he must have worried that no matter how quietly Katherine and the Paynells tried to keep the proceedings, it would be talked about all over York and beyond once the testimonies were heard. It was already 'the rumour of the county' that he was impotent. If such an intimate detail was already widely gossiped about, how much more would Katherine's testimony be discussed if it was heard so formally? The Cantilupe name was going to be held up for ridicule, his family could hardly have been thrilled that he had failed to keep his highly-prized Paynell wife for longer than twenty-four months after all the effort the match had taken, his father had been passed over for the lordship in his favour, and the relationship with the Paynells was breaking down as a result.

In defiance of the ecclesiastical court's ruling and risking excommunication, a penalty that was actually imposed upon him as a result, Nicholas ignored the fact that Katherine now had every right to leave his house and did not wish to be his wife. He resorted to more desperate measures, preparing a prison for his wife in Greasley castle and sending out armed men to abduct her from her father's manor. Lady Katherine was dragged back 'weeping and wailing' to Greasley where a 'grim-faced' Nicholas met her at the castle gate.

This was before Sir William had left for Calais, and it is improbable that he did not know what was going on between his brother and sister-in-law, although it isn't clear if he was involved in dragging her back to Greasley with his brother's men or if he himself was at Greasley during this time. If he did know and especially if he was an active participant in the strife, then the source of Sir Ralph's enmity towards both brothers becomes far clearer.

In court, Nicholas brought his defence that Katherine's claims were nonsense, and that she had sworn an oath before three witnesses to the effect that they had consummated their marriage successfully. In support of Katherine, Master Robert Bekeby testified that this oath had been made after Nicholas had sent his men to abduct her from Caythorpe, and therefore should be discounted because it had been made under duress. Master Robert told the court that when Nicholas met his men and weeping wife, he said to Katherine, 'You are a cursed woman among all women.'[65]

What he actually meant by this, we cannot know. As the defendant, Nicholas could swear that it meant she had lied about his impotency, and that she should suffer the wrath of God for those lies and her abandonment of him. On the plaintiff's side, it could also be construed as a statement masking his own self-loathing, implying that Katherine was 'cursed' to be his wife, and his wife she would remain regardless of her wishes. Master Robert did not elaborate on what he thought Nicholas meant by it, but continued with his narrative of what came next.

In a turn of events that to modern readers may sound worthy of a gothic horror novel, Master Robert swore that Nicholas then showed Katherine the room in the castle where he planned to incarcerate her if she did not agree to whatever he told her to say. Margaret de Halton also testified that he had ankle-irons and handcuffs ready to use on Katherine if she disagreed, and that he fully intended to make her his prisoner.[66] This was not a far-fetched or unheard-of strategy. Nicholas was not the only husband to threaten his wife with this kind of forced incarceration: another irate husband, Robert Person, went as far as to actually bind his wife (or ex-wife) in irons to retain her, and there are other cases of husbands abducting their wives in order to prevent separation and annulment proceedings from taking place.[67] This testimony was neither the first nor last time such threats would be heard in the ecclesiastical court at York, and was taken seriously.

Under these conditions and evidently convinced that her husband would make good on his threats, Lady Katherine was dragged to the chapel with three witnesses, to swear the oath before them that Nicholas had consummated their marriage. There, Nicholas allegedly said, 'You know well that I am sufficiently potent to copulate with you, having genitals that are good enough,' to which Katherine (quite understandably, argued Master Robert) answered, 'Yes.'

Nicholas then made her swear before his three witnesses that he had already known her carnally and was capable of having sex with her, emphasising that he had 'sufficient natural instruments' to do so. He added that he also wanted her oath 'that you henceforth do not leave my company without special permission and that you do not reveal this counsel in any way.' To this, Katherine told him, 'I will swear to whatever you said.'[68]

From that time on, Katherine became Nicholas's prisoner by virtue of that oath, subjected to what amounted to house-arrest.

Six months later in February 1368, Sir Ralph learned the truth about his daughter's situation. He assembled a group of rescuers lightly armed with bows, short swords and sticks, and mounted her rescue with the aid of his kinsman, Sir Robert Raufchamberlain Paynell, John de Hanover and Katherine's *socia in lecto*, Margaret de Halton of Holland herself.[69] Since Margaret was already with Katherine at Greasley, she is probably named here because she helped the armed band gain access to the castle from the inside. Their mission was a success: Lady Katherine packed her bags and finally went home. She was now free to pursue the annulment of her marriage and was promptly appointed a proctor, one Master John Stanton, who was her legal representative by 25 March 1368. Stanton knew his business and immediately applied to the court for protection for his young client, and on 22 April 1368 the court granted that Katherine could live separately from her husband while the case lasted.[70] The Paynells decided to take no chances this time and arranged for Lady Katherine to move north, as far away from Greasley as she could reasonably get. She spent the duration of the case living in the care of her kinswoman Lady Margaret, wife of Sir Edward Hastings, in the fortified Roxby castle, North Yorkshire.[71]

The road to annulment was not an easy one and would take another year. After all, at first she had struggled to get her own family to believe her story, hence the long delay in proceedings and the attempts made to reconcile the couple in the early years of their union. Nicholas also complicated things and created difficulties for the Paynells regarding the rescue. Well-versed in the law and not having given his consent for Katherine to leave his home, Nicholas lodged the complaint of ravishment against Sir Ralph and an allegation of theft of goods and chattels that went with Katherine's 'abduction'. The theft amounted, Nicholas claimed in court, to £2000 worth of goods and chattals, or the equivalent of around £980,000 in today's money, comprising mainly silverware and jewellery.[72] This could well be an exaggerated estimate of the cost to further entangle the Paynells in court proceedings, discredit their testimony at the annulment and paint Nicholas as the severely wronged party, and it is likely that the things Katherine took from Greasley were items she had brought with her upon her marriage or that had been gifted afterwards. Since technically all that a wife owned, including her clothes, belonged to her husband,[73] Nicholas was cynically pressing his legal advantage here to the detriment of the Paynells. It would be fair to say this is a 'cynical' push, since the thirteenth-century legal treatise *Bracton* suggested that things given and granted to a wife for her personal adornment, such as robes and jewels, could be said to be her own and could be bequeathed by her in her own will.[74] The court action indicates the extent to which relations had broken down between Nicholas and Katherine, that he was willing to formally pursue in court (and possibly inflate the cost of) the items she took with her when she left his house.

It should also be noted that in accusing his father-in-law of 'ravishing' his wife, Nicholas was not accusing him of sexual assault. 'Ravishment' in this context did not necessarily have overtones of sexual violence but was a charge that could be levelled against 'abductors' who carried the wife off without her husband's consent, even if she was taken away at her own request and of her own free will. For example, when a woman named Isabel, the wife of one Robert Bull, returned to her father's home 'of her own free will' after catching her husband 'misbehaving with other women', her father found himself up before the king's courts on a charge of 'ravishment' since her philandering son-in-law had not consented to his wife leaving home and wanted her back.[75] In another case, Beatrice Herring, forced into marriage with Henry le Welye against her will when she was underage, also endangered her family by attempts to escape. Henry pleaded a case of 'ravishment' against Beatrice's mother Sabina and against Beatrice's uncle, both of whom had helped Beatrice leave his house.[76] The punishment, should someone be found guilty of this charge, was a jail term and a payment of damages to the plaintiff, although in practice the threat of this punishment and continued use of jail over payments were used to coerce a defendant into compliance with the award of court.[77]

With this law suit against his father-in-law going through the courts, Nicholas hoped it would discredit Sir Ralph and Katherine's key witnesses. This was important: as the defendant in the annulment case, Nicholas was tasked with the unenviable challenge of disproving Katherine's story and discrediting her witnesses. The charge of theft and ravishment helped with that, but he had to discredit all of them to the court's satisfaction and prove that his wife was lying. While a physical examination would have been the easiest and most obvious way of doing this, and arguably far better than threats, violence and spousal abuse, Sir Nicholas refused. Such an examination was highly intrusive and embarrassing, as one church legal expert laid out the procedure:

> The man and woman are to be placed together in one bed and wise women are to be summoned around the bed for many nights. And if the man's member is always found to be useless and as if dead, the couple are well able to be separated ...[78]

In York, 1433, one wise woman took the procedure into her own hands with an unfortunate man called John:

> The ... witness exposed her naked breasts and with her hands warmed at the said fire, she held and rubbed the penis and testicles of the said John. And she embraced and frequently kissed the said John and stirred him up in so far as she could to show his virility and potency, admonishing him for shame that he should there and then prove and render himself a man. And she says, examined and diligently questioned, that the whole time aforesaid, the said penis was scarcely three inches long ... remaining without any increase or decrease.[79]

A proud man from a noble family may well refuse such a procedure even if he had 'typical' genitalia, but at the same time Nicholas's refusal to undergo this humiliating exam was suspicious but meant that Katherine's allegations could neither be proved nor disproved. It all came down to witness testimony, and whether or not Katherine could provide witnesses to testify firstly that she was not given to lying and could vouch on oath for her good character, and secondly that Nicholas's impotence was common knowledge or 'the rumour of the county'. Nicholas, as the defendant, had to rebut this by discrediting the witnesses and giving evidence against their characters, telling the court why these witnesses should not be believed.

Katherine eventually won her case on 1 April 1369, having begun proceedings on 15 March 1367, but Nicholas, unable to bear the ignominy of her allegations, appealed. In 1370 he travelled to Avignon to seek an audience with the pope, where he fell ill. The symptoms of his illness bore strong resemblance to arsenic poisoning, and when he died, the authorities were immediately suspicious. His brother Sir William the younger was in Avignon at the time and stood to gain the title and lands his brother had held, and so, in another twist to the Cantilupe tale, he was promptly arrested for murder.[80]

The Exchequer Roll records the following (misdated in the printed edition to November 50 Edw. III, that is, November 1376, by which time William had been dead for a year and Nicholas dead for six):

> To John Vendour, of Newark, coming by command of the council from Lincoln to bring Sir William de Cantelupe [sic], knight, to the Tower of London, upon suspicion had against him for the death of Nicholas de Cantilupe, his brother, slain; and there safely and securely to keep him in the King's prison until otherwise respecting the same William it should be ordered by the said King and his Council. In money paid, &c., in discharge of 100*s* which the Lord the King commanded to be paid [to Vendour] for the wages and expenses of himself and his men going with him in his retinue for the safe custody of the aforesaid William.[81]

Sir William's military career was cut short: under arrest for poisoning his own brother, he was taken back to London to face his own trial. If Sir Ralph believed that Sir William was guilty, this would hardly be a reason to wait until 1375 to procure the murder of Sir William himself. The news of Nicholas's death would have come as a relief to Katherine, who was now completely free from the spectre of Nicholas's legal action and appeals, not to mention the threats of physical violence. She was now free to remarry, which she had done by 1371 – to another neighbouring noble, Sir John Auncell. This match may have been arranged for Katherine in 1370 and lined up to take place after her annulment, but Nicholas's appeal was a potential legal block to this marriage taking place. Once he died, this was no longer an issue.

Frederick Pedersen believes that Nicholas exhibited the symptoms of the final stages of Congenital Adrenal Hypoplasia, a condition that would account for his sexual characteristics and other symptoms one must read between the lines of the evidence to identify. The final stage symptoms apparently mimic acute arsenic poisoning, and Pedersen believes it was this condition that was the most likely cause of Nicholas's death.[82] It seems that there was not enough evidence against Sir William to convict him of the apparent murder of his brother, or that Sir William at least managed to prove or persuade the king of his innocence, for by the end of 1371 he had been released from the Tower and his lands restored to him.

By 1371, his step-grandmother Joan had also died, and the letter close was addressed to the escheator for Nottinghamshire and Derbyshire, Robert de Twyford. This was the order to deliver Nicholas the younger's manors of Greasley and Ilkeston to Sir William.[83] In December 1371 it was noted that three manors in Lincolnshire, namely Lavington, Withcall and Kinthorpe, were being jointly claimed by Katherine and her new husband, Sir John Auncell of Spalding, Lincolnshire.[84] A member of parliament for Lincolnshire in 1378 alongside his fellow shire knight (and another kinsman-by-marriage to the Paynells), William Bussy,[85] Sir John was a good match as far as the Paynells were concerned, and her swift remarriage indicates that she was an equally good prospect for him regardless of her previous situation. Since Katherine and John could not produce a deed that proved they were jointly enfeoffed of these manors, but Sir William, the deceased's brother, *could* prove that he was the next heir, Edward III ruled that these manors should be handed over to William rather than to Katherine and her co-claimant.[86]

By the end of 1371, Sir William the younger had been acquitted of murdering his older brother, was released from the Tower, and inherited all Nicholas's estates and lands, the title of Lord Cantilupe, and managed to keep hold of the manors Katherine and John sought to retain. Not only had Katherine been subjected to abduction, verbal threats and physical violence, but now her [ex-] brother-in-law was denying her the manors she felt were rightly hers. Sir John Auncell re-appears in the records a few years later in connection to Sir William's death: as one of the knights of the county willing to mainprise[87] Lady Maud for her husband's murder.

Sir William's Marriage, Knighthood and Military Career

While all this was going on at home, following his sister-in-law's abduction from her father's manor, William VII de Cantilupe travelled to Dover to make the crossing to France. Nicholas may not have had a military career, but William did.

What did William's career look like, what experiences had he had, and how did this affect his relationships with others? What about his own marriage, and the impact that his brother's crisis had upon him and his wife Maud Neville, left behind in Lincolnshire to face the consequences of her brother-in-law's actions against her sister-in-law and friend?

These are the obvious questions to ask, but they are also the most difficult to answer. It is not even known when his own marriage to Maud Neville took place. It is most likely that they were married in the mid-1360s, given Maud's close relations with the Paynells, which would make more sense if she had maintained close links with her sister-in-law. With Sir William away for three to four years on campaign, they would not necessarily have spent much time together beforehand, and, as with many experiences of life after war, the man who returned in 1371 may not have been the same as the man Maud had married.

Marriage was an important rite of passage for young people, and it is likely that William's own marriage to Maud Neville came not long after they both were of 'full age', which generally meant 18, but it is possible that Maud was older than he was, and had been waiting for him to reach his majority so that their marriage could be formally contracted. They could not have spent much time together if the marriage took place before 1370/1 – William left on campaign in 1368, and only returned from Aquitaine under arrest, following the death of his older brother.

While it is difficult to assess Sir William the younger's career due to a lack of evidence for his activities in these years, we can instead look more broadly at what it meant to be a knight and the kind of military service he was required to perform.

There is a clear framework for understanding the concept and context of knighthood at this time, which had its roots in previous centuries. In earlier England and Normandy, the Latin term '*miles*' or its Old French equivalent, '*chivaler*', meant a mounted warrior and could be applied to nobles possessing various degrees of wealth and land. By the thirteenth century, the poorer nobility, or emergent gentry class who were almost exclusively tenants of greater lords, could be classed as '*miles*' and bore this as a badge of aristocracy. Poorer, non-landed knights were squeezed out of this bracket, since only families with landed interests could serve the Angevin government in a practical capacity.[88] By the fourteenth century, the landscape of the nobility was still stratified, with greater lords, middling lords and lesser lords within it, but they all had some form of land-based wealth in common, even if they were renting it from those above. This created socio-political networks of nobility across the country, and the more lands that a lord held, the wider they looked for alliances that would pull them closer into the king's orbit, where greater shares of political power and more opportunities to receive patronage could be found. The fewer the lands, and the more concentrated they were in one area, the more limited the family's scope. They would look to the greater lords of their area and those social climbers around them for alliances to boost their own holdings or consolidate what they already held. If they felt that one or more lords were particularly rapacious, or had personal grudges against them, then alliances with other families who could support them in their legal battles and ensure a more influential future for their offspring, at least locally, were sought. Working their way into the households of the great lords as knights would ensure that they met, befriended and fought alongside the sons of other great and middling elite families, and that afforded them a wider scope and greater chances to marry well. In the same way, these middling nobles would take on armour-bearers or squires from the younger sons of the lower, poorer nobility who would otherwise have nothing to inherit or at most very little, ensuring them a place in a household where they too could distinguish themselves in battle and meet those of a much higher standing than themselves.

The Cantilupes had been a far more influential family in the previous century than they were in 1375 and were still trading on their ancestors' collective and individual reputations. William's grandfather, Nicholas II, was a man with extensive lands in Lincolnshire and Nottinghamshire. His career was notable and a great attempt to restore the family to some measure of their status as great magnates, but in practice he had fallen short of this goal. His grandchildren were the hope of the dynasty to continue this upward trajectory, so the pressure on Sir William the younger can be imagined. His older brother did not engage in military service or campaigns, and this left him with these responsibilities to shoulder.

Sir William the younger does not appear very frequently in the records, but in 1368, when he was around 24 years old, he left with the king's licence to go overseas, nominating local gentry Sir Robert Roos of Ingmanthorpe and William de Dalton as his attorneys in his absence.[89] The licence was granted in December 1367, giving William some time to get his administrative affairs in order before his departure. At this time he would have been a young man with no previous military experience, but with his living father and step-grandmother to advise him, and his newly-married older brother Nicholas taking care of the lion's share of the estates, he chose two men whom he trusted to oversee his part of his inheritance while he was away. Sir Robert Roos was well known to him and had been a family friend for many years: this man's name appears in a petition to the king in 1362 as a co-petitioner with Joan Kymas, his step-grandmother.[90]

In 1367, William de Dalton was a canon of York, with benefices in Ripon and Durham. He had been a canon of Lincoln in 1353, and the senior Nicholas de Cantilupe's foundation of the Cantilupe chantry in the cathedral indicates a link between the family and this churchman.[91] There is also a Peter de Dalton, canon of Lincoln, mentioned in a papal letter of 1367, a bachelor of canon and civil law, through whom the Cantilupes could have maintained this connection.[92] Having a secular and a spiritual protector of one's estates made sense to medieval lords, since kings routinely left the country in the hands of a council of the great earls, barons, and bishops. Churchmen were also well-trained in legal matters, and so William de Dalton was a wise choice of attorney.

William de Cantilupe the younger made the crossing to Calais from Dover with the large retinue bound for northern France. He took with him 'a yeoman, 2 hackneys each under the price of 40s', and a letter of [currency] exchange from Silvester Nicholas the Lombard for £20, the £20 being for his expenses while overseas.[93] It could be that the 'yeoman' was his *armiger*, or armour-bearer, Richard Gyse, previously in the employ of Richard de Bingham, but on this point we cannot be certain. There is no mention of an armour-bearer.

Yeomen did commonly accompany knights in various capacities, as Chaucer's portrait of the Knight's Yeoman suggests, not to mention the fact that Sir William was not the only knight in the Patent Roll list with a yeoman travelling with him. Chaucer's yeoman could be read as a jack-of-all-trades exemplar or humorous exaggeration, with overlapping duties of forester, lawman, hunter, bodyguard and soldier. Kenneth J. Thompson argued that this forms the background for a 'consummate bowman', able to give his lord service in both peace and war, and if this is the kind of man whom Sir William brought with him to France then it is a shame that we know nothing about him.[94] It also begs the question of where this man was while his lord was being murdered in his bed, but it is most likely that this man was part of the household of another manor and after the war he returned to his own duties elsewhere, and did not have anything to do with the Neville manor of Scotton where Sir William met his death. A yeoman was a freeman who could be bound to service for a contracted term, and afterwards would go back to his own land to farm it or return to his duties elsewhere, and so was not necessarily a consistent household member.

John of Gaunt, Duke of Lancaster, the second surviving son of Edward III and uncle to the future king Richard II, was 29 at the time, and the 1369 campaign was his first military command.[95] Lancaster undertook to serve with one of the largest retinues of the Hundred Years' War, including 499 men-at-arms, six bannerets, 130 knights and 363 esquires.[96] Joining him was Sir Henry Percy, whose indenture of 20 June stipulated twelve knights and forty-seven esquires, as well as a hundred mounted archers.[97]

William the younger was now part of a large, homosocial group with a variety of military experience and ability, and this included their leaders. Edmund, Earl of the March, one of the leaders in the second army to make the crossing, was only 17 and equally eager to build his own reputation.[98] There is some resonance here with the observation of one of Chaucer's wise older characters in *The Tale of Melibee*: 'There is very many a man who cries "War, war!" who knows very little what war amounts to.'[99]

Many of the shire knights who sat on the Good Parliament of 1376 and other parliaments through Richard II's reign cut their teeth in this first campaign. By the time of Chaucer's *Tales* (begun around 1387), there were very few knights who were so inexperienced that they knew 'very little what war amounts to', but everyone has to start somewhere.[100] Many of the older men were, by 1369, veterans of previous campaigns, but these older knights were largely outnumbered by the younger men for whom this was only their first or second. Some would have served in Spain with the Black Prince in 1367, but William the younger was not one of these men, and the major battle before Nájera had been in 1356 at Poitiers, when he had only been 12 years old.

If it sounds like William the younger was travelling light on his crossing from Dover to Calais, with his letter of exchange, £20 of expenses, two hired carriages (under 40 shillings each) and a yeoman, it's because he was. Lancaster's army intended to live off the land, which they did by raiding the French countryside and terrorising the peasants for nearly four months.[101] Laying waste to large swathes of the countryside became a dominant feature of all three phases of this campaign. As few actual engagements with Charles V and his forces as there were, the English army did face defensive attacks from the French peasants themselves, while the French army did little or nothing to assist them. In the third phase, according to the *Chronique Normande*, the English 'cut a swathe down the Norman coastline keeping within eight or nine leagues of the sea', and the fleet kept pace with the army's advancement, 'following its trail of fire and smoke'.[102]

Such tactics were common in medieval warfare, although discussions around how to treat non-combatants and whether (or rather, the circumstances under which) pillaging was acceptable was disputed by churchmen and military men themselves for centuries.[103] Geoffroi de Charny (d. 1356) was one such military careerist, a French knight and author of several works on chivalry. He criticised knights who plundered and pillaged 'without reason', and those who plundered and stole from the church, citing these as examples of unacceptable conduct in warfare.[104] Here, however, while the conduct of the English is decried in the *Chronique Normande*, it is fairly standard behaviour.

There were further battles in the campaigns that followed: the siege of Limoges in August of 1370 and the battle of Pontvaillan in the December of that same year; the naval battle of La Rochelle in 1372, and the battle of Chiset in 1373. Of these, is likely that Sir William took part in at least Limoges and Pontvaillan in 1370, as a closed letter[105] dated 26 September

1371 said that William was still 'abiding on the king's business in Aquitaine'.[106]

It is hard to say what long-lasting effect this campaign had on Sir William, if any. The brutality of the slash-and-burn approach to the French peasantry, the razing of farmsteads and actual engagements with the French army when they came, all must have had a psychological impact even if he was never wounded or physically hurt. What did this mean for his style of governance when he returned home, after a year of riding at will through France in the company of his peers who took what they pleased and left destruction in their wake? Did the pressure put upon him and his brother translate into a sense of entitlement, or a desire to prove himself? How did he treat his servants at home upon his return? How did he treat his wife? One may hazard that, since his murder involved his entire household staff, the answer to this may well have been: not well.

The military context of the 1369 campaign and the battles of the following year have not previously been considered when suggesting motives for the murder, perhaps because it is assumed that all men take war in their stride when living in a violent society, and violence was a normalised part of life. Human experience would point to this being untrue: individuals react differently to the same stimuli, and where we cannot reconstruct the emotional worlds of those in the past, we cannot assume that they went through their own experiences entirely unaffected. The reader is invited to bear this in mind for the moment, as when alternative interpretations of the evidence are put forward centring the servants themselves rather than the elite, it will become a relevant question.

Equally, if he was away for so many years – from 1368 to at least 1371 – then the servants' loyalties were more closely tied to their lady rather than their lord, and as for Maud herself, she had had little time to get to know her husband. While building his reputation and military career overseas, Sir William was left out of the constructions of power networks at home, most of which were formed through interpersonal alliances. This would prove costly.

Then, in 1370/71, there came another twist to the tale: while at Avignon, Sir William was himself arrested for murder. The victim was his own brother, Sir Nicholas the younger and while it was eventually ruled that Nicholas had died of natural causes, nothing more is heard of William until 1375.

Sir William's Death

There is no further mention of William in the government records from 1371 until his death in 1375. The details of his final, fateful night can be pieced together from the court records that followed, although medieval records do not preserve the witness testimonies, and so we are without many details that would give us a fuller picture of the case.

Firstly, like the man's life and personality, the exact date of his death is also obscured: the witnesses could not seem to recall accurately when the murder had taken place. Estimated dates ranged from early December 1374 to late April 1375, with the majority of guesses clustered in March, from the 5th to the 31st.

It is possible that the failure to accurately recall the nearest feast-day to the murder was psychological – a case of the collective and individual trauma playing tricks on their memories. However, since everyone involved pleaded 'not guilty' on all counts, it could also have been a deliberate ploy to obscure the time of death and attempt to undermine any witnesses from the locality who might come forward claiming they had heard or seen something suspicious. If a witness came forward claiming they remembered something about a day in April, for example, then what good was that to the jurors if the murder had taken place in early March? Similarly, if someone swore they had heard suspicious hoof beats one night in the middle of March, what good was this if the murder had actually happened towards the end of April?

It is also possible that the collective refusal to agree on a date was part of the attempt to 'prove' their innocence in the matter. The household steward Robert of Cletham, who held lands in his own right and probably lived outside of the manor, claimed that not only was he in no way guilty but also that he had no prior knowledge that the murder was going to take place. In Robert's indictment, the jurors thought the murder had taken place on 14 March 1375, but when his mistress Lady Maud was indicted, first for murder then for aiding and abetting the murder, the dates given were 5 March and 11 March, putting the murder around the start of Lent (Easter Sunday that year was 22 April).[107] She also pleaded not guilty on all counts.

What we can deduce from the conflicting testimony is a rough idea of when the couple spent time at Scotton. Instead of spending Easter at the family seat at Greasley or another of the Cantilupe manors, Sir William and Lady Maud chose to go to Lady Maud's manor of Scotton and spend time there instead. Scotton was not exactly an out-of-the-way place where nefarious deeds could be easily hidden away from the eyes of the locals. Archaeological evidence suggests that at this time it was a larger-than-average settlement with two manor houses, fishponds and a church, also consisting of farms and what could have been a village green on its south end.[108] Scotton manor was next to the church, and had been subinfeudated[109] to the local branch of the Neville family by Peterborough Abbey, and upon Maud Neville's marriage to William Cantilupe it had been given to her by her father. On this fateful occasion, visiting the manor to celebrate Christmas or Easter there had probably been Maud's suggestion. Whether or not William suspected anything, we will never know, but the bustle of the large village could have seemed reassuring; he had brought his squire along, and he slept with his chamber door locked.

We can deduce that they were living there before Christmas of 1374 as this is the earliest estimated date of the murder and would not have been suggested if the household had been elsewhere at the time. It is likely that it was suggested at first because they moved to another manor for Christmas itself or spent it as guests of friends or family, and so Sir William was not seen in Scotton over this period, and that they returned afterwards in the spring around Easter. This date is suggested once and then dropped from other indictments, suggesting that witnesses had testified to Sir William being alive after December. There would have been enough people to recall that he was absent from Scotton, since traditionally lords gave out special food to their tenants and servants at Christmas time and Christmas feasts and public community activities involving carollers, mummers and other such entertainments, were common.[110]

The estimates of his death all fall from the start of Lent to the day before Good Friday, which may mean no one saw him during the Holy Week celebrations when, as at Christmas, the lord would be present in church at the solemn masses and participate in feasts and celebrations.

While the question of 'when' is obscured by conflicting testimony, the 'who' enters Agatha Christie levels of intrigue akin to *Murder on the Orient Express*, and the 'why' is a mystery, the 'how' is, at least, more straight-forward.

Whichever night it was, Sir William and Lady Maud retired for bed. Either he or Lady Maud locked the bedchamber door, which may mean that he suspected something or just that they wanted privacy without servants bustling in to light the fire or disturb them with questions and reports. Sir William prepared himself for bed, undressed and apparently said his prayers: the jury were told he died 'at peace with God and the king'.[111] This detail may seem trivial or sentimental, but for the sake of Sir William's soul, it would have been important to know whether he had died 'at peace with God and the king' because he had not received the last rites. There is also a link to be drawn with the pious reputation of his grandfather, Sir Nicholas senior, and with the saintly Thomas de Cantilupe of Hereford, protecting the family's reputation and good name. Additionally, by painting her husband as a good and pious man who had been the victim of a terrible and apparently unprovoked attack at the hands of his treacherous servants, Lady Maud could gain the sheriff's (and the jury's) sympathy at the trauma she had experienced and throw suspicion away from herself. If she had testified that he was impious and brutal, that he had locked the door in order to 'discipline' her in a violent way, a motive for murder would be obvious even if the action was more understandable, and if convicted she still faced death by burning at the stake.

She could also, of course, have been telling the truth.

The choice of murder scene was a pragmatic but loaded one. Given Sir William's military record the best opportunity to overpower him was when he was unarmed and unsuspecting, not to mention in a private space where the act would not be witnessed. Similarly, if Lady Maud was not part of the plot, it was also a space where she could be controlled and threatened, which although not recorded as part of her defence would seem to be the obvious line to take in asserting her innocence. Alternatively, if Maud herself was the killer, it was the opportune moment to attack him. The bedchamber was the ideal site for all these reasons, as other medieval killers also found: in 1400, a woman called Agnes Cran killed her husband with an axe-blow to the head while he slept in his bed, when he was in a position to be overpowered and the deed could be done quickly without the aid of anyone else.[112]

The fact that 'diverse mortal blows' were inflicted suggests that he was stabbed either in a frenzied attack, or because his attackers were inexperienced and failed to strike a clean blow in the first instance. If Sir William tried to fight them off and was harder to subdue and kill than anticipated this would also account for multiple wounds, but the surviving records do not list where on the body these were. Given the state of decomposition that his body was in when discovered, there would have been difficulty in establishing this anyway.

At this point, someone unlocked the chamber door from the outside. John Barneby the chamberlain was repeatedly listed among the primary accused, but at the indictment of the chambermaid Agatha Frere it was found that it had been unlocked with *her* key, in full knowledge that her fellow-servants were going to enter the bedchamber and murder their master.

Sir William's assailant or assailants then crept in, surprising him, and subjected him to 'diverse mortal blows' while he lay unarmed on his bed. Who his attacker or attackers were, the jurors couldn't seem to agree.

To begin with, the servant Augustine Morpath's name appears first on the list of those accused. He is the very first person that the coroner William de Kirkton appealed in his initial report, followed by [Augustine] Warner and Richard Gyse.[113] In the *Curia Regis* records, Augustine Morpath is again consistently listed first, then Richard Gyse and Robert Cook were named along with John Barneby the chamberlain, and another servant, William de Hayle or de Hole. These men seem to have been the core five, appearing repeatedly in lists of the accused, but other indictments added to their number the names of other servants, such as John Henxteman, whose occupational surname suggests he was a stable groom, Augustine Forester, Augustine Warner, John Astyn, William (or Walter, a scribal error for the same servant) 'Chamberlainman' (confusingly *not* the chamberlain in this household), and Henry Tasker, who also appears on more than one list.

It was Lady Maud's testimony that the two main perpetrators were Robert Cook the butler and William's squire Richard Gyse, and not Augustine or the other servants, who then failed to arrive at court to conclude the trial, and so were declared outlaws. This is interesting since Augustine de Morpath seems to have been the primary suspect among the servants, and if Richard Gyse was Lady Maud's lover, as some scholars have assumed, singling him out over Morpath makes little sense. Either she was incredibly callous and manipulative, or forced to name him by the sheriff and second-husband-to-be Sir Thomas, *also* thought to be her [jealous?] lover in the traditional interpretation.

The anatomy of the household will be dissected further in the next chapter, where more general servant profiles will be taken into consideration in order to paint a more complete picture of who these people were, and what part they might have played in the crime.

After the perpetrators gained access via Agatha's key and slipped into the room to subject their lord to a vicious attack, they stripped him of his bloody night clothes, while one or more of his assailants or their accomplices – again, it is unclear who – went back downstairs through the house, drew cold water from the well in the manor's courtyard and carried the bucket to the kitchen where the water was boiled. This would have taken some time. The boiled water was then carried through the manor up to his room, where the body was washed to stem the bleeding. Once sure that the wounds would not bleed and give them away, William's naked body was bundled into a sack, presumably procured from the kitchens or the stables, and carried out of the manor. At least one, but more likely two horses were brought out and saddled. The body was slung onto one of the horses and transported to a suitable location. This accounts for the stable groom being accused with the others: it seems unlikely that servants whose job revolved around the care and protection of their master's horses would not have known when one was taken.

Under cover of darkness, Sir William's body was transported from Scotton to Grayingham, a distance of 4 or 5 miles. There he was dumped in a field, where the next part of the plan was put in place. Once at a suitable location, not too close to the village to be seen or arouse suspicion, his naked corpse was pulled from the sack and completely re-dressed in his riding clothes including a belt, boots and spurs, so that anyone coming upon it would think that Sir William had been murdered by unknown highwaymen on the road.[114] The squire's job was to dress William in his armour, and so he would have been used to this task – another mark against Richard Gyse, as far as the jury were concerned.

It is no wonder that the jury was clear on the fact that it was a premeditated act, even if they had no clear idea who was to blame. It was highly unlikely that such a plan could have been carried out by only two men, and even less likely that no-one else in the house was aware of what was going on.

The manor was promptly closed up that very night, the servants dismissed and scattered. Sir William's wife Maud immediately undertook the journey to Caythorpe, some 40 miles away, accompanied by her chambermaid and Sir William's squire, Richard Gyse. Here, they were sheltered by Sir Ralph Paynell until William's body was discovered and the case came to trial.

It is a sad fact that we know more about the circumstances of Sir William's final hour than we do about most of his life. While this is not uncommon, it is difficult when piecing together the evidence from a murder trial.

Was Sir William a victim of his own absenteeism and ambition? While he was abroad on the king's business, the traditional view posits that all kinds of things were going on behind his back, including his wife's extramarital affairs, the creation and consolidation of friendship networks among his peers that would support and create the background to his murder, and the eroding of his servants' loyalties towards him, a lord they barely knew.

Was Sir William a bad master and/or husband, returning from war a changed man (or finding that his experiences had brought out latent negative traits and developed them further)? Was this the reason for Lady Maud's affairs (if she had any at all) and the motivation for either the local elite to plot and support his murder or for the servants to take things into their own hands?

In order to explore these and other possibilities, a fuller consideration of the suspects and their potential motives is required, along with some comparative cases of spousal murder, feuds between members of the knightly class, other household conspiracies and squires killing their knights.

Chapter 3

The Indicted Suspects

'*Every murder turns on a bright hot light, and a lot of people have to walk out of the shadows*'

Mark Hellinger

This chapter will look at the individuals indicted either for Sir William's murder or for aiding and abetting it. The challenges of such biographical sketches are many, particularly when the trial records are the only place some of these people are mentioned and no other records exist to tell us anything of their lives. Even Sir William himself, for all the information we have regarding the times in which he lived, is a shadowy and obscure figure.

For this reason, the offices these people held and duties they performed will be considered more broadly alongside examples of similar cases where wives murdered their husbands, nobles killed one another, and servants of various descriptions conspired against their masters. This will help to contextualise the accusations and build up a fuller picture of their daily lives.

Maud Neville: The Wife

Maud Neville was of a cadet line of the influential Neville family, whose branches are awash with Mauds, Roberts and Ralphs in the same way that the Cantilupes had a habit of passing on the names William and Nicholas. Consequently, there is some confusion regarding Maud's branch among genealogists and historians. Some take the antiquarians Robert Thoroton and John Nichols' lineage as correct (Maud as the daughter of Sir Phillip Neville and his wife Sara, a knight from a cadet line of the family settled in Lincolnshire).[1] Charles R. Young, in his study on the main branch of the family, *The Making of the Neville Family 1166–1400*, does not mention

Maud or any of her three marriages, first to William Cantilupe, then to Thomas de Kydale, then to John Bussey, and indeed the only place Maud would fit on his family tree would be as daughter of Phillip Neville, son of Phillip Neville of Lincolnshire. Other scholars, like R. Bevan, have some reservations about the ages of the respective Phillips, and believe she is instead the granddaughter or even niece of Phillip, and the daughter of Sir Robert Neville and Jane (or Joan) D'Eyncourt or Deincourt.[2] The Deincourts were knights of Lincolnshire and Nottinghamshire too, and good cross-county matches for the local Nevilles and Cantilupes.[3]

It does appear, however, that Maud as daughter of Phillip Neville is the most likely option. Sir Phillip Neville 'of Scotton' was active in 1338, providing the Chancery Inquisition of that year at Lincoln with ten sacks of wool for cloth-making, his contribution to the wool tax of 1327–48.[4] This indicates that he was of full age and possessed of his lands and rents by this time. This would make him old enough to be Maud's father if she was a similar age to Sir William and also born *c.* 1344. Phillip also held one knight's fee in 'Torryng and Westden' directly of the Duke of Lancaster, John of Gaunt, which meant that he owed the duke knightly service and would have accompanied Lancaster overseas when called upon to do so.[5]

Since Phillip is active in 1338, Maud could well have been born before 1344 and be several years older than her first husband. Such an age gap would have been beneficial to the younger knight, since Lady Maud would have been trained by her mother to run a household and have some experience while she waited for her betrothed to reach his majority. This was just the kind of wife he needed if he was going overseas for a few years to build his military career and reputation, and could have suited him very well, but it may not have suited Lady Maud.

In 1345, there is mention of both Sir Phillip Neville ('*chivaler*') and Richard Neville 'of Scotton', most likely Maud's cousin, instructed to undertake a commission of the peace along with Sir Adam de Everingham of Rockley and John de Hundon.[6] Sir Phillip is listed first followed by Sir Adam, indicating that he and Sir Adam are the two most prominent men on the list, with Richard and John following in that order, neither designated as knights. Elsewhere regarding this same commission he is listed as 'Richard de Nevill [sic], parson of the church of Scotton', and it would be highly unusual for a son and heir to go into the church rather than take over his father's manors, making it more likely that he is Sir Phillip's nephew or a cousin of some description.[7]

That this Richard Neville is required to undertake such a commission is something of a surprise: he had been the parson of Scotton since at least 1297, and his time there had more parallels with the Coterels and their nefarious clerical associates than the family may care to admit. In 1339, Richard, along with kinsmen John Neville and William Neville, were threatened with arrest for certain 'felonies and misdeeds'.[8] The king first ordered his men and serjeants-at-arms to arrest these three Nevilles and bring them to Newgate gaol to be imprisoned there by the sheriffs of London, but then several knights from the relevant counties – Simon de Drayton of Northamptonshire, William de Claworth of Nottinghamshire, William Wade of Leicestershire and Roland Daneys of Lincolnshire, mainperned them to prevent their arrest and promised 'to have Richard and the others before the king and his justices to answer for their excesses, and that they will behave themselves well'. This, apparently, was a success as far as Richard was concerned.

If Maud was Phillip's daughter then she had lost him by 1366,[9] meaning that unlike her sister-in-law she had no father to whom she could appeal if her marriage proved unsatisfactory or if her husband was cruel to her. As her father had no sons, Maud and her younger sister inherited everything between them.[10]

Another kinsman, Roger Neville of Redburn, Lincolnshire, was also dead by 1357, and Peter Neville was his heir – this is potentially the branch to which Richard the parson of Scotton belonged.[11] What is interesting here is that although there were other Nevilles active in Lincolnshire through these decades, Maud's closest friendships were with the Paynells, her neighbours, with Sir Ralph acting in a fatherly capacity after Sir William's murder.

The relationship between these branches of the Nevilles and the Paynells goes back to at least the previous century. When Phillip Paynell, the son and heir of John Paynell and Katherine his wife, wanted to claim his inheritance in the December of 1290, the inquest held to determine if he was of full age to inherit featured testimony from a William Neville who supported Phillip and testified that he was indeed of age.[12] It is therefore unsurprising to see the proceeding generations still moving in one another's circles, supporting each other and the historic bonds of alliance between their families. Crucially, Phillip Neville, the son and heir of Robert Neville lord of Scotton, enfeoffed his own son Phillip (Maud's father) with the manors and advowsons of Scotton and Malmeton, Lincolnshire. The grant was witnessed by several knights of the shire, including Sir Ralph Paynell.[13] This is the grant that confuses the issue of the dates. The grant claims to date from 1316 although it is torn and in a poor condition, and the one immediately above it is dated from the fourteenth regnal year of Edward III (1340–41). The one immediately below is dated from the sixth regnal year of Edward III (1332–33), so it makes more sense that this date is an error. Positioned between the fourteenth and sixth year of Edward III, it is likely that this grant dated from somewhere between this period, and the torn fragment and poor condition of the grant is responsible for the mistake. 1316 was the ninth or tenth regnal year of Edward II, which ran from 8 July (the date of his coronation) to 7 July. It would make more sense that this was the ninth or tenth regnal year of Edward III which ran from 25 January – 24 January, so either 1335 or 1336. This solves the problem of the relative ages of the two Sir Phillips of Scotton, and if Lady Maud's father was of full age by 1335, i.e. 21, then she could have been as much as nine years older than her husband, Sir William.

While on the surface this does not make a lot of difference in adulthood (she would have been 39 at the time of his death in 1375, when he was aged 30), Maud would have spent her entire adolescence waiting for her prospective husband to grow up. By the time he was 18, she would have been 27, and perhaps, as in the case of 16-year-old Joanna Malcake, she had not been patient. If this were the case, then not only could the traditional interpretation of the Cantilupe case be correct, but the seeds of resentment could have been sown in these earlier years, waiting on just the right catalyst and set of circumstances (perhaps including the close association with a certain felonious parson of Scotton) to flower into murder.

While the parson of Scotton is not mentioned in the trial records in any aiding-and-abetting capacity, Richard Neville, who by 1375 would have been in his mid-forties to sixties, did not abandon his kinswoman after her husband's death. He and Robert Constable were the two men who gave pledges for her appeal against the murder charge.[14] Robert Constable seems to have been a kinsman of Sir Marmaduke Constable, a sheriff of Yorkshire in the 1360s and in the same socio-legal circle as Sir Ralph Paynell, but this connection will be considered more fully later on.

Being an heiress or co-heiress, even of a modest inheritance, made a young lady a valuable asset to another family, but also enabled them to participate in the elite gentry culture that had been forged throughout the preceding centuries. Unfortunately, where Lady Maud is concerned, we have even less biographical detail than for her husband, and must draw upon more general examples of life as a fourteenth-century lady to get an idea of her quality of life and the lifestyle available to her.

Elite women like Maud could engage in various pastimes, become patrons of art and literature, and develop their own iconography for their personal seals.[15] Some men adopted the surnames of their more illustrious wives, while others absorbed the prestige of their ladies' families by adopting their coats of arms.[16] In this case, a cadet line of the illustrious Nevilles marrying into a cadet branch of the once-courtly Cantilupes, this was a case of a mutually beneficial marriage where both families could bask in the reflected prestige of the other. Frustratingly, no seal of this Maud survives, so it is not possible to see if she adopted her husband's arms or used them in conjunction with her father's emblems, two common choices among ladies of the knightly elite. By the fourteenth century there was considerable freedom as to which relationships were shown and how: Margaret de Umfraville's seal of 1328 depicted two shields for her parents, Thomas de Clare and Juliana Fitz Maurice, set at the right and left (dexter and sinister) of the seal, flanking a shield impaling the arms of her two late husbands, Giles de Umfraville (d. 1303) and Bartholomew de Badlesmere (d. 1322).[17] The choice of iconography on seals and counterseals offers a glimpse into the ways in which ladies chose to present their identity, and given the circumstances of Maud's first widowhood, the lack of any *representamen* of hers is a regrettable gap in the evidence around this case. Although male influence must have had a part to play in the choices of such seals, it is likely that women did have at least some choice in the way they wanted to represent themselves.

The Nevilles of Scotton were therefore lower status relations to the main branches of the Neville family, who rose to prominence in Henry III's reign. According to William Berry's *Encyclopaedia Heraldica*, the Nevilles of Scotton did have their own arms aside from those of their more illustrious kin, this featuring red, silver and gold (gules, argent and or) and three fusils (elongated lozenges).[18] Aside from the main branch who were close to Edward III and moved in royal circles, there was another cadet line who were less successful at negotiating the financial and political worlds of the upper echelons of society. A contemporary cousin of some ilk to Maud's father, Robert II de Neville (*fl.* 1344–1373) had a promising career of administrative and military service ahead of him until he ran into serious financial difficulties.[19] He married off his son Robert III (d. 1413) to the sister of the future earl of Suffolk, whose father, Sir William de la Pole, was a merchant and royal financier. The de la Poles may have been behind the difficulties that Robert II found himself in. By 1355 he was imprisoned in Newgate as a debtor and was released in 1362 after clearing some of his debts but was then committed to Fleet prison.[20] Things did not appear to improve until 1367, when his property in Kent was restored to him. His son, Robert III, also embarked on a career in royal service. Robert III entered the service of Edward, the Black Prince, and served overseas with the prince's brother, John of Gaunt.[21] He managed to keep himself out of the financial difficulties of his unfortunate father and was associated with several leading northern magnates and was employed as the steward of two Archbishops of York, Alexander Neville – another kinsman of his and part of the more influential main branch of the family – and Thomas Arundel.[22] Archbishop Alexander had two brothers, Ralph and John Neville, both of whom also served overseas with Edward III and John of Gaunt. Ralph Neville formed part of a group of councillors who were close to Edward III and was instrumental in defeating David II of Scotland in the wars against the Scots. According to the Lannercost chronicler, Ralph Neville was a powerful man, brave, cunning and much to be feared.[23] His brother John's son – another Ralph (*c.* 1364–1425) – became the first earl of Westmorland.[24]

Several of the prominent women in this family were named Maud, indicating that our Maud Neville was named in honour of her more powerful kinswomen, just as the men were named in honour of their male kin.

Maud's own branch of the family had nothing like the power or affluence enjoyed by their exalted kinsfolk in the royal court, but were respected in the county on their own merit as well as for their connection to their more powerful kin. Maud's manors bolstered Cantilupe fortunes and increased their control in Lincolnshire. It is unclear whether Joan Kymas, William's step-grandmother, was responsible for making this match: Frederik Pedersen posits that she was behind the match between his older brother Nicholas and Katherine Paynell, daughter of Ralph Paynell.[25]

After Nicholas the third lord Cantilupe's death in 1355 and with his son out of the succession, the two young co-heirs – aged 13 and 11 respectively – needed protection. Nicholas's second wife Joan evidently looked to the most powerful and influential men in the county to provide this security for her two vulnerable step-grandsons, and if she thought Ralph Paynell was one, then she may also have considered the local Neville branch with its sole heiresses as another.[26] Maud was to marry the younger brother, of course, and despite the estate being split equally between the two boys, her relative importance to Katherine Paynell was slightly less in terms of the potential manors she brought with her and the influence of her immediate kin.

Maud's position as coheiress to a minor branch of a powerful family put her in a difficult position. On the one hand, it made her a desirable match for a Cantilupe heir, and on the other, it made her vulnerable to rapacious families looking for a way to climb the social ladder in their locality. With her husband away from 1368–71, Lady Maud would have found her freedoms more curtailed by his return than she had done by his attorneys, with whom she did not have to live on a daily basis. William's absenteeism during this time is very likely another underlying factor that eroded loyalties and trust, or at least shifted them from him to his wife, who was present in the county and could therefore take an active role in its socio-political dynamics on her own merit.

Was this reason alone to have her husband murdered?

As a widow, one might expect her status to come with increased freedom once more, but in fact, her economic and social vulnerability returned.

The chronicler Jacques de Voraigne told of a rich widow who refused to remarry because she intimated that a woman with a good husband lived in fear of his death, while a woman with a bad husband lived in fear of his unprovoked violence.[27] While some widows in better economic positions refused to remarry, not all of them were given a choice in the matter, either by their kin or their own circumstances.

After William's murder, Maud married widower Thomas de Kydale, then sheriff of Lincolnshire. Sir Thomas died in 1381 during the Peasants' Revolt, killed by the rebels, leaving his son Thomas from his first marriage (then aged 20 or more) as his son and heir.[28] Maud almost immediately married John Bussey or Busshy in 1382, a relative of Sir Ralph Paynell, and John outlived her. A close associate of King Richard II, he was executed for his role in the young king's Tyranny in 1399.[29] John Bussey was already known to her, and at this time was an influential man in the county. Her progressively impressive marriages certainly increased her status in the county, with her dower from William's estate providing her with a comfortable amount of rent to live on. She did not get the king's permission to remarry either Thomas or John, and each time permission was retrospectively sought and a modest fine paid. Together, John and Maud filed for assignment of Cantilupe lands in Yorkshire which Maud argued she should have received as part of her dower. John's father, John Bussey senior, had been demised of Cantilupe lands himself before his death. In this case, Sir Michael de la Pole, who became chancellor the following year, mediated for the couple and they were awarded these lands.[30] It is worth recalling the Neville connection with the de la Poles: Michael's sister was married to Robert III de Neville, a kinsman of Maud's. Whether these men spoke to King Edward III in private on her behalf during the trial, we do not know, but it is likely that she had their support in order to be acquitted of all charges.

While her first husband was away on campaign with her own relatives, Maud was given charge of the household. If her marriages are any indication, she was a shrewd, ambitious woman with an eye for social climbing. Personally she must not have been without her charms, not least because of her lands and income and influential kin, but also something about her that attracted Thomas Kydale to her in the first place. It is useful here to note that if there was a plot between the two of them to murder William and marry, the motive was not her dower. Maud did not claim her dower after William's death, not making any plea for what she was rightfully owed.[31] This could be a sign of a guilty conscience, or just a desire to put the ordeal behind her. It was her third husband, the ambitious climber John Bussey, who would seem to be the prime mover in the successful appeal for these manors in 1382, after Richard II pardoned them for marrying without the king's licence.[32]

For John Bussey to marry her so swiftly after Thomas Kydale's death, without getting royal permission beforehand, it is likely that he knew her previously or had done for some time. In fact, he was the son of Isabel Paynell, whose kinsman Sir Ralph was up to his eyes in the Cantilupe case and had already sheltered Maud and demonstrated his concern for her in this way after Sir William's murder. Carole Rawcliffe, in her biography of John Bussey for *The History of Parliament*, assumes that Maud was the mastermind of William's murder and that she had seduced the main perpetrator (singular, so presumably meaning Richard Gyse), although no source is provided to support this theory.[33]

John Bussey's political opponents referred to him as a 'most cruel man, ambitious beyond measure' (*vir crudelissimus, ambitiosus supra modum*).[34] For the sake of his first and second wives it is to be hoped that this was either an exaggeration or referred to his professional life rather than his personal one. Either way, Maud's third marriage was the most ambitious of the three, and a definite step up in terms of influence. The Busseys were also part of the Lincolnshire elite, and John Bussey senior had held lands of William's grandfather Nicholas. The speed at which John the younger sought to marry Maud indicates that the murder of her first husband – of which he was surely aware – was of no consequence to him, and it certainly had done no harm to Maud's material prospects. Its impact upon her as a person, however, is information which is unavailable to us. It's this lack of personal information that should lead to caution in interpreting the evidence that we do have.

The Medieval Wife as Murderess
Homicidal wives killed their husbands in a variety of ways, although poison became the stereotypical form of murder. In seventeenth-century Italy, Giuila Tofana is credited with creating an odourless, tasteless

poison, 'Aqua Tofana', which she sold to women who were desperate to get out of their loveless and often abusive marriages. In the trial of 1658, she stood accused of poisoning around six hundred men by selling this poison to numerous clients over a twenty-year period.[35] One of the most prolific known serial killers, Tofana was a 'professional poisoner'. This type of husband-killer was not a Renaissance phenomenon: in late-medieval Bologna, for example, female poisoners were also active, with several incidents involving arsenic poisoning recorded in trials throughout the fifteenth century.[36] Yet cases where the wife physically assaulted the husband were not unheard of, if rarer.

In Renaissance England, the 'murderous wife' was represented and debated in an array of printed texts and was 'exposed' on stage in numerous theatrical productions.[37] Yet prior to this increasing interest and public discussion of such a subversive figure, evidence for murderous wives in the earlier centuries are surprisingly sparse given the high homicide rates.

Less work has been done on the medieval period pre-fifteenth century, but it is well-known that, just as at every other period of history, medieval wives did sometimes murder their husbands, although statistically were far more likely to be murdered by them.

In 1316, a court decided that Sir Thomas Murdak was murdered by his wife Juliana, allegedly at the instigation of Sir John Vaux. Vaux was imprisoned in the Tower of London but was acquitted of the charge and released, while Juliana was found guilty and burned.[38]

The author of an English chronicle pauses in his account of treason to illustrate his concerns with the somewhat distorted account of a woman who instigated her lover, a priest, to murder her husband, in 1388.[39] Compared with the trial record for the King's Bench, the chronicler made some key changes to the account, and placed it in the middle of a passage discussing treason. More than an aside or an interruption, it highlights the fourteenth-century emphasis on petty treason as an act undermining the social order, and the effectiveness of the household for purposes of social control.[40] The case in question actually occurred in 1387, and was the murder of Andrew Wauton by his servants with the full backing of his wife, Elizabeth.

Two of Andrew's servants, Robert Blake, *capellanus* (chaplain) and John Ball, were convicted of murder and hanged, while Elizabeth Wauton was tried and convicted for 'consent and aid' and was burned on the 24 June 1387.[41]

The trial records report that:

Robert and John ... lay in hiding at [Andrew's manor of] Hinton Daubeney in order to kill him, and did kill him feloniously and treasonably, and the same Robert and John on various earlier occasions lay in wait at a footpath called Godwinspath in a field called Compsfield in order to kill him [and others] ... and they planned to throw them into a well near Compsfield. They are common waylayers and despoilers in these fields and roads and common thieves and traitors to the king's people and to their master Andrew. Said Elizabeth gave consent and aid to the killing of Andrew her husband.[42]

It should be noted, as Paul Strohm does in his assessment of the case, that aiding and abetting male accomplices was the customary charge for women in such cases, either because this was the woman's actual role, or because the male-dominated court space could not imagine them acting in any other way.[43]

The Westminster Chronicler, referencing this trial, changes the details to focus on the adultery committed by Elizabeth with chaplain Robert Blake, a 'priest' in the chronicler's narrative. It is unlikely that Robert Blake was in fact a fully ordained priest, but more likely that he was one of the many clerks in the fourteenth century without full-time ecclesiastical employment, and his position as chaplain to the household seems to have carried the same kind of suspicion with which chauffeurs and gamekeepers are afforded in twentieth-century fiction.[44]

In the Westminster Chronicle's version, placed in the middle of an account of the 1388 treason trials, the 'priest' had an affair with 'a woman of good family' and was incited to kill her husband by her persuasive words. The chronicler alleged that 'The two were quickly seized one morning, as the dawn was just breaking, sleeping in the same bed.'[45] Here, the chronicler reveals their own thoughts on treason and in particular its moral dimension, by likening it to adultery and the breaking of both marriage vows and ecclesiastical vows. The mention of the 'crazed priest' also illustrates the belief in this case that treason was an unnatural act committed by disturbed (male) individuals, incited by others or by the devil. This ecclesiastical viewpoint underlines the ways treason was conceptualised, while the actual facts of the case indicate something more mundane: that these two men were 'common waylayers and despoilers' and thieves, willing to kill for material gain and not worry too much about the identity of their victims. Money is the implied motive in the court records where no actual motive is stated, although the Westminster Chronicle cites sex and lust. It could well have been both. Either way, as in the 1316 case of Juliana Murdak, Elizabeth Wauton was convicted and burned, although Robert and John were hanged whereas Sir John Vaux, accused of instigating Thomas Murdak's murder, was released and eventually acquitted after a period of incarceration.

Neither are these two incidents the only examples of a wife killing her husband with help: there are many other examples of women of the mercantile and crafts or tradesperson classes, if not of the gentry, being indicted or convicted of aiding in the murder of their husbands. Mary Hamel cites a case in Yorkshire, 1377, where a merchant's wife and a chaplain were indicted for the murder of the merchant, but they were not convicted in this case.[46] Hamel also cites a Middlesex case of 1379 where a cordwainer was murdered and his (male) servant and his wife were both convicted of petty treason. The servant was hanged, while she was burned. A London chronicle composed in the fifteenth century also gives an account of a 'treasonous' wife, which could well be an imagined version of the Wauton case, supplanted in this retelling to 1390 London, since it hits all the same narrative details (the adultery, the wife's incitement to murder 'a goode man' and the enlisting of servants to do the deed) and includes the same set of characters and the same outcome. This man is murdered in his bed at night, which also has strong overtones of the Cantilupe case. Paul Strohm considers the possibility that this is an imagined episode, saying that it seemed 'to be generated from within a whole culture's project of female subordination and [said project's] accompanying guilt and not to belong to any one historical moment or locale.'[47]

The Gaol Delivery Records for 1389–91 also reveal some relevant cases. Agnes Milner and three servants, who may have been members of her husband's family, slew her husband in his own home while he sat in a chair by the fire. They were drawn and hanged and she was burned.[48] Juliana Danker was burned for slaying her husband Thomas Danker with the help and advice of others; Thomas was wounded in the stomach with a knife and had his neck broken by a club, apparently by Juliana herself.[49] Alice Pyrye was also burned and her two male accomplices hanged for the murder of her husband John Pyrye, killed at night.[50]

In a case that bears some strong parallels to the Cantilupe murder, Joan Picard, wife of William Picard, procured two men, one Stephen Carter and one John Taverner of Atherstone, Warwickshire, William's servants, to murder her husband on 1 December 1379. Stephen came to William's hall at Goldington, Bedfordshire, and struck the unsuspecting William in the head with an axe while he sat in his chair, so that he fell forwards into the fire. Not content with that, Stephen then grabbed a trenchour (a knife used for eating) from the table and stabbed William through the heart, 'of which he immediately died'.[51] In this case, the plot was revealed by John Taverner, who turned approver in the presence of the sheriff, Sir Giles Dawbeny, and the coroners, William Frensch and William de Fancott, and confessed to the murder on 18 July 1380. Others with whom Joan was said to have acted, including John Clerc [clerk] of Willingham and Adam 'Irysch' [Irish] and John Irish, among others, were outlawed.[52] In this instance, Joan was pardoned for her part in the murder on 20 November 1381 and was released from prison.[53] Joan had the king's esquire John Peytevyn, to intercede for her, and the pardon was granted at his supplication.[54]

Here we have a similar case of a household group acting against their master at night when he was at his most vulnerable, unarmed and at home. That it took an axe-blow to the head, burns from the fire and a direct stab to the heart to kill Sir William Picard is evidence of the clumsy and somewhat inept way this murder was carried out, but also explains there being so many people involved. Killing someone trained in combat from the age of 14 is not an easy feat, and far less so without practice. These servants were not warriors, nor were they professional trained killers. Theirs may have been a society in which violence was normalised, but it was the violence of arguments and brawls, not the cold-blooded business of assassination. A carter and a taverner were hardly well-skilled at handling blades in this way, as they discovered when they somehow failed to kill Sir William outright with the axe.

Similarly, corralling Sir William de Cantilupe the younger and killing him in a bedroom with a blade was not the work of one person, but the work of a group acting together. What makes the Cantilupe case more interesting is the sheer number of people involved. While typically a few (male) accomplices were drawn into spousal murder plots, this case has Maud Cantilupe persuading her entire household to kill their master on her behalf. This will be considered more fully [and challenged] in following chapters when motives are discussed in more detail, and the alternative conclusions are presented.

Sir Ralph Paynell: The Angry Neighbour

Sir Ralph Paynell was among the most influential men of the county at the time of Nicholas, third lord Cantilupe's death. Knowing this, Nicholas's widow, Joan Kymas, who had custody of the lands until the two boys came of age, brokered a marital alliance between her step-grandson Nicholas, the oldest of the two coheirs, and Ralph's daughter Katherine, while Katherine was still under-age.[55] The age of consent was 12, and Nicholas was 13, so Katherine must have been a few years younger than him. The marriage itself was not formally contracted until Katherine came of full age, around 18.

Sir Ralph was of a cadet line of the main branch of the family who failed in the male line in the thirteenth century. Two branches continued: the Paynells of Broughton, and the Paynells of Boothby Pagnell, both based in Lincolnshire. In fact, John Bussey's mother Isabel was the daughter of John Paynell of Boothby, a kinsman of Sir Ralph, which may indicate that Sir Ralph had a guiding hand in Maud's third and final marriage.[56] The main branch of the Paynells had had dealings with the main branch of the Cantilupes before: William II de Cantilupe (d. 1251), as steward of Henry III, had received the custody and marriage of William Paynell, then a minor, in 1248.[57]

The family themselves were an old and well-established one, who diligently passed along the name 'Ralph' through the generations in the same way that the Cantilupes passed along the names 'William' and

'Nicholas'. While the first Cantilupes recorded in England appear in the Domesday Book as tenants of Roger de Courseilles of Calvados, holding Bruton in Somerset, and not even important enough to warrant the locative surname being recorded,[58] Sir Ralph Paynell was both a landholder and a tenant-in-chief of multiple manors across the Midlands in 1086.[59] While the Paynells were more important than the Cantilupes in these early days of the Norman pioneers, the Cantilupes spread further afield and climbed higher by virtue of their later association with the young prince John, whose ascent to the throne in 1199 guaranteed them a place in the royal household and the benefits of the king's patronage, something that the Paynells missed out on.

However, in terms of local influence, the Paynell centre of power was always in Lincolnshire and south Yorkshire, which the first-recorded Sir Ralph Paynell of the Domesday Book variously held of Earl Morcar, Grimkil of Wold Newton, Thorkil of Stoke hundred and Grimkil of Sturton, but the vast majority of manors in Lincolnshire and Yorkshire he held of the sheriff Mærleswein.[60] Meanwhile, Roger, 'the man of Ralph Paynell', was the 1086 subtenant of Stoke, Northamptonshire, which he held of Thorkil of Stoke hundred.[61] The Paynell family's historic influence in these shires left their mark on them. Moving forwards in time through the reigns of William the Conqueror, his successor William Rufus and Henry I to the turbulent days of King Stephen, the Paynells can be found in the records as supporters of the Empress Maud. Maud rewarded the Ralph Paynell of her day by giving him the town of Nottingham, and he followed her to London and Oxford in the summer of 1141.[62] Ralph and William Paynell both appear as witnesses on Maud's charters, with William Paynell of Drax having connections to Shropshire.[63] Paynell influence was spreading as the family itself extended outwards. By the fourteenth century, the Paynells retained their influence and power in their Lincolnshire heartlands, and that made this Ralph Paynell with whom we are concerned one of the most important local magnates with whom to make an alliance.

Sir Ralph had been a sheriff of Yorkshire himself and was a retainer of the Black Prince through the 1360s.[64] In 1355, he was indicted to answer for his excesses during this shrieval term alongside his associates Edward de Cornwall and Norman de Swynford.[65] This wasn't the last time: he appeared in court several times to answer for his excesses during his term as sheriff, which paints a picture of a man not to be trifled with, and, as Pedersen puts it, something of 'a loose cannon'.[66]

In November 1360, Ralph went before the king to answer for 'entertaining' John Courcy and John of Scotton who were accused of killing Roger de Keleby. On this occasion Sir Ralph surrendered himself to the king's presence, and it was soon dealt with.[67]

The connection with the Neville manor of Scotton is worth noting. On the surface, it appears that Ralph already knew men from the manor well before 1375 and had sheltered killers before, ultimately with little or no consequences. Digging deeper, a more interesting picture emerges. In this case, Roger de Keleby had been Sir Ralph's own servant, and was travelling by night to Broughton (North Lincolnshire), near to the Cantilupe-held manor of Raventhorpe, when a quarrel broke out between himself and John Turgy [of Scotton]. Roger, thinking John to be an enemy of Sir Ralph's because of a previous disagreement, drew his baselard (described in the inquisition as a 'long knife', but is more commonly described as a dagger or short sword), and chased John and his servant Walter as far as 'Calwehulles', which was located near Broughton, about an hour away on foot. They fought, and John of Scotton was maimed. Realising that he had nowhere left to flee, John pulled out his own knife and stabbed his assailant in the stomach in self-defence.[68] Roger de Keleby died of that injury.

Sir Ralph appeared to be forgiving under the circumstances, since he 'entertained' John at his manor later and was willing to come before the king to explain his reasons for doing so.

How to square this picture of a forgiving and apparently fair-minded master with the idea of a man willing to mastermind a murder, as Pedersen has suggested?

Firstly and most obviously, forgiving someone for killing your servant in self-defence is a very different scenario to dealing with the family of a man who once incarcerated and threatened your daughter. Sir Ralph was not likely to treat the kin of Sir Nicholas the younger in the same way, when his wound was more personal. Sir Ralph was far more likely to support Lady Maud in the same way that he had supported Katherine, and it is possible that he felt guilty for not believing her at the very start of the marriage. Had the marriage simply been quietly annulled at the start then none of the later trauma and unpleasantness need have occurred. If Lady Maud was unhappy in her marriage to the younger Cantilupe brother and begged Sir Ralph for help, this was a raw nerve that she could attempt to use in her favour.

Feuds between Members of the Knightly Class
Feuds between members of the elite were most common in the borderlands of Wales and Scotland, where the Cantilupes' ancestors had themselves been embroiled in bitter, violent disputes over castles and lands. Such disputes in the twelfth and thirteenth centuries were not only between the Anglo-Normans and the native Welsh and Scottish rulers and leaders, but also between the Anglo-Normans themselves who could and did wage private war upon one another.[69] Arguably, lords behaved in this way because they knew they could get away with it, and when given the chance in lands under the king's firmer control, behaved in very similar ways, as far as they were able.

In 1224, the Essex branch of the Cantilupes (whose descendants were still present in that county in the fourteenth century) were embroiled in a feud with the Goldinghams, another family of gentry status. The feud started when Peter de Cantilupe, then on the king's service in Scotland, had a complaint made against him by Hugh de Goldingham, recorded that year in the *Curia Regis* rolls for Trinity term (June to July).[70] In the next term (Michaelmas, October to December) another, extended entry is recorded. In this extended version, Hugh de Cantilupe (Peter's father, perhaps) is the petitioner against John de Goldingham, claiming that John owed him service as a tenant. John came to court and recognised there that he did indeed owe Hugh de Cantilupe rent for the lands he held of him, agreed to resume paying the modest 12 pence per year that was due, and that seemed to be that.[71]

However, Peter de Cantilupe and Hugh de Goldingham were still deadlocked in their case. Hugh de Goldingham's case against Peter is now listed as a complaint that Peter broke the king's peace – that is, had attacked Hugh de Goldingham in some way, or committed a (usually violent) crime against him. This could be an attack on his person, or livestock theft or a form of violent trespass. The details are unrecorded in these rolls. Peter didn't show up to court but provided an excuse for his absence, so another date was set to hear the case – which Peter again failed to attend.[72] While we don't know the details, sometime between Michalemas term 1224 and mid-1225, the conflict between the two families escalated. Yet it wasn't Peter, already charged with breaking the king's peace, who committed murder: it was Hugh de Cantilupe who killed John de Goldingham, despite having had their case settled in Hugh's favour.[73] Hugh de Cantilupe's lands were taken into the king's hands as forfeit and he was hanged for this crime, but confusingly is called 'Roger' in the chronicle account of the murder. The *Annales Monastici* claims that in 1225, 'Rogerus de Cantilupo', [as opposed to 'Hugonis'] a noble knight of Essex, was accused of an infraction of the king's peace, and he was hanged while his son [unnamed here but Hugh's son was either Peter or another William] was outlawed.[74] The monastic author of this may have deliberately mis-written the name 'Roger', since another chronicle, the *Chronica Majora*, complains about Roger de Cantilupe, legate, whose authority was questioned by the bishops he was charged with reprimanding. Evidently not popular with his fellow ecclesiastics, Roger had been tasked with telling off the bishops for their closeness to the regent, Earl William Marshal, no doubt siding with the anti-Marshal faction in court headed by the young king's tutor, the unpopular Bishop Peter des Roches.

This had not gone down well. Bishop Alexander of Coventry and Lichfield had responded scathingly to this, pointing out that the king's own legal representative was himself the son of a traitor who had been hung for his felony.[75] This slur against Roger the papal legate could account for the change of name in the *Ann. Mon.* account, although 'treason' in this context probably referred to 'breaking the king's peace [by committing murder]' rather than plotting against the king himself, since Hugh de Cantilupe is the only Cantilupe who is hanged at this time. As Peter owed service to the Goldinghams, this would be a slight stretch, but clearly Bishop Alexander wanted to undermine Roger by framing the event in this way. What makes this fall from grace more tragic is that at the Seige of Bedford in 1224, Hugh de Cantilupe had fought on the side of Hubert de Burgh, who with the Earl Marshal and des Roches made up the third faction within the minority government, against his factional rivals. Hugh had received a grant of favour and respite from his debts to the Crown as a result.[76]

When considering the court rolls, the two Cantilupe *v*. Goldingham cases, both in Essex and both involving kinsmen of the same two families, seem on the surface to be unconnected. Clearly, they did have some bearing on each other. John's withholding of service from Hugh could well have provoked Peter's attack on Hugh de Goldingham, or conversely, Peter's attack on Hugh and repeated failures to attend court to sort out their disagreement [and therefore a tacit refusal to pay damages for said attack] could have prompted John to withhold his service to Hugh de Cantilupe. It has also been suggested that Hugh de Goldingham brought the case against Peter to put pressure on Hugh de Cantilupe and pursued it through the courts to make Hugh capitulate on the rent situation.[77]

Whatever actually happened, this incident shows how kinsmen could add their weight behind one another's causes, and how a feud ostensibly between two individuals could draw in other kinsmen and escalate over time.

In Sir Ralph Paynell's case, then, given his daughter's incarceration and the threats her husband apparently made against her, it is easier to see how his involvement in Sir William the younger's murder developed. But with the focus on the nobility, very little has been done to centre the servants, who were heavily involved in the crime.

The Household Servants

The servants themselves, their duties and their connections, will now be considered as a group and as individuals. Here, the lacuna of evidence is more glaring. For some of the servants we have no evidence at all, aside from their names and locatives, and must engage in lateral thinking to understand their involvement in the case. For this, psalters and commonplace books of the thirteenth and fourteenth centuries are useful in building up a picture of offices and roles within the household, although these should be approached with caution and critical thinking. Literature can provide broader themes and a way of understanding contemporary perceptions and stereotypes, albeit in a cautious, limited way.

As far as a background framework goes, there is far more to go on. Much has been written on the manorial household and its construction. There was a hierarchy of servants within it, as can be seen from the varying salaries and privileges that each type of job provided. The Luttrell Psalter is the most obvious and well-used example of gentry family life from this period, with various marginalia images of domestic activities taking place in and around the manor house.[78] Some of the illustrations include servants dressed in their tunics and aprons, cooking fowl over a large fire on a spit, chopping up piglets, and serving food at table to tonsured priests and the lord and lady. These images are often used uncritically as mirrors held up to fourteenth-century life, but the images are more complex than this. One depiction of Sir Geoffrey at table with his household, for example, has several layers of meaning: its composition deliberately reflects the image of the Last Supper that appears elsewhere in the Psalter. In this illumination, Sir Geoffrey Luttrell occupies the same physical space as Jesus, thus setting himself up both as the lord and master of his household and as a figure of grace, patronage, piety and benevolence, while a slightly smaller cupbearer kneels in the foreground, echoing the position of the smaller figure of Judas Iscariot the Betrayer.[79] Purely allegorical this may be, and not necessarily a true reflection of how feasts were conducted, but if Sir Geoffrey was setting himself up as the Christ-figure, then it is to be hoped that the cupbearer figure was an imagined addition or if based on a real had a good sense of humour, to be so subtly linked with one of the key 'villains' of the Passion narrative. This parallelism also reinforces the medieval popular connections between God-ordained hierarchies and the notions of 'petty treason': it is a trusted household servant who takes the place of Judas Iscariot, not a guest, nor a clergyman or knightly peer.

Perhaps masters were occasionally right to be distrustful of their servants. Aside from the examples we have already considered, there are many more of servants engaging in murder most foul. In 1388, the clergyman Edmund Strete, rector of 'Merlawe', Lincolnshire, and canon of Chichester,[80] was found murdered in 'the close of the Great University Hall', now University College, Oxford, at the time one of the smaller colleges supporting a handful of fellows reading theology. Edmund had been slain by his servant, John West, who had then stuffed Edmund's body into the straw of his bed and fled the scene. The body was discovered five days later.[81]

In another Oxford case, this time in 1377, a servant called Stephen Cochran of Ireland died after a falling out with his master, John le Noble. For reasons left unstated, Stephen drew his baselard (a type of dagger or short sword) and attacked John in his hall one evening. John testified that he grabbed the knife and struggled with Stephen, and in the struggle Stephen fell down the cellar steps and stabbed himself with his own knife. John le Noble had to stand trial for felony but was cleared of all charges.[82]

Within the Oxford cases, however, servants were more likely to turn up in the coroners' rolls as the slain or injured parties rather than the perpetrators of crimes like this one. They were also more likely to be robbed, slain or injured by those of their own social standing, in altercations and affrays.[83] The same is true for London, where people were in closer quarters and as a result there was more opportunity for conflict.[84] This may have a lot to do with the fact that most servants were young men with easy access to weapons, and more than a little to do with the ideal of the male warrior embedded in the collective sense of masculinity, not to mention the normalisation of social violence.

Members of the elite class could also be killed by servants in the heat of the moment, such as during street brawls. This was more likely to happen in urban centres like London: in 1326, for example, Sir John de Felton's not-yet-knighted son, John de Felton the younger, was killed in exactly this kind of scenario over a horse. Master William de Westone tasked three of Sir John's servants to take a horse from 'parts beyond the sea' (e.g. France) and deliver it safely to Master William's servant, Peter de Seyntes. The three men brought the horse to London and were met by Peter, who asked them to give up the animal. The three men refused to do so, and a quarrel broke out among them. One of the servants drew a knife on Peter, and this drew the attention of other men who rushed to Peter's defence, one of whom punched the knife-wielding servant in the face and knocked him down. John de Felton junior, hearing the ruckus, came out of his lodging house and attacked a man called Thomas de Newetone, a servant of Hugh de Depedene, whose role in the fracas is unclear (if indeed he had any part in it). This drew the attention of the others, and several of Peter's associates, most of whom were in servant roles themselves, ran up armed with balstaffs [or balgh-staffs, defined in the *Middle English Compendium* as a stout stick, quarterstaff or cudgel][85] and brained the younger John, so that he died a few days later of the injury.[86]

Servants were not the stereotypically mild-mannered, rigidly hierarchical social group that might spring to mind in the context of later centuries, but a fluctuating group from diverse backgrounds, many of whom carried weapons of their own, and for whom the concept of community or fraternity was fluid. Being bound to the same master could create bonds of friendship and loyalty between them, since living in close quarters for extended periods of time fosters these kinds of bonds, but this was not guaranteed.

The figures in the Luttrell Psalter's illuminations range in age from older, balding and bearded men, to younger, stubbled adolescents. While some servants were professionals who remained in service their whole lives, many, if not most, of the servants in a household were young men in their teens or early- to mid-twenties, hired at local hiring fairs who would be in service for a year or so at a time.[87] By the early modern period, servanthood was very much a developmental phase of a person's youth and around 60 per cent of the population aged between 15 and 24 were in service of some description.[88]

This was a typical pattern across England in the late medieval period too, and so from this we can deduce that the majority of the men on the list of servants indicted for their master's murder in 1375 were of a similar age. The steward would have been a professional, older man, as would the marshal or master of the stables, the cook and possibly the boteler or butler, but the others would have been hired locally, and most likely by Maud and/or Robert de Cletham. Scotton itself provided a number of servants for the manor, as the locatives of some of the servants suggest.[89] Additionally, it is important to note the distant relationships between masters and servants in noble households. Servants bearing a close kin relationship to their masters were very rare, since the daily realities and challenges of living together in close quarters might blur the lines between servants and the immediate noble family in problematic ways.[90]

It is not hard to imagine the domestic scenes depicted in the Luttrell Psalter taking place in the Scotton manor household with their servants, vassals, friends, associates and extended family. In fact, since such accounts are generally scarce for the thirteenth century and even rarer for the twelfth, much more has been written on the late medieval period, in recent years including essay collections such as MaryanneKowaleski and Jeremy Goldberg's *Medieval Domesticity: Home, Housing and Household*.[91] While this section is not so concerned with daily life and household culture, or its consumption and day-to-day running and expenses, such specific details would be greatly valuable in terms of exploring the expressions of status that the Cantilupes utilised.

We know who was in the Scotton household from the records, but in many cases we only have their names and not their positions or any other information about them. Of the several thousand names that survive in numerous household records between 1350–1600, we have biographical information for only a quarter of them, and this information varies in quality and quantity.[92] The household was a typical one of modest size, comprising of the following men and one woman:

1. Robert of Cletham, a man who owned his own lands in the county and was a faithful man of the Neville family, did not necessarily live in the manor house itself, and the steward of Scotton manor;
2. Robert Cook/Coke of Scotton the boteler (butler);
3. John Barneby of Beckingham the chamberlain;
4. Richard Gyse, Sir William's *armiger*, or armour-bearer, who will be discussed further below;
5. Agatha Frere/Lovell, whose surname changes through the course of the trial, Maud's chambermaid;
6. John Astyn, a servant whose position is unknown;
7. William/Walter Chamberlainman, whose name appears as both William and Walter in the records, one apparently being a scribal error, and despite his surname was *not* Sir William's chamberlain;
8. Augustine Forester, whose surname might indicate his position as Sir William's forester but as in the case of Walter/William Chamberlainman it might merely indicate that one of his ancestors had once taken this role;

9. John Henxteman, whose surname again suggests that he was a stable groom, but again, this cannot be taken as positive;
10. William de Hayle/Hole, a servant of unknown position whose locative surname is similarly unhelpful, but Lincolnshire has a few places like Scots Hole and Pode Hole which might indicate he was at least native to the shire;
11. Augustine [de?] Morpath of Scotton, a servant of unknown positon whose surname seems to indicate more northern origins, namely Morpeth in Northumberland;
12. Henry Tasker, whose surname suggests he undertook piecework or threshing tasks, but again, this may not be a definitive indication;
13. Augustine Warner, given his surname a possible warrener (a gamekeeper of a rabbit warren, for which the lord had to have a royal licence), but otherwise another servant of whose position we cannot be certain.

This was a fairly typical ratio, as the household was, according to Kate Mertes, 'actively hostile to the presence of women', with numerous courtesy books and handbooks warning against the dangers of female servants (and laundresses in particular).[93] Most lords took this to heart, preferring to appoint single men to positions within the household rather than married men, even if the married man's wife lived elsewhere.[94] From this generalisation, we can suppose that the majority of these servants were themselves single men, and a household of single, mainly young, men in a strongly homosocial environment could pose its own dangers for women (single or otherwise) who had to navigate this environment. For example, Margery Kempe (1373–1438), Christian mystic and best-known for her dictated spiritual autobiographical work, *The Book of Margery Kempe*, reported indignantly that when she went to Lambeth, many of Archbishop Thomas Arundel's clerks 'and other rekles [reckless] men both swyers and yemen [squires and yeomen]' were abusive and threatening towards her, which would seem to bear out this general view.[95] However, experiences are not universal, and generalisations cannot take into account the friendships that form within a particular group, the personalities of the individuals and their dynamic when together.

The Remains of Greasley Castle. Nicholas de Cantelupe, Lord of Ilkeston in Derbyshire and Lord of Greasley in Nottinghamshire, was a man of great wealth, a fearless warrior and a friend and confidante of Edward III. He was knighted in 1326 and in 1340 he obtained the King's permission to fortify his manor house adjoining Greasley church, which then became Greasley Castle. He was a deeply religious man, who gave generously to the church and also founded Beauvale Priory. Greasley Castle Farm (on the right) now stands on the site. Remains of the old castle wall have been incorporated into farm outbuilding walls and traces of the moat and ramparts are still evident, just inside the hedge. (Text by Trevor Rickard, photo attribution: Trevor Rickard / *Remains of Greasley Castle* / CC BY-SA 2.0.)

Cantilupe Chantry (south side). A former chantry priest's house established by Nicholas II, third Lord Cantilupe, in 1355, enlarged in 1366, restored and remodelled c. 1843–5. (Richard Croft / *Cantilupe Chantry South* / CC BY-SA 2.0.)

The remains of Beauvale Priory, Greasley, Nottinghamshire. (Tina Cordon, 2007 / CC BY-SA 3.0.)

Beauvale Abbey Farm. Beauvale Priory was the last to be founded in England and the first to suffer as a result of the Dissolution of the Monasteries under King Henry VIII. The buildings fell into disrepair and the remains are now incorporated into the buildings of Beauvale Abbey Farm. (Garth Newton / *Beauvale Abbey Farm* / CC BY-SA 2.0.)

Sir Nicholas II de Cantilupe's tomb, located in the Angel Choir, Lincoln Cathedral. (Richard Croft / *Sir Nicholas Cantilupe's tomb* / CC BY-SA 2.0.)

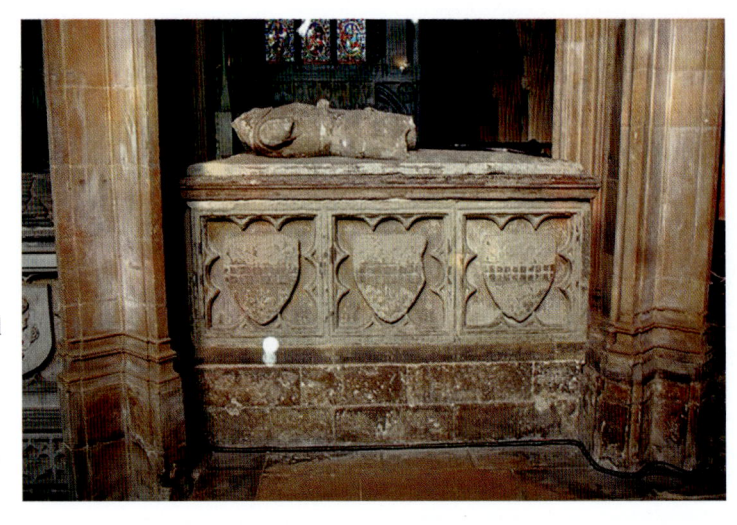

Medieval or post-medieval toy, cast lead alloy, found in North Yorkshire. Possible toy cannon or toy vase. The object is cylindrical in form with a rounded base and is hollow. Either side of the object are two attached 'strap handles' which continue above the mouth of the object. The mouth of the object is incomplete. At the base of the object is a small circular hole with an internal diameter of 2.50mm. Each face of the object is worn and there is no visible decoration. (National Museums Liverpool, Vanessa Oakden, 2014-07-22 FindID: 628757). The Portable Antiquities Scheme (PAS) is a voluntary programme run by the United Kingdom government to record the increasing numbers of small finds of archaeological interest found by members of the public. The scheme started in 1997 and now covers most of England and Wales. Finds are published at https://finds.org.uk.

A fragment of a medieval cast lead alloy toy horse, found in Essex. The item is hollow and shows the belly and part of the hindquarters of a tacked horse. The saddle, girth and harnesses are visible, though no other parts of the tack or horse remain. A casting seam is visible when viewed in plan, and runs through the centre of the saddle.(Colchester and Ipswich Museum Service. PAS Database Unique ID: ESS-B266C7. CC BY-SA 2.0.)

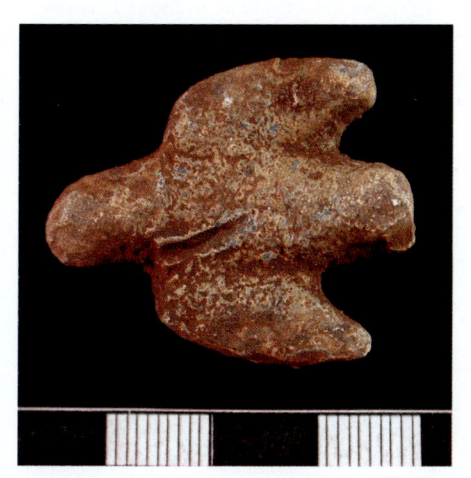

Medieval or post-medieval toy bird. Cast lead figurine of a bird in flight with a flat base, suggesting that it may be a weight or a fancy form of shy cock, perhaps based on something dug up (Geoff Egan, personal communication). Other lead shy-cocks can be seen on the database, but they are normally in the form of a cockerel, apart from SUSS-4E9687 which is more bird-like. Shy toys were designed to stand up so that they could be knocked down by having sticks thrown at them. This figurine cannot stand up, but may be missing a separate stand, as it has a recess in its base which may have formed part of an attachment. It could also have been attached as a finial to outdoor furniture, as it is lead, but it is very crudely made for this function. Forsyth & Egan (2005) explain on page 239 that shy-cocks may have derived from the Shrove Tuesday pursuit of casting stones or cudgels at a live cockerel, which was either tied down or buried up to its neck in the ground. The figurine is difficult to date from the style and could be medieval or post-medieval. (PAS Database, Unique ID: CORN-0669B0. Rights Holder: Royal Institution of Cornwall. CC BY-SA 2.0.)

Medieval posy ring found in Lancashire, dating from the fifteenth century (1400–1500). A medieval finger-ring with a slightly concave surface between two bands that enclose an inscription in French which reads: A MA VIE (To my life). Rings with inscriptions carrying romantic sentiments were sometimes exchanged as wedding rings in the Middle Ages. The words of the inscription are separated by engravings of flowers and punched decoration resembling bunches of grapes. The beginning of the inscription is identified by a six-pointed star. The ring is gold and dates from the fifteenth century. (PAS Database Unique ID: LANCUM-082840. Rights Holder: The Portable Antiquities Scheme, CC BY-SA 2.0.)

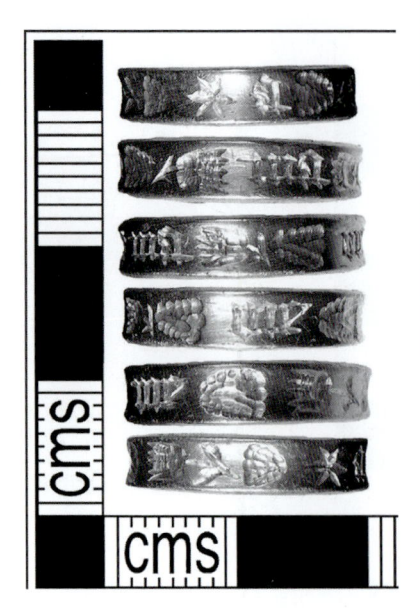

Medieval finger ring, found in Northamptonshire. A medieval finger-ring with a cabled hoop, the inside is plain with an inscription that reads: HONNE'R ET JOYE (Honour and Joy). The ring may have been exchanged between lovers or might have served as a wedding ring. The finger-ring is gold and dates from the fifteenth century. It has a diameter of 18mm and a height of 4mm. As we have no evidence that this find was discovered post-1997, we must evaluate it under Treasure Trove laws. Under Treasure Trove laws, evidence would have to point to the object having been deliberately hidden with the intention of recovery. This finger-ring is most likely to be a casual loss, therefore does not constitute treasure. (J.P. Robinson. PAS Database, Unique ID: NARC-EA0D85. Rights Holder: The British Museum. CC BY-SA 2.0.)

York Minster, York. Katherine Paynel's annulment case was heard in the Ecclesiastical Court at York. (MatzeTrier - own work, CC BY-SA 3.0, https://commons.wikimedia.org/w/index.php?curid=7305844)

A miniature depicting the Battle of Montiel, 1369 (Castillian Civil War, part of the Hundred Years' War) in Jean Froissart's Chronicles. (Public domain image)

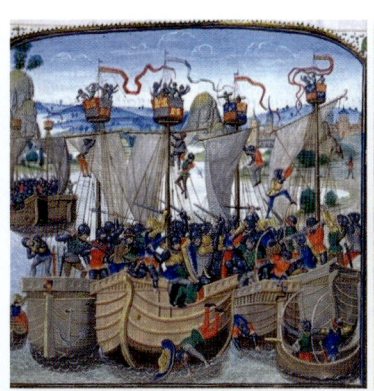

A collage of paintings representing battles of the Hundred Years' War. Clockwise, from top left: La Rochelle (1372), Agincourt (1415), Patay (1429), Seige of Orleans (1428–9). (Collage credit: Blaue Max, 2016. Public domain)

The church of St Genewys, Scotton, Lincolnshire. The church was founded before 1200 and the manor house held by the Nevilles was adjacent to this church – not to be confused with the Old Manor, Scotton, which still stands. (David Wright / *Church of St. Genewys, Scotton* / CC BY-SA 2.0.)

Dining room scene from the *Luttrell Psalter*, a book of Psalms for personal devotional use created circa 1325–35 by anonymous scribes and artists. It was commissioned by Sir Geoffrey Luttrell (died 1345), a wealthy English landowner. Sir Geoffrey is pictured in the centre with his wife, entertaining monks and clergy as well as other nobles. (British Library, Catalogue of Illuminated Manuscripts, MS Additional 42130. Public domain)

Two men threshing wheat, *Luttrell Psalter* (c.1325–35). (British Library, Catalogue of Illuminated Manuscripts, MS Additional 42130. Public domain)

Enlarged detail of a Luttrell servant, waiting on the Luttrells and their guests at table. *Luttrell Psalter* (c.1325–35), (British Library, Catalogue of Illuminated Manuscripts, MS Additional 42130. Public domain)

Folio 202v of the *Luttrell Psalter*, with part of Psalm 108 in Latin (Psalm 109 according to the Masoretic numbering). The miniature in the lower half of the folio shows Sir Geoffrey Luttrell, mounted, assisted by his wife and daughter-in-law. All three are dressed in livery bearing his coat of arms, as is the horse. The women's clothing shows the Luttrell livery 'impaled' with that of their own families (Sutton and Scrope). The Latin inscription immediately above the illustration reads Dns (the standard abbreviation of Dominus) Galfridus louterell me fieri fecit ['Lord Geoffrey Luttrell had me made'] indicating that he was the patron who commissioned the psalter. (British Library, Catalogue of Illuminated Manuscripts, MS Additional 42130. Public domain)

Sir Geoffrey and his wife playing backgammon. (British Library, Catalogue of Illuminated Manuscripts, MS Additional 42130. Public domain)

An unknown fourteenth-century knight. (Richard Croft / CC BY-SA 2.0.)

Robert Cook the butler, with Richard Gyse the squire, Augustine de Morpath, John Barneby the chamberlain, William Chamberlainman, Richard Gyse, John Henxteman and the (apparently) single woman Agatha Frere, already knew one another from this previous employment. These are the seven servants whom the trial records note had once worked for another knight, Sir Richard de Bingham.

Augustine Morpath's last name is a locative but in the trial he is also listed as 'Augustine de Morpath de Scotton', or Augustine of Morpath of Scotton (his current place of employment). This is typical for those whose family's points of origin (indicated by their original locative surname) had become their inherited 'family name' and no longer referred to where the family members were currently residing.

Bingham, Nottinghamshire, was held in the fourteenth century by the de Binghams and then by the Rempstones, and several de Bingham family members including a previous Richard (d. 1307) and his son William (d. 1349) are entombed in Bingham's parish church. The earlier Richard de Bingham (d. 1307) married an Alice Bertram who came from Morpeth, Northumberland.[96] It's likely that Alice brought servants with her to Nottinghamshire, and this would account for Augustine Morpath's presence some generations down the line with the locative surname as a hereditary one. Moreover, the distance between Greasley and Bingham is less than 20 miles, an easy distance to cover on horseback, making the Binghams and Cantilupes near neighbours. The families were linked by their cross-county associates and friends, too: Richard de Bingham of Watnow Chaworth married Anne Strelley, a member of the same Strelley family into whom the Cantilupes had married.[97]

The circumstances of these seven servants coming into Cantilupe employ are hinted at by the debtors rolls for the 1370s. Richard had gone abroad for a year in 1367, nominating John Mowbray and William Wakebrigg as his attorneys in his absence.[98] While away, presumably on campaign just as William Cantilupe was at the same time, he became answerable for a huge amount of debt to merchants and the Mowbrays. In 1372, Richard de Bingham is found owing £160 to John Philpot, merchant and citizen of London, the rough equivalent of around £78,000 in 2017 in terms of buying power.[99] This may well explain why a group of seven servants sought employ elsewhere if he could not afford to keep them on, although it isn't clear when he let them go. It could simply be that their terms of contract had expired, as servants were bound for a period of time and had to have their contracts renewed or seek employment elsewhere if they were not. Richard may have been attempting to make savings in his household bills: by 1376, he is found owing £100 – roughly £50,000 in 2017's money – to William Mowbray, kinsman of Thomas Mowbray, the second earl of Nottingham.[100] The sheriff of Nottingham found that by that year de Bingham no longer held lands or tenements in Nottinghamshire at all but had demised them to other knights.

In 1384, previous debts apparently paid off, Richard took on another debt of £128 2s, which he owed to John Burneby, citizen and armourer of London, and a bladesmith, Walter Hooper, for another military endeavour.[101] It is unclear whether this was for himself or for his contribution in lieu of his own presence. He was supposed to be travelling overseas with the earl of Arundel, but had his letters of protection revoked as the king found 'he tarries in the county of Chester on his own affairs'.[102] Some years after his death in 1387, the Calendar of Close Rolls records that an inquisition should be made regarding the lands, goods and chattels of Richard de Bingham, knight, 'deceased at the time he was outlawed at suit of Katherine Denys'.[103] In February of 1388 the Close Rolls record another pertinent entry:

> To John Briggeforde escheator in Nottinghamshire. Order to remove the king's hand and meddle no further with the manor of Byngham [sic], delivering up any issues thereof taken; as the king has learned by inquisition ... that Richard de Bingham knight at his death held no lands in chief as of the crown, but long before his death he made enfeoffment in the said manor to Robert Braybroke clerk, Reynold Braybroke, Simon de Leeke knight and Henry de Cotingdoun parson of Botelsford and to their heirs, by virtue of which the said Simon [de Leeke] entered in his own name and in the name of his fellows, taking the issues and profits for the term of four years, after which the said Richard [de Bingham] again entered and took issues and profits until his death without being enfeoffed again by said feoffees or any of them, and that the said manor is held of others than the king.[104]

This accounts for the 'Braybrokes' or Braybrookes who manumitted both Lady Maud and the steward Robert de Cletham at the trial. The Braybrookes, despite being primarily based in Bedfordshire and Buckinghamshire, were a feature of the local Nottinghamshire and Lincolnshire landscape, and neighbours of Maud and William. It is worth noting that two of the Braybrooks, one being the same Robert (clerk) mentioned in the above entry, and the other being Sir Gerard Braybrook, a knighted kinsman, manumitted the steward Robert of Cletham as well as Maud herself.

Robert Braybrooke, the clerk, was already rising up in the church, and his involvement in the trial was a minor footnote in his career. A year later he was made proctor for the archdeacon of Canterbury, in 1377 he was appointed secretary to the boy-king Richard II and was consecrated Bishop of London in 1382. Sir Gerard Braybrooke was his father, but this Sir Gerard might also have been a brother of the same name.[105]

The Braybrookes were part of a cross-county network in the same way as the Cantilupes, the Nevilles and the Paynells, and the [Cantilupe] trial highlights these connections for us by drawing clear lines between the different social groups represented by the accused. With this in mind, while the good characters of these men and their willingness to support both Maud and her steward reflected well on these two suspects, their support cannot be viewed as entirely without self-interest. The fact that these men operated in multiple counties and had their *caputs* or 'family seats' elsewhere also calls their judgement into question. How could they be sure that Maud and Robert had not committed the crime, and had no prior knowledge of it? How long had it been since they were in Lincolnshire or Nottinghamshire at all? Whose word were they prepared to accept and why?

The element of social cohesion and closing ranks when faced with a crime that fundamentally challenged the status quo – that of petty treason, rather than mere homicide – meant that they were more likely to lend their support to those within their own community.

For the servants who moved from de Bingham's service to William Cantilupe's, they found their social circle somewhat decreased, particularly Richard Gyse. William Cantilupe was a younger man and working his own way upwards through the social milieu and out of the shadow of his older brother and his grandfather. The arrangement of his father being cut out of the succession was another factor that potentially told against him. If Gyse had hoped de Bingham would reward him with land of his own or that an earl would take notice of him and allow him opportunities within his household, he was sadly mistaken. Neither was William Cantilupe the younger going to be much help on that score: Gyse owned nothing he died.

If Cantilupe's service was disappointing, or if he was not a good man to be contracted to for any length of time, it wasn't as if anyone could refuse. Since the Black Death the issue of compulsory labour for the 'idle' was addressed repeatedly in parliaments from 1351 to 1430. The Statute of Labourers of 1349 declared that:

> each man and woman (*homo et femina*) of our realm of England – of whatever condition, free or bond; able in body; under 60 years of age; not living by trade; nor exercising a particular craft; nor having assets with which to live or land to cultivate; nor serving another – shall be bound to serve anyone who requires his/her services, as long as the service is appropriate to his/her estate.[106]

They could be asked to perform any reasonable service – not just seasonal piece-work – at any time of the year, not just at harvest time. Remuneration generally included room and board, and a cash stipend at the end of the contract.[107] If a group of seven servants were forced to leave one knight's employ, or, in modern phrasing, their contracts expired and were not renewed, they could therefore be contracted by his neighbour regardless of whether or not they wanted to work for him. This meant that in such situations lords and ladies were no longer entirely familiar with the servants in their households, and that the servants themselves may not have long-standing loyalties to their employers.

Since so many servants (all of them, in fact) were indicted for the murder, but despite this we are left in the dark about what most of them actually did in the household, or who they were, we will focus on the core four. Robert de Cletham, the steward, was an important man who was manumitted (roughly equivalent of bailed out by) the same upstanding men of the county who manumitted Lady Maud, but we know very little about him. Could he really have known nothing about the conspiracy?

Robert Cook of Scotton was the butler. He was accused by Lady Maud along with Sir William's armour-berarer, Richard Gyse, but it was her chambermaid Agatha Frere/Lovell who provided them with the key. We will start with the little we know of Robert of Cletham, Robert Cook and Agatha Frere/Lovell, and then look at Richard Gyse and the role of armour-bearer in more detail.

Robert de Cletham: The Steward

The steward of the household, Robert of Cletham, was most likely from the hamlet of Cleatham in North Lincolnshire, in the parish of Manton. He was already connected to the Nevilles, as a Thomas de Neville of Cleatham appears in the *Calendar of Inquisitions Post Mortem* in 1310.[108] Thomas and his wife Maud held land jointly at Snitterby, with Ralph Neville as their next heir. This would mean that Robert of Cletham was a Neville tenant, not just hired by the Nevilles but with a longstanding and potentially generational family connection to the family. Fleming noted that in cases where the extended kin and immediate kin were distant, long-standing servants would provide greater companionship and support than one's own family could, and this would have provided Lady Maud with some comfort in the early days of her marriage.[109]

The steward role was a supervisory or managerial one, roughly equivalent to an estate manager. There was some anxiety expressed in medieval literature regarding the steward, who could prove to be either a traitor or a 'true man'.[110] The job involved supervising the lord's estates, managing them while the lord was away, checking on the taxes and rents owed by the tenants. The steward would, therefore, be knowledgeable about his lord's finances.

Robert de Cletham must have been experienced and shrewd to have been appointed. He also owned land in his own right, from which he collected rent and so had an independent income. In 1372, three years before the killing of his master, he is mentioned briefly in the available records along with two of his associates, Ralph de Thirsk and John de Kilvington. The three of them granted rent in Thonock (Gainsborough), Laughton, Gainsborough, Morton, Walkerith and Stockwith to three chaplains at the altar of St. Mary in the church of Gainsborough, with 'the said Ralph retaining land in Lincoln, the said John rent in Harmston and Wellingore, and the said Robert rent in Cleatham.'[111] Neither was his piety and gifts to the church a one-off occurrence in his family: the abbot of Humberston Abbey, Lincolnshire, acquired the land of Robert's father William in Belsby, Thurlby, Huttoft and Ingoldmels.[112] Since a lot of the evidence was based on considerations of the characters of the accused, Robert's gift of rent to the chaplains could have swung the jury to acquit him of aiding and abetting his master's murderers, his piety part of the evidence to suggest that he was a 'true man' and not a traitor. If the jurors themselves were closely connected to the Nevilles and the Paynells, they would have been more likely to take this into consideration and believe him.

Robert Cook of Scotton: The Butler
Robert Cook, the butler held responsible with Richard Gyse for William's murder, is an interesting character. The trial records call him 'Robert Coke [or 'Cook'] of Scotton' which implies that he was a native of that village.

The office of butler was a middle-ranking position within a household, in charge of the buttery where 'butts' of beer and wine were stored, although the term came to mean a general storeroom or pantry. Robert Cook's tasks would have brought him from the storeroom to the hall and meant that he was one of those servants with access to the kitchen, and the knives within it. He would have had charge of other servants in the domestic quarters, supervising their duties and serving meals to the family and their guests. As a man with others under his direction, it is no wonder that he came under immediate suspicion as a main player in the conspiracy.

Robert Cook was a man of modest means, owning an acre of land and his own moveable goods. The trial record reports that: 'The chattals of the aforesaid Robert Cook are 40 shillings ... And he has one acre of land in Northtoft which is worth 6 pence per year ... .'

Northtoft was significant, in that it demonstrates a historical connection to the Neville family. Adam de Northtoft was one of the rebels in the Second Barons' War of 1264–67, alongside his neighbour John de

Neville, both of whom are charged with other knights in their shire to do no more damage to the king in return for the recovery of their goods and a promise that no further action would be taken against them.[113] Edmund de Northtoft held the manor of Northtoft of Sir John Neville at the time of his death in 1376.[114]

This man was therefore a trusted Neville servant, loyal to Neville allies within the region, and these connections tied him more closely to his lady than his lord.

Agatha Frere/Lovell: The Chambermaid

The conceptualisation of women in society centred around their sexual and marital status (virgins, wives, widows), whereas men were conceptualised in terms of their social and economic status (e.g. knights, merchants, tradesmen).[115] While this is broadly true and forms the background to how male and female socio-economic roles were more broadly understood, individual relationships and interpersonal dynamics of specific groups should never be assumed. Women *were* conceptualised by their socio-economic status in the Statute of Labourers (1351), where they were categorised by their occupation.[116] Cordelia Beattie suggests this was an 'alternative model',[117] but there is no reason why multiple models and understandings of working women could not co-exist simultaneously in the minds of their contemporaries. Besides, models of any kind are only of limited use when attempting to uncover what people actually thought of one another in their more intimate everyday interactions, the details of which we can never know.

The role of female wage-earners in fourteenth-century England has been chronically understudied, but in recent years more historians have turned their attention to this social group, recognising their importance to the medieval economy. Their role in the cloth and brewing industries has always been known, but as Simon A.C. Penn points out, a greater and growing appreciation of women wage-earners in urban society has not been matched by a reappraisal of women in rural work.[118] The rural, agricultural labour available for women to perform was more limited and less specialised than that of men, but women could also earn a wage as part of a manorial household. Women entering service in this way also had fewer opportunities, and this led to the household dynamic being majority male. This does not necessarily mean that a woman in this environment would be ignored by her male counterparts, cause trouble between them or create tensions in a stereotypical fashion: friendship bonds and the common bonds of servants could be forged just as strongly in such mixed groups.

Agatha's position is recorded as the *ancilla*, the maid, which was a position of trust that could be abused. Her job was generally centred in the private quarters of the house, but in such a small manor house as Scotton it is likely that she performed other duties around the house, was familiar with her male fellow-workers and, given the male-dominated space she was working and living in, had to leave the manor to visit family and find the company of other women in the village and wider locality.

The French-Italian writer Christine de Pizan (*c*. 1364–1430) wrote about the dishonesty of chambermaids in urban households of the great lords or middling gentry, posing as shrewd managers:

> They get their positions of buying their food and going to the butcher's, where they only too well 'hit the fruit basket', which is a common expression meaning to claim the thing costs more than it really does and keep the change … they put to one side a little titbit, have a pie made and baked, charging it up to their master, and when their master is at court or in town, and their mistress at church hearing high Mass, a delightful little banquet is spread in the kitchen, and not without plenty to drink, and only the best wine! The other housemaids in the street who are part of the crowd of cronies turn up and God knows how they plunder the place![119]

De Pizan is best known for her work, *The Book of the City of Ladies* (1405), in which she defends women and offers marginal female groups such as domestic servants and prostitutes advice, but this class of women received a mixed response from their society. Her point here was that since female domestic servants had to earn their living from an early age, their moral education was neglected – this meant that their employers should watch out for dishonesty.[120] In other popular literature, maid servants were typically portrayed as the embodiment of 'feminine vices', namely, dishonesty, avarice, lust, disloyalty and hypocrisy.[121] Yet the term *ancilla* was also applied to saintly, cloistered women. A group of female servant-saints emerged, whose virtues of humility, hard work, loyalty, charity and firm chastity were the embodiment of the church's values.[122]

Reality itself is hardly as black and white. Since domestic service was part of the life-cycle of young men and women, offering a degree of independence and modest prosperity, but not always (and indeed not usually) a permanent post, maidservants and prostitutes could be linked in popular thought.[123] Prostitution was often resorted to at times when women could not find other employment, and Ruth Karras has shown that it was common for women, especially single women, to choose prostitution under these conditions, restricted economically as they were by their sex.[124] Even as respectable servants, these young women could be the cause of sexual tension in a household and were vulnerable to sexual exploitation by their masters.[125]

At first, when questioned and indicted, Agatha gave her name as Agatha Frere. Towards the end of the trial, Agatha was being recorded as 'Lovell', which was the family name given when her bailiffs were later indicted for her escape. There are three possible reasons for this.

1. It's a scribal error and the court scribe simply got her name wrong.
2. Agatha got married at some point during the proceedings, resulting in the change of name.
3. Agatha gave a false name at first, perhaps to protect her family from the ignominy of the trial, and this was later uncovered.

Of the three, the simplest reason – that she got married – is the most likely. There is no evidence in the trial that she was accused of giving them a false name, or of lying about her identity. While the Lovells were a very powerful gentry family, Agatha may not have married into such high circles: William Lovel was a baker from Middlesex in 1369, despite other 'Lovels' and 'Lovells' in the county being named as knights.[126] There is however no mention of anyone with that family name (whether a knightly family or an unrelated family from a lower strata of society) in connection with Scotton.

Agatha was apparently known as Agatha Frere when she worked for Richard de Bingham, presumably as a chambermaid for his wife Joan, before transferring to the Cantilupe household and becoming the maid of Maud Neville. She was very likely around the same age as Maud herself, if not younger, as most domestic servants of this kind were in their late teens to twenties. She was the only woman listed as being part of the household except for Maud, her lady, and had worked with six of the men before.

These circumstances can be considered to create a new, alternative narrative to the traditional interpretation of the evidence. Was she involved in the murder due to the unwanted advances of her master, and did the other servants come to her defence in a violent way? This question will be discussed more fully in chapter six, where revenge or communal justice will be explored as one of the motives for Sir William's murder.

Richard Gyse: The Armour-Bearer

It is worth noting that by the mid-fourteenth century, terms such as *armiger* and *esquire*, which had been military terms often synonymous with terms for valet (*vallettus*), were becoming more differentiated, militarily, socially and economically.[127] At this time, the rank of *armiger* or *esquire*, originally a servant who looked after the knight's horse and arms, became associated with a territorial and economic formulation of status rather than a military designation.[128]

There is a question mark over who exactly Richard Gyse was, and what level of society he occupied. Was he the unnamed 'yeoman' who accompanied William on campaign in 1368–69? A 'yeoman' was a man holding or cultivating a small area of land, a freeman, a freeholder. The yeomanry were able to move up the social ladder, but their rise into knightly classes came with stigma and criticism from the chroniclers and moralists, particularly in the twelfth century.[129] As a rhetorical device to express villainy and add weight to bad conduct, it continued into the fourteenth century, with Froissart levelling this charge against a squire who raped his master's wife.[130]

By the fourteenth century, the increased social mobility of the post-plague era had created more opportunities for the lower-born men once more, albeit on a smaller scale than being elevated to official positions in the royal household. Free-born men who held and farmed their own land and could turn a profit were becoming more affluent and might be able to step onto the lower rungs of their local social ladder.

While this may be the case for Richard, there was a knightly family with the same locative surname holding lands in Lincolnshire through the fourteenth century, and it just as likely that Richard was one of their younger (not to mention poorer) relations.

Around 1316, Sir John de Gyse is found complaining to the king and requesting remedy for being disseised of his manor of Bloxholm, Lincolnshire.[131] The complaint, directed against Piers de Santemareys, led to Santemaryes' imprisonment until John and his wife were satisfied.[132] Around 1327, John de Gyse made another petition to the king, not long after the fall of the Despensers. The king had taken control of the Despenser lands, including, John argued, a manor in Oxfordshire that was rightfully his, which he had gained from Thomas de Grele or Greylee (without the king's licence, for which he had been pardoned in 1308) and had in his turn given it to the elder Hugh le Despenser.[133] This was investigated, but as it was found that the manor of Pyrton had been formally gifted to the elder Hugh by John himself, nothing further was done and it remained confiscated.[134]

As an indication of family wealth at this time, in 1325–26 Sir John owed an eye-watering £120 to Henry atte Swan of St Ostyth, a merchant and citizen of London.[135] Henry ensured writs to this effect were not only sent to the sheriff of Lincolnshire but also to the sheriff of Gloucestershire, where Sir John held Elmore in Dudstone Hundred.[136] In 1333, Sir John owed £60 to the same creditor.[137] Sir John's worth can be estimated from the debts he accrued (and paid off) from 1307–10, a total of £116 12s 4d.[138]

That the Gyse family were connected to the greater magnates in this way is an indication of their relative status, but also of their ability to move in wider local circles. While this branch of the Gyse family had money and lands, that did not mean that young Richard Gyse could expect to inherit them. That Richard had to go out in service of others and was found to own nothing at the time of his death, not lands nor chattals, is indicative of his relative status as a younger son of a cadet line that needed to make his own way and find a suitable patron and wife in order to do so.

The Gyse family were baronets based in Bedfordshire and Buckinghamshire, but had other manors elsewhere, including

Gloucestershire and across the Midlands. Aspley-Guise was their seat, which was subinfeudated to Anselm Gyse by its original holder, John de Burgh. On John de Burgh's death, it passed first to his son, who died without male issue, and then to his daughter Hawise.[139] Hawise de Burgh married Robert de Gresley, which could refer to the village in Derbyshire, or (more likely) be a variant spelling of Greasley, Nottinghamshire, the seat of the Cantilupes.

The Gyse family continued to rent from the heirs of Hawise and Richard, which gave them access to their landlord's social networks if good relations were maintained between them. Given that the position of armour-bearer or squire was a trusted one, it is most likely to be the latter. Richard Gyse went to work for Richard de Bingham, whose main manor was near Greasley Castle. If he came recommended by a landowning family who had links to the locality, the de Binghams would have been more likely to take him on. When Richard de Bingham let seven of his servants go, it was not without his own recommendations, and the ill-fated Sir William was more likely to take on young Richard if he had reassurances about Richard's character and suitability for the role. It is noted that he had began as a servant of Sir Richard de Bingham, along with Maud's maid Agatha, Robert Cook the butler, John Henxteman, Augustine Morpath and William Chamberlainman. Presumably these six, including Richard himself, had come with Sir Richard de Bingham's approval.

Richard Gyse, whom we can estimate from the average ages of armour-bearers or squires at this time to be a young man of around 21 years of age or less, occupied a different position and one that arguably afforded him a greater level of intimacy with Sir William. The traditional interpretation of the evidence suggests two motives for a young squire to kill his master: money and/or sex. Both are compelling, but to explore them further, the context of knights and squires must be more fully explored, along with the background of Richard Gyse himself.

Firstly, we should consider the squire as a figure within medieval thought, and then as a murderer of their master. How often did people of this rank kill their lords? When they did so, if they did so, what were their motives? How were squires seen by others – a much harder question to answer, and not one with a satisfactory answer. To get a sense of the squire in the public eye and imagination, it is important to consider the contemporary literature where squires are concerned.

Chaucer's fictionalised, stereotypical squire, introduced in the General Prologue of *The Canterbury Tales*, is a lusty young bachelor of around 20 years of age who has distinguished himself in various campaigns to Flanders, Artois and Picardy in an effort to impress his lady love.[140] A squire would expect to be knighted at around 21, but not all squires were ultimately knighted. A squire who had grown too old to qualify for knighthood, or could not afford the expense of knighthood, was termed an *arma patrina*, that is, allowed to carry a lance and shield in battle.[141]

Chaucer's Squire is the son of the Knight, whom Chaucer paints as the ideal crusader in his introduction. Since the squire has not been to the same places that his father has been, but instead has made a name for himself in France and the Low Countries, it is clear that he is not his father's usual squire but has joined his father partly in this capacity on the pilgrimage. This was a customary practice: the sons of knightly families were often fostered out to other noble families in the locality or beyond to strengthen kinship ties and to improve the social standing of the family. Squires working their way up to be knights would have to distinguish themselves on campaigns and prove themselves in battle, but also would need means of their own. Land was, by the fourteenth century, a prerequisite for knighthood.

Also by the fourteenth century, knights were involved in both martial and administrative roles as part of a small elite stratum of society. The number of fighting knights had diminished through the previous century. Ralph V. Turner notes that other studies, such as those conducted by J. Quick and R.F. Treharne, show that there could have been no more than 2,000 of such men actively involved in administration during the thirteenth century.[142] More recently, however, Noel Dunholm-Young concluded that in Edward I's reign there were only 500 fighting knights left in England, with an estimate of 3,000 potential knights and 1,250 actual knights, figures with which Peter Coss agrees in *The Knight in Medieval England*.[143] The Great Roll of Arms *c.* 1308 listed 1,110 names, doubtless a high proportion (although not a complete list) of the knights functioning at the time, which was a small elite in light of the population estimates of five to six million.[144] In the early phases of the Hundred

Years' War, the army that Edward III took to Brittany in 1342 had 330 knights, and 1,470 men-at-arms. At Crécy and Calais in 1346–7, as many as 927 knights were identified as serving in these campaigns, and the royal expedition to France in 1359–60 included 870 knights – in each case, not all of them from England.[145] This left very few at home to perform administrative tasks and to look after their lands. This was left to those knights who could not perform their martial duties due to ill-health or age, the wives of these knights, and their appointed stewards. The elected sheriff of the county, although himself a knight or knighted magnate, would also need to remain to perform judicial tasks, as would those on the justice circuits for the court of the king's bench, and those great magnates and bishops left in charge while the king was away. For those who were absent for twelve months or more, this meant that they had to trust those left behind to manage their estates properly, to raise taxes effectively, to collect rents fairly, and not to conspire behind their backs while they were abroad.

The second phase of the Hundred Years' War, 1369–1413, sometimes known as the Caroline War after Charles V of France who resumed hostilities nine years after the Treaty of Brétigny, saw campaigns take place in 1370, 1372 and 1377, although the Treaty of Bruges was made in 1375.[146] William de Cantilupe the younger, as we have seen, served as a knight in the retinue of John of Gaunt. His grandfather Sir Nicholas had served under Henry of Grosmont in 1336.[147] It is unclear when exactly Richard Gyse transferred to Sir William's employ from that of his neighbour, Sir Richard de Bingham, and so unclear whether Gyse had the opportunity to serve on campaign with him in the year he went abroad, but Richard de Bingham had also gone on campaign and Richard could have served with him.

For young men like Richard Gyse, knighthood was not their only career path. Throughout the fourteenth century, there was an increase in opportunities to forge a professional military career regardless of knighted status, while some of those already knighted chose to remain in Europe to head roving mercenary gangs, selling their services to the warring Italian city states and whoever else would pay them, like the infamous Sir John Hawkwood.[148] Mercenaries and mercenary captains were not the only options – 'careerist' was not synonymous with 'mercenary', like

Sir Robert Knolles, freebooter and royal captain in the French wars, and John Doncaster, leader of the Calais band of adventurers who captured Guines castle from the French in 1352.[149] Yet this single-minded focus on war that characterised the military careerist was not for everyone, and if bound in service to a knight who was not so regularly abroad or called to serve, then this was another limiting factor.

Squires were limited in other ways, too. Not all were well educated or even literate, even in the fourteenth century where education was of increasing importance, particularly for the knightly (or aspiring knightly) classes, for whom administration was a key part of daily life. Lack of education could prove costly, as Peter de Panato, lord of Cupiae in the diocese of Rodez, discovered in 1356. The pope wrote to Edward, prince of Aquitaine and Wales (the Black Prince, son of Edward III), praying him to remit any penalty that Peter incurred, describing him as 'a simple, unastute nobleman'.[150] Pope Urban V claimed that Peter, 'trusting in his own innocence, the prince's justice and the pope's recommendation', had sent 'an illiterate squire' to court to plead against the excesses with which he had been charged, rather than a skilled or professional advocate.[151] This squire had his petition framed by a clerk, and, not being able to read or discern whether it was framed correctly, presented the petition just as it was. Apparently, this had been inadequate, and Peter de Panato then was forced to petition the pope and ask Urban V to intercede on his behalf with Prince Edward, denying the crimes he had been charged with.[152]

We therefore cannot make assumptions about Richard Gyse's levels of education, his social standing or his prospects. The position was occupied by a cross-section of men, and Richard's early life and any patronage he received is lost to us.

The Medieval Squire as Murderer
The Calendar of Coroners' Rolls for the City of London, 1300–78, has three instances of men and boys identified as '*armiger*' or variants of '*esquier*' involved in untimely deaths, although the third incident is the murder *of* a squire by a platemaker in a quarrel, and so does not quite suit our purposes.[153]

Squires could be decidedly unchivalrous, as Thomas atte Church, esquire to the earl of Arundel, demonstrated in 1321. The jurors said that

Thomas, accompanied by a man unknown to any of them, were riding together down 'Tamsetrete' towards the Tower of London when Thomas nearly threw a woman to the ground who was carrying a child in her arms. Challenged by John de Harwe to ride more carefully and watch where he was going, Thomas got angry and drew his sword, striking John on the side with it and inflicting a mortal wound.[154]

In 1324, also in London, another group of servants – including a squire – banded together to commit murder, but in this case it was the murder of a fellow-servant as a result of a quarrel in a brothel. The victim was a man named Nicholas, a servant of Simon de Knottingley. Nicholas was found dead in the street and the hue was raised by the householder who found his body. It was discovered that Nicholas had been assaulted, beaten and wounded by three men, two the servants of Henry Percy and one the squire of Henry Krok. These three were William de la Marche, who seems to have left Henry Percy's employ as a palfrey-man (*palefridarius*) not long before, Henry Percy's cook (another William), and Henry Krok's squire John, who had been with the ill-fated Nicholas at a courtesan's house. While Krok's squire and Percy's cook had been involved in the beating, it had been William de la Marche who had stabbed Nicholas with an 'Irish knife' and it was from this wound that Nicholas died.[155] All three fled, but only William de la Marche is recorded as being captured. The jurors found that none of these three had any lands nor chattals that they could ascertain, which was also the case where Richard Gyse was concerned. It was not unusual, therefore, to have squires involved in violent crime, and neither was it unusual for them to own next to nothing but be reliant on their lord and their position in the household to sustain them. While that position was supposed to come with responsibilities and codes of conduct, in practice, this was not necessarily how they conducted themselves in either the public or private sphere.

In the first of these cases, there is an element of privilege and arrogance attached to the squire's status, while the second case seems to be an instance of four men quarrelling while engaged in extracurricular activities. It also demonstrates that in urban centres there were many opportunities for servants of different masters to meet and engage in social activities beyond their own households, creating networks of friendships and alliances that could result in similar violent outcomes as when close-knit groups banded together in less populated areas where social opportunities were more limited.

With this in mind, it should be noted that squires deliberately killing their own lords were rare. The twelfth-century chronicler Orderic Vitalis recounts the *accidental* fatal wounding of Hugh Giroie by his squire, after which Hugh, as he lay dying, advised the hapless young man to run so that Hugh's brothers wouldn't avenge themselves upon him.[156] Such accidents were a hazard of noble pastimes like hunting and relatively rare, but could be high-profile. The most notorious in England was surely William Rufus, or King William II, who was infamously shot by one of his own companions, Sir Walter Tirel, Lord of Poix, while hunting.

Deliberate murder is quite another thing, and it is not until the thirteenth century, when the roles of knight and *armiger* were more clearly defined and the elite had established a stronger collective identity, that there are some parallels are to be found with our household conspiracy case.

In Warwickshire, 1276, Sir William de Arden was murdered in his grove (*grava*) called 'Biddesmore', near Henwood Priory. His murder was procured by two of his most trusted servants: his steward, Walter de Winterton, and his squire (*armiger*), William de Norton. Unlike the Cantilupe case, the steward and squire did not kill their lord themselves, but instead obtained the services of Richard de Bury to do the deed.[157] They appeared to be motivated by Sir William's poor treatment of them – Richard de Bury claimed that Sir William had withheld a sum of money from him and detained his service, and this was the reason why he 'hated' him enough to kill him.[158] This case will be considered further in chapter five, where material gain and loss will be considered as a possible motive for the Cantilupe murder.

An earlier case in the same county is found in the plea rolls of Henry III, relating to an even earlier incident that occurred in the reign of Richard I. This case is referenced in an assize held to discover the true heirs to some land. It was found that William Trussell's heirs should have this land (a virgate in Merton, held at that time by the Prior of Chaucombe) but the proceedings saw fit to mention a murder case connected to William Trussell in order to contextualise things for the inquiry. The jury, who had known William Trussell and were acquainted with the status of the land, said that he had gone to Jerusalem as a pilgrim after the coronation of King Richard (I) and 'he had held at that time the land in fee and in demesne, and he gave that land to farm for a term of three years to two men.' His land thus dealt with, he entrusted his wife back into the care of her father, John de Draycot, and went on his pilgrimage. Trussell left with his squire, Walter, but Walter left him a few weeks after they set off and returned to stay with Trussell's father-in-law.

About six weeks after Trussell left, his wife was killed in her father's house and buried in a marl pit.[159] William Trussell's illegitimate brother (also called William, and known as William the Bastard to differentiate him from Trussell) fled and claimed sanctuary in the church. He acknowledged his guilt and abjured the realm. William Trussell's squire, Walter, also fled for the murder of his master's wife. William the Bastard admitted that both he and Walter had killed her, although no motive is given in the records. For the purposes of the assize, this meant that William Trussell was in the clear for the murder and had not been outlawed, which meant that his heirs could still claim their land inheritance.

This kind of activity – the coveting of one's master's wife – was not uncommon. Froissart's *Chronicles* recounts the tale of Jacques Le Gris, the squire of Sir Jean de Carrouges, whom Froissart is quick to label as a 'low-born' man risen in favour to the position of squire.[160] For Froissart, this was a moral issue, and an indication of the squire's untrustworthiness: he had usurped the natural order of the social hierarchy, and nothing good could come of a low-born man becoming the favourite of a high-born man, in this case, Count Pierre d'Alençon, their master. The case that Froissart relates in a detailed narrative spans the years 1386–7, culminating in a judicial duel or trial by combat, the type of ordeal described by Warren C. Brown as a means of legitimising violence and revenge.

Froissart relates that through 'a strange and perverse temptation' the devil entered Le Gris and caused him to become obsessed with Sir Jean's wife, 'a good and sensible woman'.[161] Sir Jean went on an expedition overseas to help with his socio-political advancement, while Le Gris remained behind in the castle of Count Pierre. Le Gris caused himself to be seen at Count Pierre's castle in the morning but was sure not to let people see him leave. He rode to Sir Jean's castle, knowing Sir Jean to be away, and was admitted at once, recognised as a friend. He raped Sir Jean's wife and threatened to expose her to public disgrace if she told anyone what had happened. He then rode back to the count's castle, where it appeared that he had never left.

Sir Jean, on his return, at first refused to believe his wife's account. However, he was finally persuaded, and brought his grievance to Count Pierre, who in his turn refused to believe Sir Jean. Sir Jean, despite Le Gris' powerful ally and apparent alibi, 'had great courage and believed his wife', and appealed Le Gris before the parliament at Paris, bypassing his lord.[162] Count Pierre was so enraged by Sir Jean's stubbornness on the matter that 'there were many times when he would have had him killed, but for the fact they had already gone to court.'[163] The case dragged on for a year and a half, culminating in a judicial duel, since the lady could not prove her charge against Le Gris.

By this time the case was so notorious throughout France that when this verdict was made known to King Charles VI (r. 1380–1422), waiting to embark on his attempted invasion of England, the king asked that the duel be postponed until he could be back in Paris to watch it. This delayed the proceedings, but the duel was indeed postponed, and when the king returned to Paris a date was finally set and Sir Jean prepared to meet his adversary.

After so much time and no further evidence to prove his wife was telling the truth, Sir Jean's courage wavered a little. Just before the duel was due to start, Sir Jean went to his wife, who was dressed somberly in black and seated in her carriage, to assure him one final time that she was telling the truth. She reassured him that his cause was just and true – he kissed her, made a sign of the cross, and entered the lists. She, meanwhile, prayed to God and the Virgin. Their anxiety was entirely justified: should Sir Jean lose, it would be taken as a sign from God that the lady had perjured herself, and he was to be hanged while she would be burned.[164]

Froissart gives a blow-by-blow account of the duel, which began on horseback and ended on foot. Sir Jean was wounded, a worrying moment for their cause, but in the end he managed to knock Le Gris down and run him through with his sword, killing him on the spot. With the case ended, Le Gris' body was handed over to the executioner, who hanged it symbolically. King Charles gave Sir Jean 1000 francs and made him a member of his chamber with a pension of 200 francs a year.[165]

Froissart's distaste for low-born men rising to ranks of privilege expressed a wider social concern across France and England, one of many tense undercurrents that ran through fourteenth-century society. Squires were among the most trusted men in a knightly or elite household, and it mattered who they were and where they came from. Were they rapacious or trustworthy? Could they be given such positions of authority with any degree of confidence? Were they prone to temptations and giving in to their baser natures? To whom were they loyal – the social network of the nobility, or to the networks of other base-born men who might also rebel against their lots in life, and with what consequences for society?

Moral questions like this carried with them the desire to uphold the status quo, so threatened by the Black Death and the recurring outbreaks of plague that continued through to the seventeenth century, and the need to restore confidence and control in a traumatised population now ravaged by war and the burdens of increasing taxes and legislative curbs upon the greater degrees of social mobility that the lower status classes were now enjoying.

Here we have three cases that demonstrate the dangers one's own household could present. The role of the squire required an intimate personal knowledge of the family and household, which could lead to strained or divided loyalties, tensions and anger. Just as wives feared being tied to a bad husband, so servants feared being tied to a bad master, and that seems to have been the case in the 1276 murder of Sir William de Arden. In this latter case, Richard be Bury may have hated Arden enough to kill him, but the murder was 'procured' by the knight's own steward and squire, who clearly had their own reasons to want their master dead.

Richard Gyse would have become an armour-bearer or squire aged around 14. It is worth remembering that 14-year-olds were considered 'men' at the time, and might even be married by this age since the age of consent was 12.[166] He would already have served as a page from the age of 7, and so had most likely grown up in the service of a knight (if not Richard de Bingham, the Cantilupes' neighbour, then another local family) from that time. Although his age at the time of the murder is not recorded, it is most likely that he would have been in his mid to late teens, or, like Chaucer's Squire in *The Canterbury Tales*, 20 at most. Estimating his age as mid-teens when he entered William's service and supposing that he been with William after 1367, when William was abroad for a year, then by 1375 he would have been around 22 and taken part in at least that one campaign. He would also be too old to be fully knighted, even if he possessed the required pre-requisites, and could not expect to climb the social ladder in that way unless there were some extraordinary battlefield circumstances that made him catch the eye of the king.

To murder someone one has known and served for several years, in cold blood and with malice aforethought, is not a thing to be dismissed lightly with a trite gloss about the violence of the society as a whole. The Neville servants of Scotton could have dragged Richard into the plot for the sake of Maud's future happiness with Kydale, but this is a thin premise for Richard to get involved. Hence Rawcliffe's assertion that he was Maud's 'young lover'.[167] Naturally, the reasoning goes, the lusty squire of Chaucer's sketch would be in love with his master's wife, and this would cause him to participate in the plot to murder her husband.

To make these leaps, we must first assume that Richard conforms to Chaucer's stereotype. We can perhaps consider that he was *not* her lover, but committed murder at her request so that they *could* be lovers afterwards. We must also therefore assume (with no evidence either way) that he was both heterosexual and that it was Lady Maud that he was attracted to, rather than the chambermaid Agatha Frere, with whom he also fled the manor. Indeed, the traditional interpretation centres the trope of lady/squire forbidden love and does not consider a far more prosaic idea: that if any heterosexual romantic dalliances were going on, it may well have been between Richard and Agatha, with whom he had a history of serving within the Bingham household.

He was one of the seven servants who transferred from Richard de Bingham's household to the Cantilupe's manor, although his age is never stated. If he was a young teenager at the time, Maud could well have seen him in a maternal light rather than a lustful one. Nevertheless, it was her testimony that convicted both him and Robert Cook, but that doesn't mean that she was happy to give them up, and the circumstances of her confession to Thomas Kydale – what she was told, whether she was threatened or intimidated during her arrest, how she was treated generally

– is also not recorded. Again, the constructed narrative that leans towards Maud's testimony as an act of callousness and self-preservation is based only on the fact that she did name these two men at all.

The jury completely acquitted Maud of her husband's murder, of orchestrating the plot, and of aiding and abetting, and the case was heard before the king himself. There must have been a reason other than corruption of the jury to explain why they too did not jump to the conclusion that Maud was an adulteress and therefore guilty of *something*. If it was clear to them all that her relationship with the squire was pseudo-maternal, bearing in mind that the jurors elected were from the same social circles as the Nevilles, Cantilupes and Paynells and therefore aware of her character and the reputations of all concerned in the case, then it would not have even occurred to them that she and Richard were having an affair.

The assumption that romantic love or lust was the primary motive in this case also doesn't account for the fact that, for William to have been murdered in a household conspiracy, his entire household was more or less willing to assist in his death, which indicates at the very least he was not well-liked and had not won their loyalty. At the very least, they were willing to put aside personal moralising for the sake of a bribe. Another possibility is that William was a bad master, or a bad husband, or both. If so, we return to the alternative suggestion of domestic violence and a planned, drastic intervention. In this scenario, even if Richard had been in love with Maud, his feelings did not need to have been returned in order for him to want to 'rescue' her from her situation. Otherwise, if William was not a bad husband but a bad master, the actions of the servants could be interpreted as an attempt to free himself from his own situation, with the assistance of a household of similarly angry, oppressed young men with access to blades.

One way to consider the most likely scenario is to consider a short, telling line recorded in the Sessions of the Peace:

And the said Richard Gyse has nothing whether chattals or land, nor tenants, etc.[168]

Knighthood was an expensive profession, and knights were expected to own lands and pay taxes in order to undertake local administrative duties.

If Richard could not afford to become a knight, then perhaps the promise of land and money was enough to override any loyalty to William that he may have had. His role was meant to provide him with these things and help him to climb the social ladder in order to carve out a career and a name for himself. Yet it would seem he had not even been gifted any goods of any value by his master, nor had he been entrusted with land, nor had he inherited anything from any of his own kin. Was this lack of goods or money a motive in itself? Had Richard become embittered by his master's lack of patronage, or had he taken his situation into account and agreed to a bribe? While Maud could have offered a bribe, it seems more likely that Ralph Paynell was behind it – after all, Richard went with Maud to Ralph's manor, where he had access to Ralph's household and could have entered Ralph's service had the highwayman ruse paid off. Did Maud run to Caythorpe with him willingly? Or did he insist – at bloody knifepoint, after stabbing her husband on their bed – on going with her, to the house of another noble who may need a squire and could introduce him into a better, or wider, knightly social circle than William had done? These are questions we cannot answer from the evidence, but they are worth asking. If assumptions are to be made on the scanty circumstantial evidence provided in the trial, then it is worth pointing out all of the interpretations of these events that can be made.

Summary of Suspects and their Suggested Motives

The indicted suspects have been discussed here as fully as possible, despite the lack of evidence around the majority of their lives. While considering the question of *who* killed Sir William, they have also provided a small window into the world of fourteenth-century England, which opens the door to considering motivations for the crime.

The unhappy or mistreated wife of noble birth, the powerful neighbour slighted and seeking revenge, angry young men in a predominantly masculine, homosocial environment with access to deadly weapons, all could have played a part in the murder for a number of reasons.

Was the murder committed for material gain, and if so, who stood to benefit in this way?

Was the murder a crime of passion or a case of domestic disharmony?

Was the murder committed in the spirit of revenge or communal vigilante justice?

Each motive will be given a separate chapter where comparisons and other relevant examples will be considered, shedding light on the dark sides of medieval life. In terms of material gain, William's father, William senior, will be considered as a potential mastermind of the plot, underestimated and left out of all historical interpretations of the event. William senior has been neglected largely for good reason: filicide of this type is very rare indeed, and he already held lands and had made a good marriage, so killing off his son seems far-fetched. Nevertheless, for the sake of being thorough, this chapter will deal with the troubling question of filicide and how such fathers were represented in literature and law, and attempt to colour in some of the patchy details of William senior's life and career. It is harder to see a motive for the household to engage willingly in such a conspiracy, either, considering their loyalties to other lords, but money can be a powerful motive for people who have very little. The plausibility of this will be considered here too.

The traditional interpretation of the evidence, as we have seen, favours the 'adulterous wife with many lovers' motif, casting Maud Cantilupe and the corrupt sheriff as the villains of the piece, with Richard Gyse as the manipulated young lover and patsy. This will be considered in chapter five, where the murder will be examined from the angle of a crime of passion. An overview of the concept(s) of medieval marriage will set this motive in context, along with comparative examples of wives killing their husbands, and a consideration of adultery in the fourteenth century. Again, while this provides Richard Gyse with a motive for murder, it does not so easily explain the household's willingness to support him in such an active way, except (again) for bribery.

It is worth noting that neither of these motives adequately explain Sir Ralph's involvement, and so it must be assumed that his grudge against the Cantilupes as a family had been continually nursed over the intervening five years following Nicholas's death and was strong enough to translate into either sheltering William the younger's killers (alleged or actual), or into being the purse-strings behind the bribe, as has been suggested by some scholars.

However, there are other reasons why a wife might want her husband out of the way, and one of those is what shall be termed 'domestic disharmony', which could be anything from a dysfunctional relationship and breakdown of communication between the couple to spousal abuse. 'Domestic disharmony' as a motive for revenge or form of vigilante justice perpetrated by the household is the final motive discussed. Of course, in this case the victim does not have to be Maud at all, but rather one or more of the servants, and mistreatment is not necessarily sexual in this context, either. Other household conspiracies hinted at a collective sense of grievance against the lord in question, and a closer look at these would help in reading between the lines of the trial narrative.

Chapter 4

Motives for Murder: Material Gain/Loss

'Where there's a will, there's a family fighting over it'
Matt Wohlfarth

Since (for scholars) the case seems to revolve around (bribery and) who held the purse-strings, money is the most obvious motive to consider if only to rule it out. Sir William himself was accused of poisoning his brother in order to gain the lands and title. One of the first questions that should be asked is, who stood to gain from Sir William the younger's death, and what did they stand to gain? Could the motive have been material reward, or could it have been its inverse: anger over the withholding of money or lands or goods, another reason cited in court for violence against medieval lords?

The Calendars of Inquisitions Post Mortem were the records made by the king's investigators into the deaths of those men and women of means in the kingdom, so that the king knew who owned what at the time of their death, who the heirs were, and who had to pay for their lands to be released to them.

On 12 April 1376, the king's writ went out for the inquisition to take place across the counties of England. The inquisition for Wiltshire was heard in Salisbury, 1 May 1376, and the findings reported. Sir William, at the time of his death, held one manor in Wiltshire, namely the manor of 'Ambresbury', held as a gift of the earl of Salisbury by knight's service. He held it in fee tail (that is, it reverted to his heirs at his death), by gift and enfeoffment of Sir Thomas Newemarche, Sir John Bussey the elder (husband of Isabel Paynell) and Hugh Cressy. These were the three knights that his grandfather had demised several manors to, but now they would revert to his heir – named in the inquisition as 'William de Cantilupo, knight, aged 40 years and more', that is, Sir William the elder.[1]

The inquisition at Aylesbury for the county of Buckinghamshire was held on the 22 May 1376, and found that the manors of Middle Claydon and 'Eselburgh' both belonged to William, inherited from Sir Nicholas the elder his grandfather. Again it was found that his father, Sir William the elder, was his heir.[2]

On 22 June 1376, the York inquest was heard at York castle. Here it was found that Sir William the younger had held the manor of Ravensthorpe and 'diverse lands' in Ferham, Stanlay, Azerlowe, Braithwaite, Rydner and York, but it was found that he had, on 6 August 1373, given all of them by charter to Sir Marmaduke Constable who had served a term as sheriff of Yorkshire in 1362,[3] Sir William de Aldeburgh, William de Bradeston who was the parson of the church of Wynfield, and John de Felicekirk who was the parson of the church of Scotton, Lindsay.[4] Therefore, he held no manors in Yorkshire at the time of his death, and these men continued to hold them under the terms of the 1373 charter. These men appear again in 1378, when a commission was ordered to discover if they really were in possession of Ravensthorpe and the other manors as they claimed. The commission was required by John son of John Hastings, a minor in the king's custody, and William de la Zouche of Harringdon, the Cantilupe cousins-by-marriage who were apparently still very interested in the lands of their cadet kinsmen.[5] William de la Zouche was also connected to Sir William the younger's erstwhile attorney, Robert Roos of Ingmansthorpe, as de la Zouche was pursuing a suit of court with Roos' son Thomas, which in 1378 was pending in Chancery.[6]

This is a telling paragraph, as it indicated the Nevilles and their networks had already benefitted from Maud's marriage to William before 1375. The Neville parson of Scotton's church had already gained Cantilupe lands by this 1373 charter, and the Constables, part of the local gentry network of which Sir Ralph Paynell was another major player, were also connected in this material way. Sir Marmaduke's kinsman Sir Robert Constable appeared with Sir Robert Neville (most likely Maud's father) as a pledge for Maud when she was indicted for murder.[7] It is also to be remembered that Scotton was never a Cantilupe manor: it belonged to Maud, not to William, and it was not listed among the manors he held at his death.

The Nevilles and Paynells seem to have been far more closely connected to one another than they were to the Cantilupes, or at least after Sir William's death were prepared to take sides and protect Lady Maud during the trial. With the backing of such powerful men, this put the sheriff in a difficult position. Marrying Lady Maud may have been more about advancement for Sir Thomas de Kydale than actual affection, especially if he wanted access to these social circles and did not want there to be hard feelings from such quarters for his part in arresting Maud in the first place.

For Lincolnshire, the inquest held at 'Ancastre' heard that Sir William held the manor of Lavington in Kesteven, which his grandfather had enfeoffed to the same three knights: Sir Thomas Newemarche, Sir John Bussey the elder and Sir Hugh de Cressy. As with the Buckinghamshire manors, this reverted to William's heir – his father, Sir William the elder.[8] This was one of the three contested manors that Katherine Paynell had claimed Nicholas the younger had given to her, but she had been unable to support her claim with documentary evidence.

At the trial, it is notable that none of these three men appear in any capacity, which would imply they did not come to testify against Lady Maud's character or give any evidence that might have implicated her or Sir Ralph in the incident.

Also in Lincolnshire, Sir William was found to hold Kinthorpe and Withcall in Lindsey, the other two manors contested by his ex-sister-in-law. These also passed to Sir William the elder.[9]

Greasley castle and its lands in Nottinghamshire were also inherited (finally) by Sir William the elder, as was the Derbyshire manor of Ilkston.[10]

In fact, the only person to gain materially from Sir William's death was his father, and there is no indication of the kind of relationship they had, in the same way that there is no recorded evidence regarding the state of William and Maud's marriage. Maud never claimed her dower after the trial, and so did not receive anything from her husband's estate until her third husband, John Bussey the younger, a favourite of Richard II, helped her claim her share. While Maud and her second husband, Thomas de Kydale, did grant the Paynells some lands to hold until Maud's death, these were Neville lands not Cantilupe lands, and the Paynells did not benefit directly in any material way from Cantilupe manors, rents or castles after Sir William's murder.

William the elder has been left out of every interpretation of the evidence and was not recorded as present at the trial. Neither was he called as a witness, nor did he appear in any of the recorded testimony. Yet he gained the most from the deaths of his sons, even though Nicholas's untimely demise was deemed to be natural. If anyone bribed the servants for a material motive, it would be the only person who did stand to gain from Sir William the younger's death. Therefore, if only to be ruled out, William the elder must also be considered.

Could William the elder be behind the murder of William the younger?

It is difficult to piece together anything about the elder William from the records, since he appears even less than either of his sons, and hardly ever in the years between his father's death in 1355 and the death of Nicholas the younger. Where he does appear it is usually in relation to his inheritance, and what he had and had not received. In 1352, three years before his father's death, he is found owing £60 to William de Clinton, Earl of Huntingdon and £200 to John Hilltoft, goldsmith and citizen of London.[11] He also owed £400 to John de Bures and Robert Picot, citizens and merchants of London that same year: both debts were recorded in December.[12] By March 1353, William owed his father Nicholas an enormous amount of money, namely £1000, possibly because Nicholas had consolidated and paid off his debts the year before, but the records do not tell us what the debt was for.[13] It is likely that debts this eye-watering (£1000 had the rough buying power equivalent of nearly £600,000 in 2017, according to the National Archives Currency Converter),[14] were accumulated for military expeditions. Of course, passing the succession straight to his grandson meant that William the elder's capacity for debt was limited, or this could have been part of an agreement father and son reached to write off this enormous amount. In 1356, William VI, still listed as his father's son and heir although Sir Nicholas senior had died the year before cutting him out of the succession, owed John de la Porte of Northamptonshire £100.[15] It would seem that he was listed as the 'son and heir' here either because he held his father's part fee in Friskney and Elkington in his own right, or because he was jointly holding his father's lands in trust for his two young sons with his stepmother Joan. Or, of course, he simply hadn't told his creditor and the witnesses to the debt that he had not in fact inherited his father's lands and title.

In the first set of debts to the merchants, incurred while his father was still alive, William was also called 'the son and heir' of Nicholas Cantilupe (my emphasis), even though his two sons had already been born. This would mean that the arrangement could only have happened after the debts were incurred, and that Nicholas senior did not correct the creditors' assumption that William senior was to inherit.[16]

With his eldest son disgraced and dead by the age of 28, and William the younger still childless by 1375, William the elder could well have decided he had two disappointing sons, and if his debts privately increased, unrecorded in formal documents, then he may well have arranged to have his younger son killed for the Cantilupe estates and rents that would return to him.

Moreover, with the arrest of the younger son for the suspected murder of the older, it is possible that the father did not quite believe that Sir William was not responsible even though he was acquitted.

This kind of conjecture is, like the traditional interpretation, essentially unprovable. Imagined debts are required to be as concrete for the motive to work as Sillem's imagined affair. Procuring murder was a very difficult thing to prove unless someone confessed to it, and there was no whisper or rumour that this was the case, just as there was no suggestion recorded to suggest that Maud and Thomas were involved before the murder.

Still, if we are to consider one seriously, we should also consider the other. Unfortunately for William the younger, money was not the only possible motive, and his father was not the only possible suspect.

Filicide in the Middle Ages

Filicide was a common theme in classical literature, although in medieval narratives and English versions of classical, Celtic and German tales, it is usually an infant that is killed, and often by the mother rather than the father.[17] Eyre rolls from medieval England support the pattern, with more cases of filicide being a case of infanticide, including infant exposure, and was recognised primarily as a single woman's crime.[18]

Nevertheless, literature traditions still recognised and represented fathers killing sons, sometimes conceptualised as 'sacrifice' rather than 'murder', a designation that was very rarely applied to a mother's killing of her child. Some of these paternally-perpetrated filicides include Arthur's slaying of his son-nephew Mordred, and fathers killing their adult sons in the Old Irish *Cath Maige Tuired* (*The Second Battle of Mag*

Tuired) and *Fingal Rónáin* (*The Kin-slaying of Rónán*).[19] The father-killing-sons motif appears in various sagas, such as Snorri Sturluson's *Ynglinga saga*, the first part of his immense *Heimskringla* (*Circle of the World*), which includes the tale of King Aun, 'who sacrifices his sons, one by one, to Odin in order to prolong his own life.'[20] Where it is not so commonly represented, however, is in the Anglo-Norman literature tradition. Anxieties here feature the fates of children in foster-care, a common practice whereby families gave their sons to other families to raise as their own, in order to create and strengthen the bonds between them.

Romances and tragedies dealt with issues of cruelty and mistreatment of such fostered children, and in Chaucer's *Clerk's Tale* infanticide is used as a test of a mother, Griselda, by her husband Walter, who is also the biological father of the children. As it turns out, the murders never actually occurred: Walter takes away Griselda's children to test her resolve never to say 'no' to him, and pretends to have them killed. They are not, but Griselda believes her children are dead for eight years. Barrie Ruth Straus, focusing on Walter's motivations for such a test, argues that this shows the father's right to commit infanticide, and suggests that 'psychologically he may desire to be rid of the child that makes his own death implicit.'[21] Chaucer does not go as far as making Walter a murderer, however. More often in medieval literature, where such a crime is committed, it is the mother who is depicted as both the giver and destroyer of life, as the church counted contraception and abortion as forms of murder.

While the perception was that such a crime was a single woman's, this was not the case. In practice, fathers were regularly indicted for filicide and may have 'sometimes escaped conviction because society expected a good father to discipline his child.'[22] Fathers were also treated more harshly than mothers because, for a mother to kill her own child, the jurors believed she must be insane and often went to great lengths to describe her state of mind before and after the murder(s), but did not go into such detail when the accused was the father.[23] Conversely, deaths caused by fathers were more likely to be ruled as death by misadventure or accident than when the mother was to blame.[24]

There was clearly a framework for thinking about filicide, but in this case, it simply wasn't suspected. Fathers killed sons with their own hands, by excessive discipline or by accident in the fields or during some other strenuous activity, and in the vast majority of cases the son was still a child. Such a framework did not have much room for fathers calculatedly hiring servants to murder their adult sons.

Additionally, none of the servants admitted to being bribed or coerced by anyone, not even Maud or Sir Ralph, and not even Robert Cook the butler or Richard Gyse the squire tried to pin the blame onto their social superiors when accused outright by Lady Maud herself, but stuck resolutely to their plea of 'not guilty'. Maud did not give a reason for the murder, at least, not one recorded in the trial records. She merely pointed the finger at Gyse and Cook, and this testimony was eventually accepted. Some scholars believe Sir Ralph had been holding the purse-strings to bribe the servants into the deed, although there is no evidence for this. With the same amount of evidence – or rather lack thereof – why not consider Sir William the elder, ensconced safely elsewhere, miles away from Scotton and not likely to be suspected? We know absolutely nothing about the relationship between father and son, as nothing was settled in court between them or reported to the justices, and there are no debtor or creditor records that might illuminate their financial relationship.

Material Loss

The inverse of this motive, that of material loss or detained service, does not implicate the father unless William the elder was exceptionally unhappy with the arrangement from the start. It would implicate the servants themselves, but not necessarily the servants already attached to Scotton through the Nevilles, but rather the servants who were more mobile and had already come to the Cantilupes after being released from their previous lord's employ. Since all the servants stuck to their 'not guilty' pleas and refused to implicate one another, we do not know whether William had promised any of them money, lands or anything else that was not delivered. The only servant this would fit would be the accused Richard Gyse, the squire, who had no lands of his own. Being promised a career or material reward that could greatly improve his status, and then not receiving it, would certainly add a reason for him to want his master dead.

The murder of Sir William de Arden is a key example of a household conspiracy around a material motive – the murderer himself bore a grudge based on the detaining of his service and withholding of money – but given the number of servants both within and outside de Arden's household involved in his murder, it would seem that this was the tip of the iceberg. Sir William de Arden's steward and squire, apparently unwilling to get their own hands dirty, found a man to do the deed who hated their master as much as they did. The murderer Richard de Bury, 'hated William because he detained his service, and [withheld from him] a sum of money acquired in the war time.'[25] On 17 April 1275, Richard de Bury met with Sir William in William's grove called 'Briddesmor' by Henwood Priory and killed him there. It is not recorded if the steward and squire were present, but they hardly needed to be: Richard was supported by eight other men who were present at the scene to aid him in his crime.

These men were: Robert, whom the jury knew to be a servant or tenant of Sir Hamon de Vielest; Richard de Hockley; Alexander Carles of Alcester; Nicholas son of Nicholas de Kingley; Robert de Woodville a sumpter-man (*sometarius*, that is, a driver of a pack horse or beast of burden); Richard Brid and William his brother, and Richard son of Alice of Solihull, who was a goldsmith of Bristol.[26] All these men were said to be present at the time of the murder, implying a similar conspiracy to the Cantilupe case. Not all of them were members of William de Arden's household, and it is hard to say what motives they had for aiding and abetting, although the goldsmith may indicate that the main motivation was similar to Richard de Bury's, that is, the withholding of or perhaps cheating out of money, or the detaining of service.

In order to throw suspicion away from themselves or to kill two birds with one proverbial stone, the blame for the murder was thrown onto Sir Richard de Insula, who was arrested and imprisoned in Shrewsbury.[27] Richard de Insula languished in prison until a royal writ was issued to the sheriff of Shropshire in 13 December 1276. The king learned from the sheriff of Warwick that Richard de Insula had been charged with the murder 'out of malice and hatred and not because he was guilty thereof', and that twelve knights of the county had mainperned him so that he could be released from gaol and attend the sessions of court.[28] It is unclear whether the guilty parties had cast the blame onto Richard, or if this had been done by the sheriff or other law enforcement officials in the county, or some other party who simply saw an opportunity to make trouble for the knight.

William de Arden's brother Richard was his next heir but was found to be mentally incapable of holding his lands, so the lands were taken into the king's hands and granted to his consort Eleanor.[29]

The loss or withholding of important possessions could be a powerful motive for murder, but in this case the only thing that we know Sir William VII de Cantilupe withheld from anyone were the three manors that Nicholas gave to Katherine upon their marriage, and they were never really hers in any case. These were three manors held by fee in tail, so that when Nicholas died they would no longer belong to his wife but to his next heir – should that be his son, this wouldn't have mattered, and his wife could have theoretically held the lands on behalf of her child if he was a minor. Nicholas and Katherine obviously had no children, and so Katherine couldn't prove that he had given her these manors on any other conditions. It seems more likely that this was pushed into court by her new husband, Sir John Auncell, out to capitalise on his new wife's history if he could with nothing to lose if their case was rejected.

Sir Ralph Paynell certainly had enough manors and income of his own to be unconcerned about three relatively minor manors in Lincolnshire that his daughter had no real claim to after her annulment.

Overall, material gain and material loss, while strong motives for murder, do not seem to fit this case. Revenge may be closer to the mark if William senior is put in the frame, particularly if he believed Nicholas had been murdered and suspected his younger son of the deed. Otherwise, he had not been left without lands and income, he had his wife's lands as well as those granted to him by his father even if the lion's share had gone to his children, and he was never suspected at the time or mentioned in the trial. Whether this is a fair reason to discount him, given the vast lacunae in the evidence, is left up to the reader to decide.

Chapter 5

Motives for Murder: Affairs of the Heart

'The nature of love is to kill for it, or to die'
Maaza Mengiste

Medieval Marriage

Marriage in this period changed a man's relationship to his male kin, admitting him into the circle of his elders and older brothers as a member of the decision-making, responsibility-bearing male group who controlled the family's patrimony.[1] For men as well as women it marked a transitionary period from childhood/adolescence to adulthood, and could make or break the ambitions of a social climber.[2] While the celebrated 'greatest knight' of the twelfth century, William Marshal, may have availed himself of the company and sexual favours of the prostitutes at court (or indeed, the women under supervision of the Marshal's department), he never acknowledged any bastards in the later part of his career and, it is related, desperately hung around in anterooms waiting to hear if the new king Richard I would make good on the old king's promise to give William a wife.[3] In the fourteenth century, a good match, preferably to an heiress or co-heiress with lands and dowry that would vastly improve their current standing in the community was just as important for ambitious young men as it was two centuries previously.

Marriage also created a contractual obligation to the wife's kin, particularly her father and brothers, and provided access to a wider social network that could expand the young man's horizons in terms of acquaintances, career opportunities and patronage.[4] Nicholas Cantilupe the younger had failed catastrophically in the latter area, with the breakdown of relations between himself and his father-in-law underscoring the breakdown of his marriage to Katherine. His actions and acts of aggression towards his wife can be read as an example of 'anxious masculinity', framed by Mark Breitenberg in an early modern[5] male context as male preoccupation with (male) sexual prowess, sexual jealousy and cuckoldry, a response to the contradictions within the patriarchal society engendering these anxieties.[6] This system was rooted in the social norms and developing culture of the previous centuries, and in this respect is a relevant framework to retrospectively apply to the fourteenth century. With the stigma surrounding his physical traits, leading to popular rumour and criticism of his [knightly masculine] identity, Nicholas responded with denial and 'masculine' acts of aggression, refusing to expose himself to the public gaze and settle the veracity of Katherine's allegations one way or another, but instead using legal means to fight his case. The social structures of the time arguably left him with few recourses, channelling his actions along destructive routes, and resulting in domestic abuse and Katherine's six-month ordeal at Greasley.

This, and Nicholas's explicit insistence that he was able to procreate, contrasts the official ecclesiastic position that it was consent, not consummation, that made a marriage binding.[7] Despite this official position, procreation was simultaneously promoted as the purpose for marriage, and in the popular thought at least, the conjugal act and consummation seemed to win out over consent, with a number of annulment cases citing the wife's desire for children and the husband's inability to provide them.

William VII, on the other hand, had no such problems with the Nevilles, at least, none that survive in the records. The state of his relationship with Maud is unknown, but no annulment proceedings were brought in this case, which implies neither party had sufficient grounds. Nevertheless, rumours about his brother abounded, as Katherine drew upon them for corroboration in the ecclesiastical court, and gossip could be transferred from one Cantilupe brother to another, particularly as William and Maud remained childless and therefore without obvious evidence of William's own virility or indeed his ability to procreate. His brother's personal crisis is all the more relevant in light of this, since it adds another layer of motivation to dispose of him. Reputation and tainted reputation were powerful things, particularly among families that relied upon the respect of their peers and social superiors to advance themselves. It could conceivably give rise to dissatisfaction in the marriage on Maud's part, and, if the traditional interpretation is taken as the actual version of events, then it could have given her an added impetus to look outside of her marriage for solace and for another member of the knightly elite to improve her situation.

Adulterys

Unhappy marriages seem to have been a theme among this generation, and annulment, as we have seen, was a long and often public process. Katherine Paynell won her case, but Maud had no such grounds and there is no evidence regarding the state of her marriage in the stages of its contraction or early years. Even regarding the trial, the records do not provide any clear indication of her feelings towards her husband, only that she denied any involvement in his murder. The only evidence supplied for Maud's marital unhappiness is her swift remarriage to Thomas Kydale after the trial's conclusion. How swift this remarriage was, however, is up for debate. The formal royal pardon issued to Maud and Thomas for marrying without the king's permission is dated 1379, four years after the trial.[8] Even if they had married in 1378, that was hardly rushing things.

Reasons for this assumption have been laid out in the previous chapter, and, as we are considering Sillem's traditional interpretation first, we should now consider what adultery meant in practice in a medieval marriage.

Yet experiences are not universal, and private arrangements and sexual proclivities were just as diverse as today. For example, Nicholas le Wodeward and his wife Alice, a peasant couple from the Bury St Edmunds manor of Hinderclay, in North Suffolk, were revealed to have a complicated arrangement with Robert son of Adam, with whom Alice had been having an affair for a number of years with Nicholas's full knowledge and consent.[9] Additionally, Jan Rüdiger has played devil's advocate in the face of accepted understandings of monogamy and marriage – a position he freely admits is a difficult one to take – and suggests that in fact medieval Europe was largely a polygynous society. Rüdiger takes this position by arguing that at the 'core' (if that is a meaningful simile at all) of a household was a person – usually a man – who entertained a number of social relationships with the people around him. These people occupied various positions in the hierarchy, in various degrees of dependency and/or subordination, and many of these relationships had, or were presumed to have, a sexual side to them.[10] Whether this argument is taken as reasonable or not, it still hinges upon the binary of man-woman sexual activity as a socially accepted form of interaction, and as a measurement of masculinity within the medieval European context.

To put this more plainly: Rüdiger contends that people were expected to have relationships with servants and peers, and that these relationships were usually extra-marital. While Rüdiger is playing devil's advocate here to challenge the concept of monogamy as a medieval norm, this is a relevant hypothesis for this chapter, but doesn't take into account the dynamics of particular relationships.

For a start, given the anxieties around masculinity were predominantly focused on the warrior culture and sexual prowess, William himself may have been having other relationships throughout his marriage, and that being the case, perhaps the focus should shift from Lady Maud's supposed adultery to his as a motive for murder. Just because men could take advantage of their position or could engage in extra-marital affairs did not mean their wives were happy about it. This, after all, was cited as the reason Isabel Bull ran away from her husband Robert, whom she caught 'misbehaving with other women.'[11] If the woman was in a subordinate social position and unhappy with Sir William's advances – in this case, for example, Agatha Frere – then where might she complain? Only to her mistress and fellow-servants, although there was a risk that her mistress would turn her out or mistreat her as a consequence. Or, perhaps, such a story would be listened to with outrage, and the consequence would be murder. This is an alternative to the traditional interpretation that will be considered more fully in the following chapter on communal vengeance or revenge.

As far as the traditional view goes, Lady Maud as adulteress makes just as much sense for a motive as any other. Whatever the societal expectations, monogamy was taken seriously in legal practice. The church held up monogamy as the norm, and there were severe punishments for violating the sanctity of the marriage bed when husbands or wives were thus accused in a formal manner.

One punishment for being caught in adultery involved being stripped to one's underwear and beaten with sticks around the parish church in public. In practice, the punishments were stratified by status, since there were political and socio-cultural needs to uphold the status quo. This meant that members of the knightly class and other social elites caught in adultery could receive pilgrimages and fines as punishment, rather than the humiliation of half-naked beatings, thus avoiding the embarrassment and disgrace. As Lindsay Bryan puts it, '[h]igh-ranking people were supposed to set good examples for the lesser folk, and it would be difficult to maintain respect and deference for them if they were to be beaten in public in their undies.'[12]

By the fourteenth century, this was a well-established alternative. In the early 1290s, an adulterous knight in Canterbury gave alms to paupers at the hospital 'because it is not decent for a knight to do public penance.'[13] In York, 1309, Lady Lucy Tweng was sent to Watton Priory to do her penance to avoid scandal.[14] Evidently, there was no such mutually consenting arrangement as that between the le Wodewards and Robert son of Adam in these cases.

That members of the elite could and did receive punishments and penalties for adulterous behaviours when caught and given the nature of public life and scandal in local elite culture, it would seem that either Maud and Thomas were not caught, or perhaps got William out of the way before Maud could be disciplined.

As far as popular thought was concerned, however, adultery could occasionally be justified, and adulterers could incur sympathy. Alisoun's adultery in Chaucer's *The Miller's Tale* is ingenious and comedic, positioning the old, foolish husband as the butt of the jokes (quite literally, at the memorable climax).

Marie de France's lai, *Yonec*, positions the young wife of an old, miserly marcher lord as the innocent damsel-in-distress, despite her son (the eponymous hero, Yonec) being the product of adultery with an angelic, shapeshifting knight who visits her locked tower in disguise as a hawk. In each case, as in other examples, the adultery can be justified if the husband is old, impotent, miserly, falling into the recognised medieval literary tropes of the comedy villain or antagonist. Most especially, it is the question of the cuckold's virility which is central to the jokes and the motivation for the affair. If a wife cannot be satisfied, then she may engineer all kinds of entertaining devices to trick her husband and find that satisfaction beyond the marriage-bed. Impotence carried with it a host of baggage in the medieval mind, and the picture accompanying it was one of advancing years (therefore obvious physical frailty), usually contrasted by the lusty young lover. In a society where, despite the widespread belief in the sanctity of marriage (at least theologically), extra-marital affairs were common and sexual activity was an accepted fact of life among the laity, the issue was not necessarily constrained to one partner cheating on another, but that of ability (and desire) to have sex *at all*.

Male impotence as expressed in the literature of the time invoked real concerns surrounding medieval concepts of masculinities, as expressed in the ecclesiastical courts. Nicholas and Katherine's case was just one example of suits brought to York, emphasising the seriousness of erectile dysfunction and the traumatic difficulties of being intersex in a society where procreation was a central concern to socio-cultural, economic and religious structures.

At 30 years of age with military campaigns under his belt, William Cantilupe was hardly the comedic, elderly cuckold of popular humorous fiction, but bawdy tales acted as mirrors for their society's anxieties, particularly around the issue of sexual prowess. Up to now, a picture of Maud as scheming adulteress has been presented, but William's response to his wife's childlessness and/or the desire to prove his own masculinity in ways acceptable or readily recognised as 'male' by society could equally have driven Maud to seek protection and comfort elsewhere. This consideration positions Maud as dissatisfied rather than scheming, and should William have responded to his own childlessness with some form of aggression towards his wife, as his brother Nicholas reacted, then Maud's assumed affair still fits the traditional interpretation of events but with a potentially stronger motive for murder.

Considering the traditional interpretation from this angle, the question of what happened within abusive medieval marriages and how this was policed or tackled by the wider family and community will be tackled in the remainder of this chapter.

There were two kinds of divorce that a married couple could attain, one, the annulment – a divorce *a vinculo*, 'from the bond', which was only granted by the ecclesiastical court if the marriage had not yet been consummated or if the marriage contract was proven to be invalid, so the couple had technically never been married at all. If this was impossible to prove, then the only other option was a divorce *a mensa et thoro*, 'from table and bed', which legally allowed the couple to separate and live apart, exempting them from the marital duties of sharing meals and a bed together. Neither party were allowed to remarry, as the bond was not dissolved. This kind of 'divorce' was granted only rarely and usually because of the husband's cruelty.

If a woman was unhappy with her situation, she could not just apply for a separation – men were permitted and expected to 'discipline' their spouses, and views on what discipline counted as 'excessive' was subjective. Depositions in cruelty suits emphasised the shedding of blood and risk to life, so an abusive husband who was cruel to his wife in other ways would not necessarily fit the court's definition of a cruel husband. Even if she could prove her case and be allowed to live separately from him, she could not remarry. If Lady Maud wanted both to be free of a cruel and abusive spouse but also desired to marry again, then a divorce in her circumstances was not an option and she would not be free of her husband unless he died.

Domestic Disharmony

First, we will consider the traditional interpretation that centres Lady Maud, and adjust the assumptions that she orchestrated the murder because she was in love with another man. There are, after all, other reasons why a woman would want her husband dead, as the example from renaissance Italy demonstrated. If there were many women desperate enough to use poisons like Aqua Tofana in sixteenth-century Naples, Perugia and Rome, there were also women in the same situations in fourteenth-century England without the recourse to similar drastic 'remedies'. In such circumstances, and especially in peasant communities, aggressive forms of community justice were a common factor in protecting women from excessive spousal cruelty.

At the time of her marriage, Maud Neville was likely in her early twenties. Marriages typically didn't take place until the woman was at least 16 to 18, as can be seen from Katherine Paynell's testimony in pursuit of her annulment. By the time of William's death he was around 30 years old, so they had probably been married for some years by 1375, even though we have no clear record of their marriage date, and of course William was abroad from 1368–71. Given the closeness of her relationship with the Paynells, and the almost fatherly concern shown to her by Sir Ralph, it would make sense that Maud was friends with her sister-in-law and had a long history with the family.

The drama of her sister-in-law's unhappy marriage and struggles with Nicholas would not have been totally unknown to Maud: apart from the gossip among the familial circle, there was the high-profile castle-breaking incident by Sir Ralph in 1368 to rescue Katherine from her husband. It is unlikely that people in such small circles of elite county society did not talk about this, or that the two brothers themselves had no communication with one another for the duration of Nicholas's marriage.

If Maud did indeed plot and orchestrate the murder of her own husband, as some historians believe, she was sure to find an ally in her sister-in-law's outraged family, even though by that time Nicholas had been dead for five years.

For England in the later Middle Ages, Barbara Hanawalt argued that domestic violence was infrequent, and Fletcher, while admitting it was 'unquantifiable' and 'a regrettable part of married life' gives the impression that murderous violence would prompt interventions by neighbours and authorities.[15] This certainly seems to have been the case for Katherine, who had her kin to protect her from her husband's attempts to keep her locked up.

In his assessment of spousal abuse and domestic violence in later medieval Bologna, Trevor Dean notes that it has been 'long and widely known' among historians that husbands had a legal right to use violence to 'correct' or 'discipline' their wives.[16] This right was assumed by husbands in their daily lives, although levels of domestic violence were regulated in law. In Dean's example, a Sienese man, taken to court after breaking his wife's arm, exclaimed incredulously, 'Can't a husband beat his wife?'[17] Similarly, in 1357, another man was taken to court in Bologna for hitting his wife over the head with a stone, drawing blood. He said he had done it to correct her; the judge accordingly closed the case and no further action was taken.[18]

In England, actions were generally not as extreme, and where men participated in tithing groups from the age of 12 they were prepared to engage in their communal responsibilities. This included intervening if they felt that a husband's chastisement of his wife was too excessive.[19] Regarding these incidents, family and friends may themselves take things into their own hands: a Northamptonshire coroner's roll for 1315 records the case of John Pistor of Pilsgate as one such example. John Pistor and his wife Emma got into an argument at their home, during which John began to beat her as punishment for her 'misbehaviour'. Emma raised the hue against him, and her brother, hearing his sister's cries for help, came into the house with an axe and killed John with a blow to his head.[20]

Opposition to family violence could also come from the in-laws. Again in Lincolnshire, Alice Sely was accidentally killed by her own brother, Walter Rake. Walter's wife Margery had fled to her sister-in-law's home for protection, where Alice took her in, but Walter followed her there. An argument broke out and when Alice saw him draw his dagger, she flung herself between them to save Margery, and her brother stabbed her through the heart.[21]

These examples come from the lower end of the social spectrum, where neighbours knew one another's business. For a member of the gentry it was harder to flee from manor to manor, particularly when lords with multiple possessions in multiple counties travelled between them and may not be in a convenient place at the time sanctuary was required. Instead of running from village to village or house to house within a few miles' radius, the logistics involved taking horses for longer journeys – an act of theft when taken without the husband's permission – and the risk of pursuit by armed men. This was Katherine Paynell's reality. Her husband did in fact send out mounted armed men to bring her back to Greasley Castle, and her father responded in a similarly violent way.

For Maud, perhaps she felt safer being in a Neville manor, where she could count on the loyalties of the villagers and the servants who had known her since her birth. While the household conspiracy has previously been painted as a callous, calculated plot to get William out of the way so Maud could marry Thomas Kydale, it could also be that William's isolation in the Neville manor was to check his behaviour towards his wife and that Kydale did not come into the picture at all until the trial.

Loyalties within families and communities could lead to more violence and death, but there were other options that spouses could consider, although they could face violent responses and legal action as a result.

Women who deserted their husbands and refused to cohabit with them could often face sanctions such as suspension (a minor form of excommunication) and excommunication in the ecclesiastical courts. Marital disharmony very often had a legal dimension, particularly from the fifteenth century onwards.[22] Charles Donahue's work on the fourteenth and fifteenth century courts at York showed that women were therefore more likely to pursue legal action, and that in these cases the courts were pro-plaintiff, seeing marriage as a sacrament and wanting to resolve such complaints to keep married couples together.[23] For the woman, this was preferable to braving the full social exclusion of major excommunication, which prevented participation in community life and prohibited other Christians – that is, the majority if not the entirety of their local community – from talking to them, doing business with them, entertaining them or working with them. Economically, also, women who deserted their husbands were vulnerable unless they had the full support of their kin. Should they take something with them from their homes, they could be accused of theft and dealt with in the courts accordingly. Wives who deserted their husbands risked a great deal to overcome the permanence of marriage, as did those who abetted them.

There is no evidence that Maud was similarly treated by William, just as there is no evidence to suggest she and Kydale were having an affair. However, if William had in fact been abusing Lady Maud in a similar manner, this would explain why his murder was undertaken by his entire household as an extreme form of intervention. Knowing Katherine's experience with Nicholas and the subsequent legal battles over her three manors with William, Maud could be sure that Ralph Paynell would believe the worst of the surviving Cantilupe brother. Moreover, Sir Ralph was the kind of man who listened. While he had initially dismissed his daughter's story, he came to Katherine's aid at once upon hearing that she was in real trouble. Moreover, he had once entertained the killer of his own servant, appreciating the fact that it had been a case of self-defence. If this was the Ralph Paynell his family and friends could count on, regardless of whether or not he was willing to abuse his power in an economic and political capacity, then this was a man that Maud felt she could trust to protect her and believe her.

If he really knew nothing about the premeditated crime that had taken place, which was what the jury decided, it was probably because Maud had told him she had fled William (omitting that he was dead) and put herself, Agatha and Richard into his protection. If Ralph believed William was alive at this point then he did so knowing that he could be taken to court for another case of 'ravishment', just as in 1368. He was fully become suspicious, but if Maud or Richard broke and told him the truth, he still sheltered them and ensured he used his social networks to his advantage when it came to trial.

If, on the other hand, he knew exactly what had happened and managed to persuade the jury otherwise, then he was taking an even bigger risk. This would make sense if he was behind the murder plot himself, but to have his son-in-law's brother murdered so elaborately five years after the death of said son-in-law over three manors and in revenge seems a bit of a stretch.

The one problem with this is that the murder itself was not a case of self-defence and never couched in these terms. William was, by Maud's own testimony, 'at peace with God and the king' before being stabbed on his bed. It is an odd choice of words if he had been beating her savagely enough to provoke a violent intervention. This was a premeditated act, even if it was in response to something. Moreover, Richard Gyse and Robert Cook pleaded not guilty on all charges. They insisted that they had not killed William and had nothing whatsoever to do with his death. Given the fact that judges were apt to throw cases of domestic violence out of court on the understanding that men were perfectly entitled to correct their wives by physical violence, perhaps they did not believe William's treatment of Maud was a legal justification for murder. In this version of events, they could not plead self-defence: it was still petty treason.

By Maud's own testimony, William was not acting violently towards them, and they apparently acted without provocation. 'Not guilty' was the only plea they could make if they wanted to avoid a death sentence. Maud's insistence that it was only Robert and Richard is, by this logic, evidence that she wanted to do right by all her household, but knew that she couldn't save everyone. As the steward, Robert of Cletham was indicted separately and acquitted of murder, which would support the idea that he was an older man, and perhaps not physically capable of active participation in the killing.

Robert Cook of Scotton was also an older man, or at least, older than Richard Gyse, with one acre of land and chattels worth 40 shillings at his death.

While it is possible Richard Gyse the squire was also a lover of Maud's, there is no evidence for this, and his testimony does not exist. To consider the involvement of the cook and squire and chambermaid in the murder, since these three householders were the three convicted, we must look more carefully at the household itself, how it was constructed, and the types of people who were employed. By looking at the medieval manorial household more generally, we can begin to apply some ideas to the Scotton manorial household in particular and suggest why they were willing (or not) to engage in this conspiracy.

Chapter 6

Motives for Murder: Communal Revenge or Communal Vengeance?

'Revenge is an act of passion; vengeance of justice. Injuries are revenged; crimes are avenged'

Samuel Johnson

What might the household community of Scotton Manor have done if they deemed their lord to be excessively cruel? This may not have taken the form of domestic violence towards his wife, but could instead relate to his treatment of them and their fellow-servants, or those in the village. If Sir William was a hard man to work for, abusing his position consistently and with impunity, what could they do about it? And if they did lodge a complaint with the eyre court, could they trust a court of the lord's peers and higher magnates to deliver an equitable judgement, or a merely legal one?

In the traditional interpretation Maud could have appealed to this communal sense of justice for her own predicament, but there need not have been any explicit appeal.

Following the assessment of the traditional interpretation of the case and its centring of the elite figures, creating the impression of a crime driven by passion and power, or by power in response to a potentially passionless and/or abusive marriage, it is time to turn to the other aspects of the case and its reinterpretation. It should be emphasised again that this reinterpretation is built around *the same*, not additional, evidence, and as engaging an endeavour as it is to play detective with an eye to 'solving' the case and drawing a definite conclusion, without proof of either scenario it is entirely based on the preferences – and prejudices – of the historian to decide which version sounds most likely.

One major flaw with the traditional interpretation is that it paints a rather flat picture of the servants themselves, that is, as the actual perpetrators of the crime. In the traditional interpretation of the treason, they must either have been corrupted or coerced, little more than greedy drones in thrall to their social superiors. They are not permitted the agency of forming a conspiracy without any input from their masters whatsoever (but perhaps with their sympathy, consent, and limited protection when the plan was discovered and executed).

Part of the blame for this lies in the previous lack of historiographical interest in the medieval household as an organisation, with many of the recognisable heavy-weights in the field such as R.A. Griffiths, Alan Macfarlane and E.A. Wrigley stating a need for a full study of the royal, ecclesiastical and secular noble households of the Middle Ages.[1] As Kate Mertes has pointed out, servants did not exist in a vacuum or pop into existence as fully grown adults, ready to serve, but were born somewhere, raised somewhere, shaped by their own communities, personalities and individual experiences.[2]

These are real people rather than abstractions, and what we are considering here is a group of people with no clear chain of command despite the steward's theoretical, if not actual, household-wide powers.[3] While the steward was a *major domus* of some sort, we do not know the extent of his authority over other servants such as the kitchen clerk, or whether the kitchen clerk had control over other servants like the chief larderer, or the degrees of the latter's independence across all kinds of households and, of course, the variations in individual household dynamics.[4] Allowing for these inevitable variations, it should make the conspirators less plot devices or puppets and more a group requiring deeper consideration on their own terms.

The idea that individuals would not participate in violence on their own terms due to their age or social station is clearly erroneous. With this in mind, a second interpretation should centre the servants themselves.

Firstly, in a general sense, the servants were not necessarily locals of Scotton, although the majority of them had spent several years there. Free tenants of Scotton, including some of the locals who worked at the manor, would have been prevailed upon to act as jurors for the manor court, and have strong opinions on and a working knowledge of societal norms and legal frameworks. Lloyd Bonfield's thesis on the nature of customary law argues that manorial courts were not based on substantive law drawn from the legal texts and precedents of the king's court and the kind of training given to professional lawyers. Rather, the jurors, being local and knowing the parties involved in various cases (not to mention being party to the circumstances surrounding the case, including the local gossip and what was already common knowledge), would look for an equitable solution for the parties involved, irrespective of actual legal precedent.[5] As a corollary to this debate, John Beckerman adds that community norms and shared values could lurk in even in the equitable and particular responses of the peasantry to disputes, especially in the application of customary law.[6] He points out that 'harmful actions done negligently, wantonly, or intentionally, broken commitments and misunderstandings, and slights and injuries merely imagined were then, as they are now, ordinary by-products of human social intercourse. Any of them could occasion dispute or controversy, whether or not legal relief was available.'[7] Then, as now, such negative social interactions could lead to more violent resolutions than legal means of satisfaction.

With this attitude to dispute-resolution in mind, an apparently typical one regardless of where the servants came from, and the communal response to instances of domestic abuse as discussed in the previous chapter, this alternative possibility presents itself as an equally likely scenario. James Buchanan Given has argued from his study on murder in the thirteenth century that the bonds between servants who served a common master were also strong.[8] An incident that occurred in London in 1276 demonstrates how something as minor as a quarrel about noise levels in the street could escalate and involve an entire knightly household.

After curfew on Sunday, a certain Richard Moys came to the door of John le Chaloner who lived next door to Agnes of Essex, near Fanchurch. Richard Moys tried to gain entrance to the house, wherein lodged Sir Robert de Munceny and Sir Robert's son, Arnulph, with their household. Richard made such a racket that four of the householders told him to stop, and the argument brought the knights and the rest of the household outside, all of them armed, to chase Richard off. Richard Moys fled to the house of Alice the Official, where many people were drinking but had left the door open – Richard concealed himself between two wooden vessels there, and the de Muncenys and their household burst in after him. Arnulph de Munceny was first in, and met a confused man at the door of Alice's house (a certain Richard de Parys). Seeing an armed stranger trying to force his way in, Richard de Parys exclaimed, 'Who are these people?!' and was promptly struck by Arnulph's drawn sword. In an apparent case of mistaken identity and plain confusion, the pursuers rushed in after Arnulph and struck poor Richard de Parys in the back, a deep wound 'between the ribs, two inches in breadth, penetrating the intestines', and gave him another small wound 'under the left breast'. Richard de Parys died of these wounds on Thursday that week.[9]

In February 1323×4, an altercation arose when a certain Roger the cook of the archdeacon of Winchester, turned up at Robert de Holewell's house for supper where a group of friends and associates, including a married couple, Guy 'Fulberd' and Agnes, were also dining. Roger tried to take Agnes off to see the archdeacon (for reasons left out of the official record, but probably not for the good of her soul) and her husband, 'moved with anger on that account frequently told the said Roger to depart thence,' but Roger refused to go and a quarrel broke out. Roger was driven from the house by the furious Guy Fulberd, Robert de Holewell and John de Holewell, William de Dene, and Peter, William's servant.

Roger's friend, Gerard Andrieu de Golbiak, came to Roger's assistance at the door of the house but was driven off with staves and arms, and ended up being fatally struck on the head by John de Holewell with his ballstaff at the 'assent and assistance' of Guy Fulberd.[10]

The escalation of violence and the mob-mentality shown by the householders in these examples is an indication of the kind of dramatic acts relatively minor infractions of the peace might cause. After the fatal attack on Richard de Parys, two of the servants fled, while Arnulph and the remainder of the men returned to the protection of Sir Robert. Similarly, after the fact, the householders in the Cantilupe murder also scattered, and had to be rounded up for the trial at Lincoln. The traditional interpretation has them bonding around Maud as the central figure, and loyal to her over Sir William, but it's equally possible that they were demonstrating their loyalty to one another only, and that the murder was not orchestrated by Maud at all.

Neither should a relatively young group of servants be considered less likely to get involved in the violent acts of others simply because of their age. In mid-fourteenth-century Marseilles, during a street battle between Durant Batuto and Johanet Guis, Johanet's younger brother Guilhelm came out of their father's house with a knife to chase the wounded Durant down the street. Durant died of his wounds: Johanet was tried for his murder, and Guilhelm was fined £6 for his part in the fracas. Guilhelm was 11 years old.[11] Guilhelm only joined in near the end of the battle, and did not inflict any wounds himself. His fine was given because he drew a weapon and threatened someone with it in public. In this kind of situation, his loyalty to his brother and desire to be involved in his fight was not the result of coercion or bribery. Other motivations, including, perhaps, a desire to be 'a man', were at play in this example. Therefore, when looking at a large group of men and one woman, some if not most of them in their teenage years, why should we assume that their motives were uniform and devoid of interpersonal loyalties?

The fact that in the Cantilupe case Richard Gyse and Robert Cook stuck staunchly to their 'not guilty' plea and refused to bring testimony against one another is a strong indication that they had bonds of loyalty to one another that outweighed the pressures to give each other up or to prove their own innocence at the expense of someone else. Similarly, the other servants indicted didn't come to court on the dates they were summoned, except for Agatha Frere who was arrested with Richard and Lady Maud and imprisoned for aiding and abetting.

The Cruelty of 'Great Men'

Lords did abuse their positions, and there were complaints brought to court regarding heavy-handed actions, ranging from theft of goods and livestock to imprisonment without just cause. A good lord was expected to look after the interests of his servants, uphold their complaints against others and support them in their litigation, as well as help them, his tenants and other clients to resolve their disputes.[12] But abuses of power were rife and difficult to curb, again because of the reliance the king on his nobles to keep the peace, enforce the law and administrate their localities. At the opening of the 1328–30 eyre of Northamptonshire, the county justice for the court of the King's Bench explained that the reason for holding the eyre court was related to complaints heard at the 1328 Northampton Parliament, regarding the suffering caused by the 'manifold oppressions of the magnates and from the extortions of the maintainers', other wrongdoing by those in positions of power, and a failure to keep the peace.[13] In 1377, royal statutes were issued with the aim of curbing such abuses, with limited effect.[14] 'Bad' lordship, where the 'middling' sort found themselves between a rock and a hard place regarding various unscrupulous actions, was a regrettable theme of the fourteenth century, and there was very little anyone could or would do about it.

Many of the worst complaints against lords and royal officials came from the frontier lands of Wales, Scotland and Ireland, where the king's reach was weakest. Another member of the Cantilupe family, Richard de Cantilupe, sheriff of Kerry, Ireland, was brought before the justices in 1295 accused of extortion, corruption and various other offences including the dismemberment of Thomas Obrochan [sic] in revenge for the murder of his kinsman Ralph de Cantilupe.[15]

On the Welsh border with Shropshire, the Corbets of Caus found their power waning from 1300 when Peter I Corbet inherited his rapacious father's manors. In a complaint apparently made in the 1290s that may have been misfiled to a later eyre court or brought at a later date deliberately when Corbet influence in the county had deteriorated to such a degree that it might be taken seriously, Thomas FitzPeter of Aston Rogers, Shropshire, complained of being detained unjustly in 1272 by Peter I's father Thomas. Additionally, he complained that in 1286 two of Sir Peter's own men, Thomas Gow and another man named only as Badekyn, had come by command of a certain Adam Hagar and seized two of his cows and detained them until he obtained the king's writ for their deliverance, which cost the wronged Thomas FitzPeter 20 shillings.[16]

Such complaints were rarer in the Midlands and in England in general, where lords were less likely to get away with such extreme behaviour except in times of civil unrest and civil war, and weak kingship.

In October 1376, King Edward III heard a complaint by the 'commonalty and poor men' of Great Yarmouth, Norfolk, that 'a great number of great and powerful men' had 'threatened them in life and limbs'. The list of these men is long – thirty-five in total, including several members of the same families – and the reason for the violence towards the townsmen is not given. The sheriff was given strict instructions to seek out each of the perpetrators, but they were mainperned for £200 and had to give an oath that they would not hurt or procure others to hurt the plaintiffs under pain of imprisonment.[17] A number of these men, including Hugh de Riston, the Elyses and the de Fordeles, were landowners paying significant rents each year in the area.[18] Many had been bailiffs and chamberlains of Great Yarmouth through the 1360s and 70s.

Townsmen, especially those in positions within the ogliarchy of a town, closed ranks and defended the rights of the town from 'outsiders' and merchants, but factions could also arise within the commonalty regarding markets, unfair taxation and monopolies on town offices (among other things) that created internal conflicts. These could turn violent, and were difficult to smooth over. In this latter instance, although King Edward demanded the offending 'powerful men' come to explain themselves, Stephen Alsford notes that there is no sign of a satisfactory conclusion to the complaint by the 'poor men', and it appears that there was some partisan interest from London merchants regarding the issue, whatever it was.[19] The fact that no satisfactory outcome is recorded does not mean that a words were not had privately or that the king's verbal chastisement didn't have an effect, but it also suggests that only the more extreme cases went as far as this in the courts, and that there was greater safety in numbers as far as the plaintiffs were concerned. Individual complaints heard before the king's justices were rarer because, as defendants, the lords and royal officials had more power and leverage against the plaintiffs and could make life extremely unpleasant for them if a case was brought. As the murder of William de Arden showed, murder was sometimes seen as the better option when lords were unfair to their subordinates and these things were left to fester.

Treatment of tenants and freemen could also be excessively harsh. In Somerset, nobles ordered beatings of tenants that resulted broken bones, resulting in the nobles themselves being indicted before the justices.[20] In another incident, a lord and his squire abused the hospitality of a village and murdered one of the villagers. This event occurred in 1274, when Sir John de Rushall and his squire, Henry de Hastings, were entertained at the parson of Melchbourne's house on 4 December. Since Sir John was hardly travelling light and had his household with him, his squire went into Melchbourne and procured all the necessary provisions for his lord's use 'from many men of Melchbourne'.[21] When they were ready to go, the men of Melchbourne came to the house to ask for the money they were owed. Sir John and Henry said they had no money with them at Melchbourne, but, if the villagers elected one of their number to travel with them to Cambridge, they could pay him there and he could return with the money. The villagers discussed this among themselves and unanimously elected a man named Ellis de Astwood. Ellis went with them as far as 'le Rode', where Sir John, Henry de Hastings and Sir John's household turned on him and cut his throat. Sir John himself was acquitted of the killing at the Bedfordshire eyre.[22]

Given this context and the capacity of 'great men' for cruelty and violence against the lower and 'middling' sort, does Lady Maud have to be the ringleader or instigator of the murder at all? She may have supported the perpetrators as far as she was able, but that does not mean that the plan was hers or that they were bribed. If they had their own reasons for wanting their lord dead, then the household conspiracy had nothing to do with the nobility involved in the case, but instead revolved around the servants themselves and the community they had established.

Following on from this, an alternative interpretation of the evidence, looking at this group as a whole, would centre them as the primary instigators of the murder, not bribed or coerced, but acting as a 'community' to bring a form of vigilante justice upon their master for some undisclosed reason. This might be in defence of their own rights, or in defence of one or more of their number who was singled out by their employer.

One plausible alternative narrative supposes that Sir William, now a man of 30, married but still with no children, was determined to prove that he was not like his brother and was capable of getting a woman with child. The addition to his household of another young woman as his wife's chambermaid would have presented him with another opportunity to prove his virility.

If this was the situation then Agatha, through loyalty to Maud or simply not consenting to William's advances, called upon her mistress and her friends in the household for help. They decided, in response to Agatha's situation, that their only course of action was to kill William and make it look like robbers on the road had done the deed. One reason for her change of name could be not because she was actually married but that she was found to be pregnant and *claimed* she was married, choosing a name that would not be associated with anyone who had been part of the murder trials. In medieval thought, a woman could only conceive through orgasm, and orgasm was not considered to be a mechanical reaction to stimuli but proof of consensual sex. Rape cases were therefore invariably thrown out of court if the woman had borne a child by her rapist.

If Agatha was pregnant by William, but Maud had not yet conceived a child, then no matter how badly Agatha wanted to escape, William was unlikely to allow her to leave his employ. Nicholas had sent out armed men to fetch Katherine back, a noblewoman with the support of her powerful father, but Agatha had no one of that level to uphold her cause. Whether trapped and desperate, or angry and vengeful, or a bit of both, the result was a conspiracy to kill William one night and get rid of him.

Richard Gyse, a young man himself, could well have been in love with Agatha rather than Maud, or had purely brotherly affection for her. Maud's fury at her husband's conduct meant that she not only understood but she was willing to help them escape and give them both entry into Ralph Paynell's household, where, if their ruse was believed by the sheriff, they could find alternative employment and career advancement. Richard, after all, had nothing, and could not hope to protect Agatha or provide for her if they married. As an older and more experienced servant, Robert Cook may have looked upon Agatha as a daughter and Richard as a son, willing to help them because of the deep bonds they had forged during their time of service together. However, everything went wrong. When their ruse failed and Maud was herself arrested, she had no choice (or so she saw it) but to tell the sheriff everything that had happened, naming Richard and Robert as the main perpetrators but leaving the other servants out of the story. If she or Ralph bribed the bailiffs and rescue Agatha from Lincoln gaol, this would explain her escape, or managed to assist her knowing the bailiffs were negligent in their duties.

Again, there is as much evidence to support this interpretation as there is for the traditional view, and the motive did not have to have any sexual component at all – it could be a simple case of householders having enough, as in the murder of Sir William de Arden.

Chapter 7

Justice, Law Enforcement and Cross-County Networks

'*People demand a lot of the justice system and they demand things it can't deliver*'

Helen Garner

In the fourteenth century, the structure of peace- and law-keeping depended heavily upon the affinity of lords and gentry within each shire. Each lord had their own social network and landed interests that often encompassed more than one shire or county, so even if their *caput* or primary seat of power was in one, they could well be asked to serve in another place where they also had interests.

Justices of the peace were elected in each shire from among the most powerful and most affluent lords, as well as 'three or four of the most worthy of the shire, with some learned in the law'.[1] The 1361 statute confirmed their powers of restraint and arrest, the power to chastise and imprison law-breakers and rioters, and to be able to inquire and be informed about malefactors, outlaws, pillagers and robbers. They could also 'hear and determine at the king's suit [of court] all manner of felonies and trespass done in that shire, according to the laws and customs; and that writs of oyer and terminer[2] shall be granted, but judges would be chosen by the court and not by the party bringing the suit.'[3]

Looking at the names involved in the trial, it is possible to reconstruct the socio-legal affinities of Lincolnshire and how they interacted. By considering the names of those involved in the practical elements of the trial and the nobles indicted, particularly the powerful connections of Sir Ralph Paynell, we will get a better idea of the way the trial was conducted and who was making the judicial decisions.

As discussed previously, the jurors of a medieval trial were not neutral parties. The knights tasked to stand on the jury of a trial like this were those who knew the parties involved and who could testify to the judge and justices regarding the wider context of the case, the character of the parties involved, and any other pertinent information. They may well have relevant testimony to bring, sometimes based on 'the rumour of the county', and sometimes their own understanding of the circumstances of the crime.

While we don't know the names of the jurors, we do know the names of many of the men charged with manumitting the accused, and it is possible to look up these names in other surviving documents to see who they were in contact with.

The Sheriff and Shrieval Corruption

Fourteenth-century government faced a difficult conundrum: while the Crown had a centralised bureaucracy, its control over local government was weaker and relied upon the election of local officials who were taken from the very community they policed.[4] Officials therefore had a double allegiance and were open to corruption. This is a long-recognised trend in fourteenth-century society,[5] and leads us to look more closely at the sheriff, Sir Thomas de Kydale, and the other officers involved in the case, like the coroner.

At the time of the murder, the sheriff of the county, Sir Thomas de Kydale, was a widower with a young son, also named Thomas. He was a local Lincolnshire man and would have known the families well. He was in charge of the case, along with the five king's coroners of the county, William de Kirkton who had performed the investigation, Richard Groos, Robert de Holm, William Haxay and William de Wyhum, all of whom appeared at the trial in Lincoln.

These offices were not necessarily given to men with special knowledge of law enforcement, but rather to men of high standing in the community who at least had a reasonable working knowledge of the law and could be trusted to fulfil their duties. They all had to be men of substance (less prone to bribes and able to fund their own travel and expenses to fulfil their roles, which were unpaid and for which they were not compensated) and could be dismissed if their personal wealth did not meet the required threshold.[6] Coroners were generally considered to have been of a higher character than sheriffs, less oppressive and extortionate, and less prone to corruption.[7] This was generally due to them having their own money to qualify for the position, but as the office was unpaid, coroners did practice extortion on a regular basis throughout the thirteenth century, with no deliberate campaigns against such practices before 1274.[8]

By the late fourteenth century, the rising mercantile class was muscling in on the office of coroner (not to mention mayoral offices), since the more successful among them easily met the wealth threshold at a time when the knightly elite in England were declining in number and were often engaged in other duties, particularly during the Hundred Years' War. For example, William de Kirton was, as his locative surname suggests, a Lincolnshire man. He was of the lower Lincolnshire gentry, a fishmonger by trade and merchant and citizen of London, found in debtors rolls with John de Kirton – most likely his brother – in that city in 1368. The Kirton brothers had loaned Adam Waryner and Roger de Buckingham, citizens and pepperers of London, the princely sum of £93 6s, which Adam and Roger could not repay.[9] This had roughly the buying power equivalent to around £46,000 in 2017's money.[10] This is, of course, a general guide to historical value, and not to be taken as definitive, but it gives a good idea of how much money de Kirkton had to spare just a few years before this trial, and with him, his fellow coroners. These were men of the elite circles, who associated with others of a similar station in their localities and further afield.

Therefore, the coroner for West Lindsey was rich enough that any bribe would have to have been of a considerable sum to be worth his while. This was not always the case, of course; in return for favours or relatively small sums, coroners could still empanel juries with biased jurors, or with those who knew nothing of the matter and so could be easily swayed or make their judgements in ignorance of the wider knowledge of local contexts. They might also falsify their rolls and accounts, but the justices were always on the lookout for these kinds of offences, and coroners found guilty of corruption were committed to prison and could have their lands seized as forfeit.[11] Kirkton does not seem to have been a corrupting influence in this case, as his inquest unravelled the threads of the household conspiracy and pushed the case into the limelight. Kirketon's impartiality seems to have been recognised as a problem for the conspirators, but one that might be overcome with some ingenuity and attempts at concealment of the location of the murder and therefore of its true motivation. The attempt was good, but not good enough.

First of all, it must be recognised that the fourteenth-century sheriff had less power than the sheriff of previous years: both William Stubbs and F.W. Maitland identified the fourteenth century as the time when sheriffs were emasculated by the annual replacement of appointees.[12] Sheriffs were part of the local social milieu, but they also had interests in multiple counties and shires like other landed gentry. Since this office often came as a joint shrievalty of two counties (Warwickshire and Leicestershire came as a pair, for example), the appointed sheriff usually had interests in both, and had a much wider-reaching socio-political network than one which stopped at the borders of a single county.[13]

Sheriffs often formed part of an 'office-holding community', that is, they were elected from a subset of men who held an office in their county or counties before.[14]

Sir Thomas de Kydale came from the ranks of the middling local gentry of Lincolnshire, and could not claim such an illustrious lineage as the Cantilupes, Nevilles or Paynells. Yet the fourteenth century offered opportunities for social climbing, as difficult a feat for those of the baronial class as for those free peasants just below, but certainly not impossible. The wars offered rewards, and the English were in a better position to profit from them than the French.[15] Those who profited – the already-wealthy captains doing much better than their followers – could take advantage of the decreasing prices of land after the Black Death's ravages in 1348 to increase their own holdings.[16] Fighting for a great magnate as a retainer also offered opportunities to expand one's social circle and impress other knights who could help to boost their lesser fellow's social position. As far as his military career went, Kydale was a knight in the service of Humphrey de Bohun, Earl of Hereford, and was part of his expeditionary force in 1371.[17] In Earl Humphrey's force that year were thirty-one knights, forty-six men-at-arms and 100 archers. Earl Humphrey likely sub-contracted a fair number of these knights into his service to make up his numbers, so these men were thrown together in his service where they would not otherwise necessarily mix in a socio-political context. Contracting themselves to great magnates in times of campaigns was an opportunity for knights to consolidate and expand their social circles, and these connections could be maintained and exploited later once their contract had ended. Among the knights listed with Kydale is Maud's own kinsman Robert Neville, and Lewis Clifford, whose kinsman John Clifford, a clerk, is found manumitting Maud in 1375.[18]

In terms of gentry breaking the law, Kydale was no stranger to conspiracy and violence: he had been on the receiving end of it. Local knight John Thorley of Barton, a leading resident of the city of Lincoln, was involved in protracted disputes between the civic and ecclesiastic authorities regarding their respective jurisdictions.[19]

A group of London craftsmen mainperned John Thorley of Barton in September 1373, and had to answer for him 'on pain of £20' that he would not inflict harm, nor procure others to inflict harm, upon a group of fourteen men, namely:

Thomas Kydale (not yet elected sheriff),
Hugh and John de Ferriby (or Feryby – we will meet these men again later in the trial of 1375),
William Smyth of Barton,
Richard,
Robert Toddy of Barton,
John Kent of Barton,
John Frost of Barton,
John de Legburn of Barton,
John Baudewyn of Barton,
John de Feryby of Barton (possibly the same man as above, listed twice in error, or a close kinsman with the same first name),
John de Seton,
John Danyel
and Walter Stippyng.[20]

A jury found Katherine wife of William de Whitton guilty of receiving the said John Thorley although she knew of his felony: it is likely that this Katherine was a close relative, perhaps John Thorley's sister.[21] On the day of the sessions, the townships of Whitton and Barton failed to come and give evidence before the jurors of the grand jury, 'delaying the king's business on that day'.[22] Given that John Thorley had threatened violence against Kydale and several men 'of Barton', then taken shelter with Katherine 'de Whitton', it is fairly clear that local allegiances and his previous threats were behind their unwillingness to come and testify.

Thorley was often involved in civil unrest throughout his political career as a member of parliament and one of the leading men of Lincolnshire, frequently challenging civil and ecclesiastic authority after this incident. In later cases before the courts his resistance to ecclesiastic incursions on secular matters took the form of rent strikes, and in August 1384 he was distrained by officers of the dean and chapter of Lincoln Cathedral for allowing arrears of almost £5 (the equivalent purchasing power of roughly £3,500 in 2017's money) to build up over the previous eight years.[23] The distraint enraged the mayor and the bailiffs, who had the dean's agents imprisoned. On the same date as the distraint, Thorley was involved in another outbreak of civil unrest against John of Gaunt's unpopular mistress, Katherine Swynford. On these later occasions, although a commission was set up to handle the complaints made against him, there were no negative consequences for his actions.[24] This example again underlines the power of local lords in their locality, and the difficulties in successfully prosecuting even persistent troublemakers of their type.

Thorley's attack on Kydale and his associates in Barton in 1273 certainly has the flavour of civil unrest about it, particularly as it involved so many people. Similarly, the concern with gaining Thorley's assurances that he would not harm nor procure others to harm the men on the list would indicate a depth of personal feeling too. The Close Roll entry says that Kydale and his associates petitioned the king about Thorley's threats, averring that he had 'grievously threatened them in life and limbs,' but the London craftsmen – including a tapiter (weaver of worsted cloth), a dyer and two cordwainers, potentially implying they were part of a guild and were connected to Thorley through dealings with him when he came to parliament in London – mainperned for him 'under pain of £20' that he should not carry them out.[25] The cause of Thorley's rage is not recorded, but it indicates that procuring others to inflict harm on his behalf was a possibility, and a pertinent one in context of the conspiracy to murder William Cantilupe. The following year – 1374 – Thorley's foe Thomas Kydale was made sheriff of Lincoln.[26]

If the traditional interpretation of events is correct, then it might have been Sir Thomas de Kydale himself who abused his shrieval office and 'procured' the servants of Scotton manor to do the deed, since they were on the spot and had easy access to both the bedchamber and to blades. As sheriff, he was in a better position to not only procure others to inflict harm, but also to impanel a sympathetic jury of local knights who owed him favours or who were easily bribed or manipulated.

It seems somewhat odd, however, that Kydale would not procure men unconnected to Maud, his lover, to kill her own husband – if the ruse was to make it look like he was murdered on the road by strangers, why not actually have him killed on the road by hired strangers? His position as sheriff had brought him into contact with nefarious individuals like Robert Neuland of Humberstone and others, for whom bribery would be as strong a motive for murder as any other.

Comparative Case Study of Shrieval Corruption

To understand the general distrust that existed around the shrieval office, some examples are required. Attempts to curb excesses and bad behaviour in office were made throughout the thirteenth and fourteenth centuries, but progress was slow and success was limited in practice due to the delicate balancing act within the localities that the king was forced to undertake. Things were especially bad in the frontier regions where royal power was weakest, and even the Cantilupes themselves were not exempt from bad behaviour.

One branch of the Cantilupes went to Ireland, aided by the marriage of William III (d. 1254) to heiress Eva de Braose, daughter of Eva Marshall. William III played a semi-active role in the administration of his wife's Irish inheritance, but the family were not well regarded. Richard de Cantilupe, sheriff of Kerry at the end of the thirteenth century, was best known for his skill at packing juries, extorting payments from men of the county by various underhanded means, murder and coercion, nepotism, taking advantage of the sick and hacking an Irishman's limbs off to avenge the death of his kinsman.[27]

Richard is an extreme example of the bad sheriff, and he got away with most of his excesses by virtue of being in Ireland, where the representatives of English royal authority were limited by distance from the centralised base of power.

A good example of shrieval jury-packing and suspect behaviour in a case comes from the previous century with one of William de Cantilupe's more illustrious forebears, the saintly Bishop Thomas Cantilupe of Hereford. This is one example of several, but the principle was not unusual, and the kinship connection makes it a fortuitously appropriate example to explore here.

By 1276, the time of the case as recorded in detail for us in Bishop Thomas' episcopal register, he had gained a degree in canon law from Paris and a degree in civil law at Orleans, as well having a term or two as chancellor of Oxford University under his belt.[28] He had also served in the baronial government as Exchequer, and maintained friendly relations with Henry III that earned him a pardon when that government was overthrown and the king regained control after the Battle of Evesham. He was also personal friends with Prince Edward, later Edward I, again despite his allegiance with the Montfortians in the Second Barons' War.[29] He knew his rights, he knew the law, and he knew how things worked in the circles of his elite kin. One of his first acts as bishop was to regain rights that had been lost by the negligence or mistakes of his predecessors, particularly in regard to lands annexed from the diocese by rapacious marcher lords such as Sir Thomas Corbet of Caus (d. 1274). His son, Peter I Corbet (d. 1300), had inherited the annexed land and was not willing to return it to Hereford. As far as he was concerned, his father had taken it successfully from Bishop Peter d'Aigueblanche, and it now belonged to the Corbets. Bishop Thomas de Cantilupe did not agree.

On 8 May 1276, Bishop Thomas made a formal complaint, accusing Sir Peter's father Thomas of unlawfully disseising Bishop Peter of 100 acres with appertenances.[30] Another writ was sent out ordering the sheriff, Bogo de Knoville, to take view of the hundred acres of pasture with its appurtenances and to send four of the viewing knights to the Justices at Westminster.[31]

Sheriff Bogo seemed to have some difficulty during this time getting enough knights together to perform the viewing, probably due to the relative power the Corbets of Caus had in Shropshire and the complex socio-political networks in the region. This was a perennial problem for sheriffs of lesser social status than the greater men in their shires. Even though Ralph Paynell was arrested in Kydale's case, it is unsurprising that he was able to assure the jury of his good character and innocence in the matter. Sir Ralph had himself served a term as sheriff of Yorkshire and had a wide-reaching network and influence.

In the earlier Shropshire case, Sir Bogo de Knoville was himself a part of these socio-political networks and occupied his own social position in the shire. This can be seen by his relative position on witness lists, where the witnesses on gifts and grants made by other lords are listed in order of their status, rather than alphabetically or in any other order. On the 15 May, 1278, a grant of land of Sir Robert Blundel to Nicholas his son and heir was witnessed by Bogo de Knovill, sheriff of Herefordshire, in the company of not one but four members of the Corbet family – Sir Peter Corbet, Sir Robert Corbet, Sir Roger Corbet and Thomas Corbet.[32] Peter Corbet would be Peter I Corbet of Caus, since there does not seem to be any other Peters in the cadet line; Robert, Roger and Thomas are all cadet Corbets, either of the Moreton Corbet (Shropshire) or Chaddesley Corbet (Worcestershire) branches. The branches were closely related; Peter (II) Corbet (d. 1322) of caus, Roger Corbet of Chaddesley his 'beloved nephew' (*nepotis*), although *nepotis* may in fact refer more generally to other close kin such as younger cousins related by various degrees of kinship, and illegitimate children.[33] Bogo, despite his shrieval office, is listed sixth, after three royal justices, Sir Peter I Corbet, and Sir Robert Corbet.[34]

This put the sheriff in a difficult position: his relative status was not as great as others in his locality, whether he was an office-holder or not. Similarly, a hundred years later, when the power wielded by the shrieval office-holder had been in steady decline, the perceived status of the sheriff as a member of their society was an important factor in being able to perform their role effectively.

Some nineteen months passed before the issuing of a further writ on 30 December, 1277. This writ directed the sheriff 'to secure by distraint the service of the knights who failed to act on the perambulation of the border-lands of the Bishop and Peter Corbet.'[35] Three months later, the details of the perambulation were duly reported.[36] However, it appears that this perambulation was not good enough; a writ dated 4 June of the same year was issued to the sheriff, 'directing him to appear at Westminster to answer for his neglect to make the perambulation ordered in the suit with Peter Corbet, and to bring the names of the four knights concerned,'[37] The writ states that the sheriff was meant to have taken twelve 'wise and lawful' knights 'towards the land of Thomas, Bishop of Hereford, in Ledbury North, and the land of Peter Corbet in Caus'.[38] It would appear that the previous perambulation had not been completed to anyone's satisfaction. The sheriff responded to this writ with a letter, explaining that the jury had indeed been duly summoned, giving eleven names. It appears that only five of these were armed, belted knights (*milites gladio cinctos*), and that the jury also consisted of freemen, *liberos et legales homines*, whose inclusion Peter Corbet had challenged.[39] It was not unheard of or unusual for free men who were not knights to serve on juries, especially given the fact that knights could be unavailable to serve and were generally in short(er) supply. Technically, however, this was not the procedure, and it was a loophole that could be used as an effective delaying tactic.

Two writs were received in reply; the first is undated but says that since he failed to inspect the boundaries at Lydbury North as instructed, he was to report to the justices with twelve knights. The second, dated 14 July 1278, tersely informed him that he had been amerced (fined) for his neglect and would be fined more heavily unless he complied.[40] This was Knovill's required incentive; he managed to solve his manpower problems, despite previously insisting that there were simply not enough belted knights in Shropshire to make up a full jury unless freemen were permitted to stand.[41] The jury, whose composition had changed for a third and final time, duly reported the boundaries between the lands of the bishop and Peter Corbet.[42] The final writ in this legal saga is dated 3 November 1278; since Knovill's term as sheriff had ended eight days previously, this must have been meant for his successor Walter Hopton.[43] It simply returns the report of the boundaries to be amended.[44] In all, this case had dragged on for two and a half years, and seems to have concluded in the bishop's favour.

The dispute between the baron and the bishop was at the mercy of the contemporary state of the judicial and administrative systems, and the outcome depended on the men within those systems. At least some of these *milites* had prior dealings with both the sheriff and the Corbets, but since Thomas Corbet was not known for his amenable qualities, this was not necessarily a point in Peter's favour. For example, two of the jurors, Thomas Boterel and John fitz Aere, appear as witnesses on a deed in 1270 alongside a William Corbet, likely Thomas Corbet of Caus' younger brother, or William son of Robert Corbet of Moreton Corbet.[45]

The sheer lack of knights may have been a great difficulty for the sheriff, but it proved a great convenience to Peter Corbet as it allowed the baron to mount his objections and delay the outcome of the suit. Bogo de Knoville reports that he did try to fulfil his duty, but he found it difficult to put a jury together that the defendant would accept since there was 'a great deficiency' of belted knights in Shropshire at the time.[46] The deficiency of his shire left Knoville with the problem of putting together twelve men of whom Peter Corbet could not legally object. His first attempt had include four freemen (later termed *liberos et legales homines*, although in this original list they are specifically referred to as *milites* which could imply that they were of the knightly class but had not been knighted in the first instance, or had chosen not to be knighted).[47] It appeared that Peter Corbet had objected to their inclusion and mounted a legal challenge to ensure their perambulation was void.[48] Nevertheless, Bishop Thomas was tenacious, and refused to allow technicalities to stand in the way of justice being done. The second list of jurors, as named in the letter of June 1278, has only three freemen (this time specifically termed *legales et liberos homines*) and eight knights, with Knoville himself making up the twelfth man.[49]

Consequently the sheriff had to draft in an alternative trio who happened to be Brian de Brompton and his sons Walter and Brian, Peter Corbet's relations; Brian senior was in fact Peter's brother-in-law, the husband of his sister Emma.[50] These men could not have been completely pleasing to the bishop, however, and the final report by the jury reveals that the de Bromptons were not included in the latest composition of the twelve good men. Presumably the shortage of knights in Shropshire had been successfully overcome, since by including himself and his own son John, sheriff Bogo (erroneously rendered 'Hugo' by the transcriber) managed to put a group of twelve different knights together. Despite

Peter I Corbet's best attempts to forestall the inevitable and Sheriff Bogo's difficulties, particularly the pressures brought to bear on him from Corbet's side, the outcome was ultimately decided in Bishop Thomas's favour.[51]

Fast-forwarding a few decades, such practices were still prevalent among the English sheriffs and other royal ministers when they were able to get away with it. When Edward III came to the throne in January 1327, the start of his reign was marred by the manner in which he had become king: his father, Edward II, had been deposed by his mother, Isabella of France, and her lover, Roger Mortimer. Edward, born in 1312, was only 15 at the time and as a minor he depended on them as his regents. Isabella and Roger ruled England in his name until 1330 when he turned 18, and on taking control in dramatic fashion he executed Roger and banished his mother. The royal ministers had been able to get away with a great deal during Edward III's minority, so from 1330 onwards Edward sought to stamp his own authority upon the machinations of royal bureaucracy, administration and power. Edward III heard many cases of excesses and trespasses made by various officials (not only sheriffs) in the early decades of his reign, which seems to suggest that while in legal theory and practice the sheriff's role had been restricted and the sheriffs' power in their locality had declined, they would press their advantage whenever possible if so inclined.

Given the importance of the jurors and the wealth of information their names alone can provide, it is frustrating that in this case (1375) the names of the jurors do not appear, only that they were elected and made to swear the sacred oath. Without the names of the jurors, it's not possible to explore their connections to the Nevilles, the Paynells, the Cantilupes or the Kydales. Nevertheless, historians have found it easy to believe that Kydale pulled similar tricks to Sheirff Bogo in the thirteenth-century case study simply because this was long-established frequent practice among the elite.

Role of the Elite Community

When Maud came to trial, she was manumitted by a number of knights of the county who were responsible for her and for bringing her back to court at the appointed times and dates. The network of local knights and unknighted landholders is revealed in the lists of these men, which were as follows: Sir William Hawley, Sir Thomas Kydale (sheriff), John Boys, William de Spayne, Oliver de Barton and Gerard Sodhill. These men also manumitted the steward, Robert de Cletham, who was acquitted of aiding and abetting the murder of his master.

On the second occasion, she was manumitted by John de Rocheford, Sir Gerard Braybrook, Sir William Bernak, Sir Robert de Braybrook, Sir John Auncell, Sir Thomas Kydale, Sir John Dimmock and John Clifford, clerk. The order that these names appear in the records has been preserved here. Since names are generally written in order of relative importance, it is worth noting where the sheriff's name appears in the list each time.

The first group included two knights and four men who had not been knighted but still had an important and respected status in the county. The lack of knights in this group seems to have been rectified in the second, but these men are not families primarily based in Lincolnshire but were also men of the Welsh borders. The list of local knights also reveals the internal spectrum that existed within the community of knights themselves, insofar as such a group can be said to have formed their own community. The sheriff of Lincolnshire, Sir Thomas Kydale, appears both times.

In 1382, following the Peasants' Revolt, Sir Ralph Paynell appears in a list of three magnates and thirty-six men named in a writ to keep the peace within Lincolnshire. Among the other names were Robert de Willoughby, head of the guards who brought Maud Cantilupe to court; John Cressy, on whose kinsman Hugh Cressy some Cantilupe lands had been demised; John Rocheford, William Hawley and William de Spayne, who were three of the men who manumitted Maud Cantilupe and her steward Robert of Cletham; John de Bussey, kinsman of Sir Ralph (his mother was a Paynell) and Maud's third husband; and members of the Pinchbeck family, all of whom appear in connection with the trial itself or in wider connection with key figures like Sir Ralph or the sheriff Sir Thomas. This kind of list demonstrates who was influential within the county and who was likely to be in contact with each other, but such connections were not necessarily guarantees of alliance.

More evidence of the nature of Sir Ralph's relative importance in the county and his relationships with the men in this group is implied in another entry in the Calendar of Patent Rolls for the following year. On 12 July 1383, a commission of oyer and terminer was brought to Robert de Willoughby and his associates, Philip le Despenser, Ralph de Cromwell, Robert Tresilian, William de Skipworth, John Holt, William Burgh and Walter Tailboys. A complaint had been made by the king's clerk (also archdeacon of Lincoln), a man named Richard de Ravenser, that despite being taken into the king's protection, a number of men led by Sir Ralph Paynell (apparently the only knight among the group, which included a cleric and several with occupational surnames, implying that they were a group of Sir Ralph's servants or connected to his household in some capacity) had lain in wait for him with the intent to kill him, carry away his goods and assault his servants.[52] Richard de Willoughby and his fellows, however, did not follow this up with Sir Ralph: a note below this entry states that the judgement was 'vacated by surrender because nothing was done.'[53] This highlights the issues of leaving law enforcement in the hands of those who were closely interconnected with those they had to bring to justice, and further investigation of those who came out in support of Maud reveals further connections across the counties.

William Hawley, knight
The Hawleys settled at Grisby around the start of the fourteenth century and quickly came to exercise considerable influence in the county. Sir William's father served as sheriff of Lincolnshire from 1363–8, while Sir William himself was a loyal retainer of John of Gaunt and served as chief steward of the northern parts of the duchy of Lancaster for seven years.[54] Sir William Hawley was already a well-respected man in Lincolnshire, and so his decision to manumit Maud Neville and stand surety for her entangled his reputation with hers. It did his no harm, but his support of her and her steward must surely have stood them in better stead.

William de Spayne
William de Spayne was a responsible man and affluent merchant of Lincoln with a respected standing in the county.[55] He was mayor of

Lincoln from c.1356–9.[56] In 1361 he was with John Vendeur of Newark, making an account for corn for Calais.[57] The two men also made an account for victuals for Calais in that same year.[58] Both men had been appointed in 1356 'to buy and provide' 500 quarters of wheat, 50 quarters of barley, 200 quarters of oats and 200 quarters of peas and beans in Lincolnshire, Nottinghamshire, Huntingdonshire and Cambridgeshire for the king's use. They were also to convey this food to Calais 'for the sustenance of the King's subjects' and deliver them safely to the appointed keeper of victuals there. The same letters also ordered that they were to provide ships at the ports and places which seem most suitable to them.[59] According to a writ to the sheriff of Lincoln, he was from Boston, and of considerable personal means: in 1369, Amandus Sourdewale of Thrickingham, Lincolnshire, owed William de Spayne the princely sum of £40.[60]

William de Spayne's father, another William, was son of Adam de Spayne of Croydon, Surrey. William senior was similarly affluent and of the emergent merchant class, with enough capital to lend his brother Ralph £15 in 1311.[61] William junior seems to have suffered a reversal of fortunes sometime after this murder case was concluded. He appears to have moved to Yorkshire, and in 1393 'William Spayne of Yorkshire' is listed as a debtor to Walter Dautry, merchant of London, and Richard Broke, citizen and goldsmith of London, for the sum of £25, a loan taken out in 1391.[62] This writ carries an endorsement by John Dependen, sheriff of Yorkshire, to Thomas de Horneby, Roger de Ruston, and John Bouche, bailiffs of the liberty of the city of York, because William Spayne was not found, and had no lands or chattels outside their liberty. The previous year he is found owing an alien merchant in London, Simon Pedelowe, a citizen of Amiens, £65 10*s*, a debt he incurred in 1365, which may account for why he couldn't pay the debt incurred more recently.[63]

This case seems to have come during the zenith of William's career, but mercantile ventures were not guaranteed to have good outcomes. He maintained his good standing in the county and was elected sheriff of Lincolnshire in 1379, following Sir Ralph Paynell in 1377 and Sir Thomas de Kydale's re-election in 1378.

In 1383 during the troubled reign of Richard II, when the aftermath of the Peasants' Revolt of 1381 was still reverberating around the country in waves of unrest, a commission was sent out to all the counties appointing men to keep the peace and break up meetings of rebels, and for Lindsey, Lincolnshire, the list included both William de Spayne and William Hawley. The magnates in charge were John, Duke of Lancaster and Henry de Percy, Earl of Northumberland, and these men were joined by Robert de Willoughby, William de Skipworth, John de Hanburgh, Thomas Pynchebeck, William Pylet, Robert Comberworth, John de Ferriby and William Topcliff. John de Ferriby is another familiar name: he was an associate of Thomas de Kydale, mentioned in the complaint brought by Thomas in 1373. The circle of 'worthy men' in each county was not a large one where associates would get lost in a crowd, but rather one where factions could arise from personality clashes and conflicts of interests, kinship links and links by marriage had to be taken into account, and associates connected each other to wider socio-political groups.

William de Spayne was re-elected as sheriff of Lincolnshire a final time in 1385.

Oliver de Barton
Oliver de Barton held lands in Derbyshire, Lancashire and Staffordshire, but was not knighted.[64] It appears that Oliver was not knighted by 1390 either as he appears in a writ of Sir Nicholas de Longford, appointing William atte Walle, chaplain, as his attorney to deliver lands and rents to a number of men listed in order of rank. Oliver de Barton is one of these men, and while the ones above him are explicitly named as knights, Oliver and those following are not.[65] Since all his dealings – or at least, the vast majority of them – seem to be in the neighbouring county, it appears that on the occasion that they needed a number of men to manumit Maud, Oliver was asked by an associate to step in and lend his support. There are several 'Bartons' in England, but one such Barton is in Lincolnshire, where Adam de Kydale, kin to sheriff Thomas de Kydale, can be found in the early decades of the 1300s.[66]

It would seem that Oliver de Barton was a member of the landed gentry but not part of the knightly class, with lands across several counties gained by gift and marriage. His family were most likely well-to-do farmers or yeomen, rather than merchants.

Gerard Sodhill / Sothill

Identified as Gerard 'Sothill' in other documents, Gerard was a younger son of a gentry family who set about establishing himself in the local community.[67] He acquired the manor of Redbourne, Lincolnshire, and this was to become his power centre in the region. He was still working on building his reputation and connections in 1375, which may have contributed to his decision to stand surety for Maud Neville and her steward Robert of Cletham in such a high-profile case, in the company of other high-profile men. The Nevilles and their allies and associates, particularly Thomas Kydale and Sir Ralph Paynell, would look favourably on him in the future. A supporter of Henry IV, Gerard was one of forty-six men knighted on the eve of the king's coronation in 1399.[68]

On 22 May 1379, the Calendar of Patent Rolls recorded that a pardon was granted to Robert de 'Southill', potentially a kinsman of the 'Sothills', for the death of Richard de Ferreby who had been the chaplain of Henry de Barton.[69] In this case, the Ferrebys (associates of Sir Thomas Kydale) and the Bartons are connected by this unfortunate episode, and links the three families in a deeply personal way. The pardon was granted at the request of Sir Ralph Paynell.

John Boys

John Boys is an elusive figure, and again, not knighted at the time. There were several men named John Boys operating in the south-east of England in the latter part of the fourteenth-century and it is not always easy to distinguish between them. John Boys does appear in 1378, where he, along with Sir Ralph Paynell, Sir Thomas de Kydale and seven others, was granted a commission of oyer and terminer 'touching felonies and other excesses in the city of Lincoln committed by certain [people] of that city.'[70] Again, he is part of the socio-legal affinity within the county and in particular in and around the city of Lincoln itself, working with the sheriff and Sir Ralph, took on the shrieval office after Thomas.

That same year, he appears again with Sir Ralph and four others in a commission of oyer and terminer to hear the complaint of Sir Thomas de Roos of Hamelak, whose family had been close associates of the Cantilupes and whose kinsman had been one of the attorneys appointed by Sir William in his absence abroad. Sir Thomas de Roos complained that a large gang of men (all known to him and named in the complaint) had broken into his closes and houses at Wragby and Freston, Lincolnshire, carried away his goods, and assaulted his men 'there and at Boynington'.[71] Despite the men being listed and the complaint being a serious one, the six men commissioned were apparently unable to do anything about this, and nothing was done.

John de Rocheford

John DE Rochford was based in Boston, Lincolnshire, but was not knighted for some time. Married in 1375, he was knighted by 1399, but his career took off when he was appointed as commissioner of inquiry regarding civic disorder in Boston in 1379, the first of many offices he was to hold until his death in 1410.[72]

The Rochefords were a powerful family, close associates of the Hastings family, into whom the Cantilupe main branch had married in the previous century. The wardship of Henry de Hastings, a minor at the time of his father's death in 1250, belonged to Guy de Lusignan, who sold it and the marriage rights of his sisters to William III de Cantilupe in about 1252. Guy and Geoffrey de Lusignan and Guy de Rocheford had received the lion's share of the Hastings estate, which had been vast, and was divided between eight grantees. Young Henry, about 15 at the time, was worth about £600 a year, and so his marriage to Joan de Cantilupe, William de Cantilupe's daughter and the brother of the ill-fated George, was an increased bonus for the Cantilupes alongside the Zouche and Lacy marriages made by Joan's sister and brother respectively.[73]

The Braybrookes, Gerard and Robert

Similarly, the Braybrooke family were prominent politicians, and Gerard Braybrooke was a member of parliament in 1377. His social standing and that of his family had increased exponentially thanks to shrewd marriages and their participation in campaigns during the Hundred Years' War.[74] It was common for younger sons to go into the church to pursue a career, but even then because of their social standing and family connections could be called upon to participate in local courts.

Robert Braybrooke, here listed as a clerk (i.e. a churchman), rose up through the offices in the church and became Bishop of London, appointed in 1381 and consecrated in 1382. He was still building his reputation and career in 1375, and his involvement in this trial, with his support of Maud Cantilupe, gave him access to the Nevilles, Maud's kin, and to the wider kinship networks of the Paynells.

These men were all prominent men from high-profile families, building their own careers and so attempting to make the right friends, or already well-established in the cross-county networks that spanned the Midlands and beyond. With these men backing the accused, it is no wonder that the jury, made of other men from the same backgrounds and linked to the same networks (a fact we can safely assume even though we don't have their names), it is no wonder that Lady Maud, Sir Ralph and Robert of Cletham were acquitted. It is also not a surprise that the convicted servants were harshly dealt with on the basis of one eyewitness testimony – Lady Maud's – even though there was no proof she was telling the truth.

Chapter 8

The Trial's Outcome and Aftermath

'Executions are so much a part of British history that it is almost impossible for many excellent people to think of a future without them'
Viscount Templewood (1951)

The Verdicts and Sentencing

Lady Maud and Agatha faced death by burning if found guilty of killing Sir William, while the men accused would be publically drawn to their place of execution on a wooden frame or cart, and hanged there. Hanging was a common form of execution in Britain at this time, appearing in legal documents as early as the fifth century. Post-1066, William the Conqueror (who had to make examples of rebels and law-breakers, and struggled to consolidate his military victory with uniform, grassroots control) decreed that hanging should be reserved for poachers of royal deer, and otherwise should be replaced with blinding and castration. Henry I, who succeeded his brother William Rufus in 1100 after that king's infamous hunting accident, reinstated it.[1] It was commonly used for many kinds of crimes from this point onwards.

Over the course of the trial, Kydale stood surety for Maud with other upstanding men of the county and helped to pay the equivalent of her bail (manumission). The group swore to produce her for the next court date and could be held responsible if she did not arrive. She told the sheriff that Richard Gyse the squire and Robert Cook the butler were the men responsible: she had nothing to do with it, and neither did her steward, Robert de Cletham. The charge of murder was dropped and instead she stood trial for aiding and abetting the murderers, of which she was also totally acquitted.[2] On the charge of accessory to murder, the jurors could not find her guilty since there was no evidence to prove that she knew about the plan or was behind it. Those accused all pleaded 'not guilty', and so to accuse Maud of being behind a murder that they persistently maintained they neither knew anything about and had certainly not committed would have undermined this plea. Therefore, since there was no 'not proven' verdict, as in Scottish law, Maud went free.

Having the support of her kin and of her influential neighbours was a great boon for Maud in this case, and it can be inferred that she had the sheriff's support from the start. Kydale not only helped to mainpern her with other knights of the county but had married her by 1379, when they both gained a royal pardon for marrying without the king's license.[3]

Sir Ralph too flatly denied having any knowledge of the incident despite having sheltered Richard Gyse and the others for months. He was also totally acquitted.[4]

Maud's steward, Robert of Cletham, too walked free, acquitted of aiding and abetting the crime.[5] Wanting a new start, and unable to find that in the county where he was connected with the murder of his master, he travelled to Scotland and seems to have lived out the remainder of his days there.[6]

If Maud and Ralph were trying to protect the people involved – with the exception of Richard Gyse, who seems to have been something of a sacrificial lamb in this scenario – then Agatha was more difficult to absolve. She had been the keeper of the bedchamber key and the only one who could have given it to Gyse and Cook. While the first record of the trial indicates that Sir William's chamberlain, John Barneby, was indicted alongside Gyse and Cook and another servant, William de Hayle, for the murder, it would seem that Barneby was quick to pass the blame for unlocking the chamber door onto Agatha instead.[7] Since the charge was petty treason, for which the penalty was being drawn and hanged, (although not quartered, which was reserved for high treason), it's not surprising that the chamberlain insisted he had not given the killers the bedchamber key.[8]

Agatha was found guilty of aiding and abetting the killers and incarcerated in Lincoln gaol.[9] She was put into the care of the bailiffs, Thomas de Thornagh and John Bate. While her fate was not to be drawn and hanged, the fate of the unfortunate Richard and the butler Robert, imprisonment was not exactly the soft option. However, not long after her conviction, Agatha – now recorded as Agatha Lovell, not

Agatha Frere, as in the earlier trial records – managed to escape her cell and disappeared from the records. She was never caught. The bailiffs, Thomas de Thornhagh and John Bate, were accused of letting her escape on purpose, but Thomas was acquitted of deliberately abetting her flight as the jurors found she had escaped through his negligence. John Bate's indictment is longer – he seemed to be responsible for several escapes, and was seized by the sheriff and handed over to the marshal.[10] He was manumitted by several citizens of Lincoln for allowing Agatha to run away, including one John de Feryby, an old associate of Sir Thomas de Kydale's. John de Feryby had been one of the men involved on Sir Thomas's side of the feud with Sir John Thorley of Barton in 1373. John Bate was also acquitted of allowing her to deliberately escape, although his connections in the city of Lincoln may have had some sway over the jury in this decision. Should Sir Thomas's sympathies have lain with his (now new wife, Lady Maud), it is conceivable that he helped Agatha to escape and then ensured the bailiffs were acquitted of deliberately aiding in the escape, but it's equally likely that the friendship networks of law enforcement officials crossed over. In such a community, it would be more surprising if they did *not* have mutual friends and allies in the citizenry of Lincoln.

In the indictments of the bailiffs for her escape (and the escapes of various others), it was recorded that the murder had been committed by Augustine Morpath, who did not attend his court date and was outlawed with the other servants. It would seem that even though Gyse and Cook were accused by Maud fairly early on and were hanged for the crime, the jurors were not entirely convinced that they had been the main perpetrators, and Agatha seems to have escaped before the trial's conclusion.

As for the other servants, whose part in the killing was never properly ascertained, none of them returned to court for their next court date, and all were declared outlaws. They too disappear from the records.

Being an outlaw in this period was not quite the romantic life the ballads made it out to be. For a start, living in the greenwood was a seasonal occupation, since in winter when all the trees were bare, an outlaw camp could be spotted easily from some distance away, and being outside the law meant that anyone could do what they liked to you with impunity, from theft and all forms of assault to murder. Only men over 14 could be declared outlaws, and the female equivalent term was 'waived' but in practice had the same outcome.

The verdict for Richard Gyse and Robert Cook is recorded in typical terse form:

> Therefore the aforesaid Richard Gyse and Robert Cook ... were asked separately about the felony and aforesaid sedition of which they wish to clear themselves. They said separately that they were in no way guilty and that for good or evil they put themselves on the [mercy of] the country etc. Therefore let it go to judgement, etc. The jurors came after being chosen and sworn [in], and they say under oath that the said Richard Gyse and Robert Cook the butler, servants of the said William de Cantilupe, are guilty of the aforesaid felony and sedition. Therefore they are to be drawn and hanged.[11]

Such a trial highlighted the anxieties of local fourteenth-century English society in much the same way that the notorious nineteenth-century murder of a young child at Road Hill House revealed the domestic anxieties of Victorian England, as explored by Kate Summerscale in her book and dramatised in *The Suspicions of Mr Whicher*.[12] In both cases, the servant-master relationship came under scrutiny, and the questions of whom to trust within your own household find their uneasy parallels. Similarly, in both cases, while the lady of the house came under suspicion – in this case, the widow, and in the Victorian parallel, the child's sister – neither were found guilty of any wrongdoing despite the suspicions surrounding each of them, albeit for different reasons.

Life After the Trial

Maud Cantilupe married the widower Sir Thomas de Kydale by 1379, becoming the stepmother to his son, Thomas the younger. She had no children by him, either, and he was killed in the Peasants' Revolt of 1381. Neither she nor Thomas claimed the dower owed her as Sir William's widow; it was not until a decade later that she was granted her lands from the Cantilupe estate, for which her third husband Sir John de Bussey helped her sue with the support of the chancellor of the Exchequer.

The lack of dower, and therefore lack of means, would have put Maud in a vulnerable position after the trial had concluded. In such a position, it does not follow that Maud had to have been having an affair with Thomas Kydale at all prior to the murder: the swift remarriage may well have been one of economic necessity on the young widow's part. The stigma and stain on her reputation would have been a real concern even though she was formally acquitted: the jurors acquitted her of murder but could not find any evidence for or against her being an accessory. Rumour and gossip must have been rife in the county and further afield. Sir Thomas's offer of marriage therefore made a lot of practical sense, even if there was no affection between them whatsoever.

On 9 February 1377, an agreement was made between Sir Ralph Paynell and his wife Katherine (after whom their daughter Katherine was named) and Lady Maud and her new husband, Sir Thomas. The agreement was regarding the manors of Scotton and Manton, and one messuage, one toft [homestead] and 20 shillings of rent in Lincoln, and 'the suburb of the same city and the advowsons of the churches of the same manors':

> Thomas de Kydale and Maud have acknowledged the manors, tenements and advowsons to be the right of Richard, and have rendered **the manor of Scotton'**, the tenements and the advowson of the church of the same manor to Richard, Henry and Thomas de Pynchebek' in the court, to hold to Richard, Henry and Thomas de Pynchebek' and the heirs of Richard, of the chief lords for ever. And besides Thomas de Kydale and Maud granted for themselves and the heirs of Maud that the **manor of Malmenton'** [sic] and the advowson of the church of the same manor - which **Ralph Paynell** and **Katherine**, his wife, **held for their lives of the inheritance of Maud on the day the agreement was made**, and which after the decease of Ralph and Katherine ought to revert to Thomas de Kydale and Maud and **the heirs of Maud** - after the decease of Ralph and Katherine shall remain to Richard, Henry and Thomas de Pynchebek' and the heirs of Richard, to hold together with the aforesaid manor, tenements and advowson of the chief lords for ever.[13]

Here we have the Paynells materially benefitting from Maud's inheritance (this is not her dower but the inheritance from her father, either Sir Robert or Sir Phillip Neville). The manor of 'Malmenton' (Manton) was another Neville manor in Lincolnshire, close to Scotton and Cleatham, their steward's place of origin.

Thomas de Kydale 'of Ferriby' was re-elected sheriff of Lincolnshire the following year in 1378, followed by William de Spayne in 1379, one of those who manumitted Lady Maud and Robert de Cletham.

After Sir Thomas' death, Maud swiftly remarried without the king's permission, for which she and her third and last husband, John Bussey, received a formal royal pardon. Sir John was another man well-known in Lincolnshire elite society: his mother was Isobel Paynell, kinswoman (probably sister) of Sir Ralph Paynell, and it would appear that the Paynells continued to look out for Maud's best interests after 1375. John Bussey was a knight by 1391, when he was also elected sheriff of Lincolnshire, but he and Maud had no children either. Maud predeceased him, and he was executed in 1399 for supporting King Richard II when Henry Bolingbroke, crowned King Henry IV, usurped the throne.

Apart from the records of her marriages and the fact that she had no children, we know nothing more of Lady Maud or her life.

Sir Ralph Paynell was untainted by his indictment. He became sheriff of Lincoln in 1377. He died in 1382, by then probably in his mid-fifties, and his widow Katherine remarried, to Sir Henry de Redford.

That the steward, Robert de Cletham, had been supported by Ralph Paynell and aided in his acquittal, also seems likely. Robert disappears from the records until 1380, when he is found again as 'Robert de Cletham, living in Scotland', cited as the co-owner of lands being granted to Goscelin, vicar of the church of Gainsborough.[14] Ralph Paynell appears as a witness to the grant. Robert of Cletham clearly wanted a new start after the trial and it is possible that he already had connections there, perhaps through the Nevilles who were earls of Westmorland, or via some other well-placed connection.

Agatha Lovell/Frere escaped Lincoln gaol and so was waived (the female equivalent of being outlawed). The bailiffs in charge at the time were tried for aiding and abetting her escape, but it was found to be due to their negligence rather than their deliberate cooperation. She was never heard from again.

John Barneby of Beckingham, the chamberlain, received a royal pardon in 1387 at the petition of Queen Anne, although it's not recorded why the queen put this petition forward.[15] John Barneby of Beckingham was now going by the name John Taliour of Barneby. John Bussey, Maud's third husband, was one of King Richard II's favourites (a fact that ensured his execution when Henry Bolingbroke took the throne) so it is possible that his wife had access to the queen through her husband's friendship with the king. Did the petition come from Maud herself, knowing John Barneby was innocent? Why John and not Augustine Morpath or any of the others? These are questions we may never learn the answer to.

Murder in the Middle Ages still looms large in the modern imagination, and even historians must occasionally rely on their imagination to fill in the gaps and form some conclusions. In this instance, it is up to the reader to decide which they believe to be the most likely and why, much like a 'choose your own adventure' story where the ending is always the same.

The tale of Sir William de Cantilupe, his life and death, and the context of his world, has been a long and twisting tale full of surprising turns. The interpretations of the patchy evidence are still debated, and we will never truly know what happened or why. The pardon issued to the chamberlain John Barneby, the acquittal of well-connected Robert de Cletham, the escape of Agatha and the disappearance of the other servants implies that some measure of protection was being afforded by the nobility involved in the case. Whether this was because they were truly innocent, or because William's murder was perceived as justified, or they had been paid off, is impossible to know for sure. Several scenarios have been put forward that fit the evidence, and the wider context.

Was it, as Sillem and others believed, a conspiracy cooked up by the local nobility, Sir William's wife and neighbours, with the servants doing the actual work –taking the bribes, performing the deed (or, if Maud herself had stabbed her husband in bed, then at least helping her to cover it up) and providing the scapegoats to be executed? Or was it a community action undertaken by the servants as an act of revenge or vengeance, where Lady Maud was forced into complicity and protected by her father-figure? Or, was it a perfect storm where the grudges and hatred of Lady Maud and Sir Ralph coincided with the servants' own desire to do away with their employer?

With such gaps in the evidence, we should be careful in assuming one version of events over another, but by examining all the possibilities, a far fuller picture of their life and times emerges than if we consider only one interpretation. Without looking more closely at the servants and following other threads of the story, the fourteenth-century English ways of life are not so easily seen. It is only by questioning further and digging into the background of the people involved, comparing incidents and looking at the wider context of the time, that we can truly scratch the surface of a lost, rich world filled with social and political drama, and rediscover lives once lost to the dust of the archives.

Appendix

Richard de Cantilupe, Sheriff of Kerry

Calendar of the Justiciary Rolls or Proceedings in the Court of the Justiciar of Ireland, Edw. I, vol. 1 (1295–1303), pp. 25–6.

Richard's career has been included here more as a point of interest, and an example of shrieval corruption in a region where there was more opportunity to perform, and get away with, these and other offences. The Cantilupes in England were unable to get away with crimes like these, but that doesn't mean that they, and their noble neighbours, didn't push the boundaries of what was possible. Here is an example of the extremes that sheriffs could get up to when largely unchecked.

All spellings have been left as they were transcribed: there was no standardised way of spelling personal or place names at this time, although some spellings were becoming more common than others.

1295

Ric. de Cantelup was charged that when Adam de Cantelup, Patrick son of Robert de Cantelup, Henry son of Craddock, David son of Richard de Cantelup, Fonercath Ogenenan, Maurice Carnely, Thomas son of Maurice de Cantelup, Thomas son of Meyran de Cantelup, robbed John le Oysillour of chattels to the value of 21*d.*, said Ricard [sic] received them. And that he received Meyler Macgorgenech a felon for the death of Richard Sabin, merchant of Cork. And after Thomas Obrochan (in the time when the said Ricard was sheriff of Kerry) was taken for the death of Ralph de Cantelup, he caused the limbs (*membra*) of Thomas to be cut off.

And that he held all pleas, except pleas of replevy, out of the county, and amerced free men of the county without judgement of the suitors of it; and in pleas of debt of 40*s.* and more, pleaded outside the county, he was accustomed to be a *particeps*. And that he took the lands of John son of Henry son of Rys of Lysgennan, for lack of a syllable omitted from a writ.

And when he asked Nicholas, bishop of Ardfert, to confer the precentorship of that church to Thomas de Cantelup his brother, and the Bishop refused, and the Bishop refused, the followers of Ricard then sheriff, by his direction slew certain faithful men, Irishmen. Afterwards when Ricard was sheriff, the attorney of the escheator in Kerry falsely acquainted John Rys, attorney of the Escheator in Ireland, that said Bishop, when he obtained the temporalities of the bishopric, was not confirmed by the archbishop; said John commanded Ricard to take the temporalities into the king's hand, which he did, with other goods of the said Bishop, and disposed of them at his will, to the Bishop's damage of 40 marks.

When William de Fodeuile replevied a certain Irishman, his man, with his cattle, 33 cows, and within the day, he directed Thomas son of Daniel to slay the Irishman, which he did, so that the cattle should remain to the said sheriff.

And that his lands which he has of purchase, he has by money of the King and money which he wrongfully obtained in the county by extortion, by which the county is impoverished. And by oppression, Thomas de Fremantel was constrained to sell his land of the Keyr to the Sheriff. And when he had levied one mark of Daniel son of William, by summons of the Exchequer, he levied the same again. And imputing to Daniel that he said the Treasurer of Ireland sent a false summons, he attached him at Dublin where he was charged but acquitted.

And when he took general inquisitions, he with his clerks was accustomed to disclose the indictments of felons. And when Alexander Stake lay for two years sick in bed, said Ricard as sheriff caused him to be named in writs at Dublin, for which he was amerced in 20s. And when Maurice Stake found pledges to come before the county court of Arcdart, the Sheriff, before the day assigned, came to Maurice and Alex. Stake and Robert Stake, who likewise found pledges, and took their goods to a value of 40s. for which in fine he obliged Maurice to give him a horse value 4 marks and Alexander and Robert a pledge to come before the Justiciar. Also the said sheriff took 10 cows as a gift from Gilbert Broun which he [Gilbert] robbed from Alexander Stake. And he [Ricard] levied William son of John son of Alexander, and of William son of John son of Robert, half a mark in which they were not bound to the King, for William son of John of Cloncalech, who owed that money to the King.

And that Adam de Cantelup and Ric. son of William de Cantolup [sic], and Ph. son of El. le Clerk, by direction of the sheriff, murdered William son of Adam son of Yue [William FitzHugh son of Adam FitzHugh] upon the bridge of Limerick, because he feared that William would implead him of his land in Balyronan.

He [Ricard the sheriff] comes and gives to the King 66*l*. 13*s*. 4*d*. that suit of peace may be pardoned to him and to Patrick son of Robert de Cantolup, Thomas son of Meyran de Cantelup, El. and Thomas sons of Maurice de Cantelup, of the aforesaid trespasses and all others in Ireland to 10 June, so that they answer in the King's court if any will to question them.

Pledges: Maurice son of Thomas, Andrew Braun, Gilbert Braun, Richard Lonechest, Reym. Stakepol, Ralph son of Ricard, Hugh le Hore, John le Hore, Ric. son of Alexander, Simon Stakepol, William Rudel, John Rudel, Maurice son of John, John de Carryg, William son of Thomas son of El., Richard Keer [sic] de Cantolup, Ralph de Cantolup, Andrew de Cantelup, Simon de Cantolup, and William de Cantolup.

Peace Rolls Appendix to Roll LL: XXIX

Gentry Involved in the Case

Charge of Murder: Maud Neville

Robert Constable	Pledge for Maud's appeal
Richard Neville	Pledge for Maud's appeal

Charge of Murder: Maud Neville

John de Rocheford, knight	Manumitted Maud
Gerard Braybrooke, knight	Manumitted Maud
William Bernak, knight	Manumitted Maud
Robert de Braybrooke, knight	Manumitted Maud
John Auncell, knight	Manumitted Maud
Thomas Kydale, knight	Manumitted Maud
John Dimmock, knight	Manumitted Maud
John Clifford, clerk	Manumitted Maud

Charge of Aiding and Abetting: Maud Neville

William Hawley, knight	Manumitted Maud
Thomas Kydale, knight	Manumitted Maud
John Boys, knight	Manumitted Maud
William de Spayne	Manumitted Maud
Oliver de Barton	Manumitted Maud
Gerard Sodhill	Manumitted Maud

Charge of Aiding and Abetting: Robert de Cletham

John de Rocheford, knight	Manumitted Robert de Cletham (first charge)
Gerard Braybrooke, knight	Manumitted Robert de Cletham (first charge)
William Bernak, knight	Manumitted Robert de Cletham (first charge)
Robert de Braybrooke, cleric	Manumitted Robert de Cletham (first charge)
John Auncell, knight	Manumitted Robert de Cletham (first charge)
Robert de Braybrooke, cleric	Manumitted Robert de Cletham (first charge)

(*Robert de Braybrooke appears twice, and it's possible that Sir Robert (knight) and Robert the clerk were two different men: this may be a scribal error where 'clerk/cleric' was erroneously written twice instead of designating one as a knight*).

Charge of Aiding and Abetting: Robert de Cletham

William Hawley, knight	Manumitted Robert de Cletham
Thomas Kydale, knight	Manumitted Robert de Cletham
John Boys, knight	Manumitted Robert de Cletham
William de Spayne	Manumitted Robert de Cletham
Oliver de Barton	Manumitted Robert de Cletham
Gerard Sodhill	Manumitted Robert de Cletham

Appendix   173

Indictment of Richard Gyse and Robert Cook

(i) Trial in the King's Bench of Richard Gyse and Robert Cook, imprisoned on an appeal in the county court and indictment before King's Bench for the murder of Sir William de Cantilupe; delivery of Lincoln gaol, Michaelmas, 1375.

Richard Gyse of Scotton and Robert Cook, butler, servants of lord William de Cantilupe, knight, the charge was [made] in full in the county [court] of Lincoln held there on Monday the day following the Birth of St John the Baptist, in the forty-ninth year of the reign of the king of England in suit of Maud [Maud], who was the wife of the said William de Cantilupe, before Thomas de Kydale then the sheriff of Lincoln, William de Kirkton, Richard Groos, Robert de Holm, William Haxay, and William de Wyhum, coroners of the lord king in the aforesaid county, concerning the fact that the same persons, Richard Gyse and Robert Cook, together with John de Barnaby the chamberlain and William de Hayle, servants of William de Cantilupe, on the Friday after the last feast of St Ambrose in the above year [*this isn't possible as St Ambrose's feast day is 7th December so was yet to come in 1375, and fell on a Thursday in 1374, making this date 8 December or 15 December 1374 if the Friday of the following week is meant*] feloniously slaughtered the said William de Cantilupe, husband of the said Maud, at Scotton.

And how the said Maud before the sheriff and the coroners of the said county provided pledges to prosecute the aforesaid appeal namely Robert Constable et Richard Nevill. The appeal came before the lord king, among other things, for specific reasons he has made this determination. As well as the said Richard Gyse and Robert Cook here in the same indictment before the king of the fact that where William de Cantilupe knight was in his chamber in the peace of God and the king at Scotton going to bed on Wednesday before the feast of Palm Sunday in the forty-ninth year of the king's reign [**11th April 1375**] when the said Richard Gyse and Robert Cook servants of the same William de Cantilupe did feloniously [*felonice ut felones*] and with premeditated treason [*sedicione*] slaughtered the said William de Cantilupe in the same place on his bed giving him diverse mortal blows, and to avoid the blood passing through the wounds, [at] the outpouring [of which] [people] would take offence, the wounds of the same William were thoroughly washed with boiled water and the (naked) body laid in a sack and they carried it up to Grayingham by horse and in that same place they abandoned him in a field; and they [arranged] the same body in respectable clothes and spurs and with his belt around him – thus it was, that, concerning this new arrangement, men [would think that] [William] had been pierced through by strangers and had not been [killed] by them, and in this way they falsely and mutinously slaughtered and murdered their lord.

Presently, they came before the lord king's court here by means of the constable of the aforesaid castle's command. And the aforesaid Maud, who was in the custody of the aforesaid constable, came for some of the indictments on the aforesaid death, and she committed to the same facts. And the aforesaid Maud was asked whether she appealed against the aforesaid Richard Gyse and Robert Cook and wished to pursue it or not, and she said that she did not draw back from the appeal above.

Therefore the aforesaid Richard Gyse and Robert Cook are to go at the suit of Maud without day etc, and by the lord king's suit thus to appeal the said indictment they were asked separately about the felony and aforesaid sedition of which they wish to clear themselves. They said separately that they were in no way guilty and that for good or evil they put themselves on the [mercy of] the country etc. Therefore let it go to judgement, etc. The jurors came after being chosen and sworn [in], and they say under oath that the said Richard Gyse and Robert Cook the butler, servants of the said William de Cantilupe, are guilty of the aforesaid felony and sedition. Therefore they are to be drawn and hanged. The chattals of the aforesaid Robert Cook are 40 shillings for whence the vill of Scotton is to respond. And he has one acre of land in Northtoft which is worth 6 pence per year, where the lord king escheats in the said county *oneratur*.[1]

And the said Richard Gyse **has nothing** whether chattals or land, nor tenants, etc.

(*Margin: Distrahitur distrahitur suspendetur suspendetur. Catalla forisfactorum (xls.*^{c}.) *terra et tenementa (vj d.*^{c}*).*)

Afterwards, the day after the purification of the Virgin Mary in the 51st year of the reign of our lord king the said Maud who was the wife of

the William de Cantilupe came before the king's court at Westminster in person (*in propria persona sua*) and made a fine with the king on the above occasion as shown by the fine rolls for the end of Hilary Term in the fifty-first year aforementioned. So she is without a day [i.e. she has not been given another court date to follow up on this matter].
(*Margin: Finem fecit. Sine die.* A fine has been made. Without a day.)

Indictment of Maud de Cantilupe, née Neville

(ii) (a) Trial in the King's Bench of Maud de Cantilupe on indictment before justices of the peace for the murder of her husband (p. 82 in Sillem, no. 362); Michaelmas 1375, at Lincoln.
Maud who was the wife of William de Cantilupe knight was taken by indictment to the court by Robert de Willoughby and his fellow guards in the peace of the lord king in the parts of Lyndsey concerning that which the same Maud with others on Friday after the middle of the [forty-ninth] year of the reign of the king of England at Scotton did feloniously kill Sir William de Cantilupe her lord. This indictment, among others, has come to be determined before the lord king in the same term at court.

And also the said Maud who has been indicted at the lord king's court here for the same term concerning the fact that she and other servants of the same William, on the Friday after the middle of the fortieth year [sic] of the reign of the king of England now the forty-ninth at Scotton, feloniously killed the aforesaid William de Cantilupe knight. And now Maud has come to the lord king's court here by the constables of the said castle where she is entrusted to the Marshal. And immediately the Marshal came and addressed her regarding the aforesaid felony and treason [of which] she wished to be acquitted. She said that she was in no way culpable and she put herself for better or worse upon the [mercy of [the king and?]country.. Thus it was done by the jury etc. The jurors come, who, being chosen, tried and sworn in, said on their very sacred oath that the said Maud was not guilty of the said felony or treason now imputed nor of the occasion she retracted. So she goes quit [of court] etc.

(b) Trial in the King's Bench of Maud de Cantilupe on indictments before justices of the peace and King's Bench as accessory to the murder of her husband (p. 79, no. 344; p. 81 no. 358; p. 85, no. 377, above); Michaelmas, 1375, at Lincoln (K. B. 27/459, Rex m.39).

Margin: Lincoln

The jurors of diverse wappentakes in the said county presented in the same term at the king's court at Lincoln that Richard Gyse armour-bearer, Robert Cook **and Henry Tasker**, servants of William de Cantilupe knight, on Tuesday last before the feast of Meatfare [*Quinquagesima Sunday, the last day when eating meat was permitted before Lent*] in the forty-ninth year of our lord king of England's reign [**11 March 1375**] for the felonious slaying of William de Cantilupe knight at Scotton in the night in his bedchamber. And Maud who had been the wife of the said William de Cantilupe was in the same place as an accomplice aiding and abetting that felony.

And that when Richard Gyse servant of William de Cantilupe knight feloniously slaughtered the said William his lord on Monday last after [i.e. the Monday before] the feast of St Gregory [the Great], pope, in the forty-ninth regnal year of the lord king of England [**5 March 1375**] at Scotton, and Maud the wife of the said William de Cantilupe was present in the same place helping and an accomplice to the said felony that was done.

And that Robert Cook, Henry Tasker and Richard Gyse feloniously slew William de Cantilupe knight on Tuesday last before the feast of [Quadregesimo Sunday] in the forty-ninth regnal year [**11 March 1375**] of the king of England at Scotton, at night in his bedchamber. And Maud who was the wife of the said William de Cantilupe was in the same place as an accomplice aiding and abetting the felony that took place.

And that when William de Cantilupe knight was in the peace of God and the king at Scotton in his own chamber going to his bed on Wednesday before the feast of Palm Sunday in the forty-ninth year of the king's reign [**11 April 1375**] when the same Robert Cook of Scotton, Richard Gyse of the same and John Barneby of Beckingham, servants of the same William from the assent and the ordering and abetting of Maud the wife of the same William and Agatha her maid, did feloniously [*felonice ut felones*] and with premeditated treason slaughter the said William de Cantilupe in the same place on his bed giving him diverse mortal blows, and to avoid the blood passing through the wounds, which outpouring would [give away] the offence, the wounds of the same William were thoroughly washed with boiled water and the (naked) body laid in a sack and they carried it up to Grayingham by horse and in that same place they abandoned him in a field; and they [arranged] the same body in respectable clothes and spurs and with his belt around him – thus it was, that, concerning this new arrangement, men [would think that] [William] had been pierced through by strangers and had not been [killed] by them [the servants], and in this way they falsely and mutinously slaughtered and murdered their lord.

And that Richard Gyse of Scotton, Robert Cook and Augustine Forester of Scotton, lately the servants of Sir William de Cantilupe knight on Monday last after the feast of St Gregory (pope) in the forty-ninth regnal year of the lord king of England [**5 March 1375**] at Scotton did feloniously slaughter their lord William de Cantilupe. And that Maud who had been the wife of the said William and Agatha who had been her servant were accomplices and helpers of the felony that was done.

And that Augustine Morpath of Scotton and Richard Gyse servants of William de Cantilupe knight on Monday last after the feast of St Gregory [the Great], pope, in the forty-ninth regnal year of the lord king of England [**5 March 1375**] at Scotton, feloniously slaughtered Sir William de Cantilupe their lord. And they say that Maud de Cantilupe wife of the said William de Cantilupe, Agatha Frere the maid of the said Maud and Robert Cook butler of Scotton were present in the same place aiding and abetting the aforesaid felony that was done as accomplices. And that the said Maud [orchestrated/attended to] the said Augustine Morpath and Richard Gyse to commit the said felony etc.

And that Richard Gyse, Robert Cook, and Augustine Warner (warrener?) the servants of William Cantilupe knight on the Friday after the feast of St Gregory in the forty-ninth regnal year of the king of England [**5 March 1375**] at Scotton feloniously killed the said William Cantilupe at night, who had been their master. And that Maud who was the wife of the said William Cantilupe and Agatha the servant of the said Maud were accomplices, aiding and abetting the said felony.

178 *Murder During the Hundred Years' War*

And that Richard Gyse, Robert Cook, John Barneby the chamberlain, John Astyn, and Agatha the maid feloniously killed their lord William de Cantilupe knight on Thursday after the Passion Friday on the forty-ninth regnal year of the king of England [**26 April 1375**] at Scotton. And that Maud who was the wife of the said William was an accomplice aiding and abetting the said felony that was done.

And that Richard Gyse, Augustine de Morpath and Robert Cook feloniously slew William de Cantilupe knight then their lord and existing master at Scotton, on Saturday after the last annunciation of the blessed Virgin Mary in the forty-ninth regnal year of the current king of England [**31 March 1375**]. And that Maud who was the wife of the said William and Agatha her maid were accomplices and aided the said felony that was done.

And also in court Robert de Willoughby and his fellow guards in the peace of the lord king in the parts of Lyndsey presented that Augustine de Morpath, John Barneby chamberlain, William Chamberlain, Richard Gyse, Robert Cook, John Henxteman and Agatha lately the servants of Richard de Bingham knight, servants of Sir William de Cantilupe knight, on Friday before the feast of the annunciation of the blessed Virgin Mary in the forty-ninth regnal year of the current king of England [**30 March 1375**] at Scotton treasonously slew the said William de Cantilupe their lord at night in his bedchamber. And that Maud the wife of the said William on the day and year aforesaid was an accomplice and abettor to the aforesaid death.

And that Richard Gyse, Augustine de Morpath, Walter Chamberlain, William de Hole, Robert Cook [hanged] [*sic*] of Scotton, Agatha maid of Maud de Cantilupe, servants of Sir William de Cantilupe, knight, feloniously and treasonously slew their lord the aforesaid William de Cantilupe on the Friday before the last feast of the annunciation of the blessed Virgin Mary in the forty-ninth regnal year of the current king of England [**30 March 1375**].

And that Augustine de Morpath, Richard Gyse of Scotton, Robert Cook of the same and John Chamberlain [i.e. John Barneby] feloniously slew Sir William de Cantilupe knight on Friday before the last feast of the annunciation of the blessed Virgin Mary in the forty-ninth regnal year of the current king of England [**30 March 1375**], at Scotton. And that Maud wife of the said Sir William and Agatha the servant of the said Maud were attending accomplices and conspirators in the death of the said Sir William in the forty-ninth regnal year of the current king of England.

And that Richard Gyse and Robert Cook servants of Sir William de Cantilupe knight on Friday before the last feast of the annunciation of the blessed Virgin Mary in the forty-ninth regnal year of the current king of England [**30 March 1375**] at Scotton treasonously slew the said Sir William their lord at night in his bedchamber.

This, among other things, is the indictment to come here before the lord king in this same term at court, to be terminated. And now certainly on the next Monday following All Souls [**6 November 1375**] the said Maud came here to this same court of the lord king by the constables of the said castle committed to the Marshal. And immediately by the Marshal she arrived. And because the aforesaid Richard Gyse and Robert were the principal factor[s] in in the aforesaid felony and treason they were previously convicted of, just as it appears below in the same roll: the said Maud was urgently questioned about her presence and abetting and helping the aforesaid Richard Gyse and Robert Cook to do the aforesaid felony and treason [of which] she wished to be acquitted. She said that she was in no way guilty and for better or worse she places herself etc. Therefore let a jury etc. The jurors came who had been chosen and tried and sworn in, and they said upon their most sacred oath that the said Maud was not guilty of the consent or aiding and abetting the aforesaid Richard Gyse and Robert Cook and so therefore she is without a day [in court].

But because the said Henry Tasker, John Barneby of Beckingham, Augustine Forester, Augustine Morpath, Augustine Warner, John Barneby, [William] Chamberlain, John Astyn and Agatha of the principal aforementioned treasonous and felonious deed of which the above are indicted are not yet outlawed nor is it proved in any other way, the said Maud is forgiven and manumitted by William Hawley knight, Thomas Kydale knight, John Boys, William de Spayne, Oliver de Barton and Gerard Sodhill who manumitted the said Maud *habendi corpus eius* at the king's court on the octave of St Michael at the king's court in Westminster wherever etc.

Margin: Manucap[t]io – [bailed]

180   Murder During the Hundred Years' War

And the said Maud came on the octave of St Michael [*the first part of the Michaelmas term, that is, the business of the court in the eight days before St Michael's day on the 29 September*] to the king's court at Westminster by means of the aforesaid bail. And because the said Henry Tasker, John Barneby of Beckingham, Augustine Forester, Augustine Morpath, Augustine Warner, John Barneby, John Astyn, William Chamberlainman [sic], and John Henxteman, concerning the principal deed of the felony and treason aforesaid, and already those indicted above are outlawed as shown by the king's writ in Michaelmas term in the forty-ninth regnal year of the present king of England, and the aforesaid Agatha concerning the principal deed of the aforesaid felony and treason already indicted above is waived[2] as shown by the above writ.

The said Maud was urgently asked how her presence and support of the aforesaid Henry Tasker, John Barneby, Augustine Forester, Augustine Morpath, Augustine Warner, John Barneby [of Beckingham], John Astyn, William Chamberlainman [sic] John Henxteman and Agatha aided [in the murder] if she wishes to clear herself. She said that she was in no way guilty and that for good or ill she places herself on the mercy of the country etc. Therefore, the jury will come to the court of the king's bench at the next Purification of the Virgin Mary in whatever place, etc. And whom etc. And it will be recognized etc.

And those above came: John de Rocheford, Gerard Braybrook knight, William Bernak knight, Robert de Braybrook knight, **John Auncell knight**, **Thomas Kydale knight**, John Dimmock knight, and John Clifford clerk, and manumitted the said Maud to provide her in person (*de habendo corpus eius*) at the king's court at the aforementioned term [Michaelmas, that is, the Autumn term] etc. viz. *corpora pro corpore* etc.

(*Margin: Manucapcio – bailed out*)

On which day the lord king's court at Westminster, the aforesaid Maud came by those aforesaid who manumitted her, and was seen and diligently examined for the aforesaid indictment by them, at the other Michaelmas term in the forty-ninth regnal year of the present king of England, of the aforesaid death of which she was acquitted in the king's court at Lincoln as is shown on roll 39 among the lawsuits for Michaelmas term, and so by the law of the country concerning the aforesaid charge of accessory [to murder] the court was not able to indict the aforesaid Maud as an accessory, and so she goes without a day.

Indictment of Robert de Cletham

(iii) (a) Indictments and trial in the King's Bench of Robert de Cletham, for the murder of Sir William de Cantilupe ; Michaelmas, 1375, at Lincoln (K. B. 27/459, Rex m.58)

Margin: Lincoln

Jurors from diverse wappentakes in the aforesaid county presented themselves at the end of the king's court at Lincoln that Robert de Cletham of Scotton and others on Friday at the last Quadragesima Sunday in the forty-ninth regnal year of the present king of England [**14 March 1375**] feloniously slew William de Cantilupe of Scotton, knight, at Scotton. By that precept made to the sheriff, the sheriff arrested the said Robert etc. And only the named day, Thursday next after All Souls [**2 November 1375** *or, if the week following is meant,* **9 November 1375**] at the end of the term of the king's court at Lincoln the said Robert came and was returned to the lord king's Marshal's prison on the occasion that he was committed to the Marshal. And presently the Marshal led him and he came and was questioned about the aforesaid felony of which he wished to be acquitted. He said the he was in no way guilty, and that for good or ill he placed himself at the mercy of the country, etc. *Ideo fiat inde iurata etc*. The jurors came who were elected, tried and sworn in and said on their sacred oath that the said Robert was not guilty of the aforesaid felony nor of the occasion he withdrew. *Ideo ipse eat inde quietus etc.*

Margin: Quit or withdrawn

(b) Indictments and trial in the king's bench of Robert de Cletham as accessory to murder of Sir William de Cantilupe ; Michaelmas, 1375, at Lincoln (K.B. 27/459, Rex m.58)

Margin: Lincoln

The jurors of diverse wappentakes of the said county at the term of the king's court at Lincoln presented that Richard Gyse, Robert Cook and Augustine Warner servants of William Cantilupe knight, did in the night of Friday after the feast of St Gregory the Great (pope) in the forty-ninth regnal year of the present king of England, [16 March 1375] feloniously slew the said William de Cantilupe who was their lord. And that Robert de Cletham of Scotton was aiding and abetting the said felony that was done.

And that Richard Gyse, Robert Cook, John Barneby, William Chamberlain, John Astyn, and Agatha the maid of William de Cantilupe, knight, on Thursday before Good Friday in the forty-ninth regnal year of the present king of England [*Maundy Thursday was* **19 April 1375**, *while the Thursday the week before was* **12 April 1375**], at Scotton feloniously slew said William de Cantilupe knight who was their existing lord. And that Robert de Cletham was then the steward of the said William de Cantilupe was aiding and abetting them doing the said felony.

The sheriff by this precept arrested the said Robert of Cletham etc. And on the Tuesday after the next All Souls [6 November 1375] in the term of the court of the king's bench at Lincoln the said Robert de Cletham came and returned him from the prison of the king's Marshal on the occasion that he was committed to the Marshal. And at once the Marshal came. And because the said Richard Gyse and Robert Cook *de principali facto* of the said felony and the above were indicted and convicted as shown in the 39th plea roll among the lawsuits of the aforesaid term, the said Robert de Cletham was urgently asked how the said Robert Gyse and Robert Cook were aided and abetted in the said felony that was done if he wished to be acquitted. He said the he was in no way guilty and for good or ill he put himself on the country etc. *Ideo fiat inde iurata etc.* The jurors came who had been elected, tried and sworn in and said on their sacred oath that the said Robert de Cletham was not guilty of aiding and abetting the said

Richard and Robert Cook of the aforesaid felony that was done, nor this event, and is withdrawn. [Robert de Cletham goes quit of court and the suit is withdrawn].

But since the abovementioned Augustine Warner, John Barneby and John Astyn were indicted above for the principal fact of the said felony, he is not as yet outlawed nor in any way convicted the said Robert de Cletham is dismissed by being manumitted by William Hawley knight, **Thomas Kydale knight**, John Boys knight, William de Spayne, Oliver de Barton, and Gerard Sodhill, who manumitted for the said Robert de Cletham to [produce him] (*habendi corpus eius*) in the king's court in the octaves of St Michael in whatsoever place etc.

Margin: manumitted

On which day in the king's court at Westminster the said Robert de Cletham came by those aforesaid men who had manumitted him. And because the said Augustine Warner, John Barneby and John Astyn were indicted *de principali facto* of the felony and treason by the above indictment are now outlawed as is shown by the king's writ for the Michaelmas term in the forty-ninth regnal year of the present king of England, and the said Agatha, similarly indicted *de principali facto* in the said felony and treason is now waived as shown by the king's aforesaid writ. The said Richard de Cletham was urgently asked about aiding and abetting the said Augustine Warner, John Barneby, John Astyn and Agatha if he wished to be acquitted. He said that he was in no way guilty and for good or ill put himself on the country etc. Then the jury will come to the king's court at the next Purification of the Virgin Mary to whichever place etc. And whom etc. will be recognized etc. And to the above place came John de Rocheford knight, Gerard Braybrook knight, William Bernak knight, Robert de Braybrook cleric, John Auncell knight and Robert de Braybrook cleric and made manumission for the said Robert de Cletham [and will produce him] at the aforesaid term of the king's court etc.

On which day of the king's court at Westminster the said Robert came by those aforesaid [men] who had manumitted him, and the said Robert was seen and diligently examined concerning the above indictment for the death in Michaelmas term in the forty-ninth regnal year of the present king of England at the aforesaid king's court at Lincoln and he was acquitted. This is shown by the (*blank space*) roll among the lawsuits of the Michaelmas term spoken of above, and thus by the law of the land concerning the said aforesaid accessory [charge] it wasn't possible to indict the said Robert of the *accessoriis predictis* and so he goes without a day.

[*Margin: Without day*]

Indictment of Sir Ralph Paynell

(iv) Indictments and trial in the King's Bench of Sir Ralph Paynell as accessory to murder of Sir William de Cantilupe: Michaelmas, 1375, at Lincoln (K.B. 27/459, Rex m.58).

(*Margin: Lincoln*)

The jurors of diverse wapentakes of the aforesaid county came to the term in the court of the lord king at Lincoln to present that Augustine Morpath of Scotton and Richard servants of William de Cantilupe knight feloniously slew the said William de Cantilupe their lord at Scotton on the Monday after the Feast of St Gregory the Great [pope] in the forty-ninth regnal year of the present king of England [**19 March 1375**]. And they said that Maud de Cantilupe wife of the said William de Cantilupe, Agatha Frere, maid of the said Maud, and Robert Cook of Scotton, butler, were present and conscious helpers in the said felony. And the said Maud procured the said Augustine Morpath and Richard Gyse to do the said felony etc. And they said that Ralph Paynell knight received the said Maud, wife of the said William de Cantilupe, Agatha Frere the maid of the said Maud and Richard Gyse at Caythorpe after the fact of said felony in the knowledge of the said felony.

By this order the sheriff arrested the said Ralph Paynell etc. And on the Monday next after All Souls [**5 November 1375**] this same time before the king's court the said Ralph came here and returned himself to the prison of the king's Marshal on the said occasion that he was committed to the Marshal. And at once he was led by the Marshal and came and because the said Maud and Agatha were not waived nor in any way convicted, consequently Ralph was released by manumission of William Hawley, knight, Thomas Kydale knight, John Bussy, William de Spayne, Oliver de Barton, and Gerard Sodhill who manumitted for the said Ralph and [were to produce him] at the king's court in the octaves of St Michael in whichever place etc.

[*Margin: manumitted*]

And at the octaves of St Michael at the king's court at Westminster the said Ralph Paynell came by the said [men]. And because the said Robert [sic] Gyse and Agatha of the said felonies are now convicted, the said Ralph was pressingly questioned concerning his reception of the said Robert [sic] and Agatha if he wished to be acquitted. He said that he was in no way guilty and that he put himself on the country. So the jurors came thence to the king's court the day after the Purification of the Virgin Mary to whichever place etc. And whom etc. to be recognized etc. And in the interim the said Ralph is released by manumission as before etc.

[*Margin: manumitted*]

Easter Term 1376
At which day in the king's court at Westminster the said Ralph came by the aforesaid bail etc. And the sheriff returned the names of the jurors though none of them etc. So the said jurors *posita fuit in respectum coram domino rege virtute breuis domini regis iusticiariis his directi de iurata predicta* by the writ of Nisi Prius *capienda vsque a die Pasche in xv dies vbicumque....* [The writ of *Nisi Prius* follows[3]] *Ad quam quidem* Easter fortnight at the king's court at Westminster the said Ralph came by those aforesaid men who had manumitted him. And the said Thomas [de Ingelby?] at the court where etc. he sent a true record to the said jury at the court in these words. Afterwards, a day and place contained below at court the aforementioned Thomas de Ingelby associates to himself Thomas Claymond by the form of the statute etc. The said Ralph Paynell knight came by the said [men who had manumitted him]. And a proclamation

was made on behalf of the lord king, if a man in those parts wishes to describe in detail or to inform and none came etc. And the jurors above were similarly sent ahead and elected, tried and sworn in. They came and they said by their sacred oath that the said Ralph Paynell, knight, was not guilty of receiving *infracontento* and *nec unquam se inde retraxit*. Therefore it is considered that the said Ralph goes quit etc.

[*Margin: Quit not withdrawn*]

Indictment of the Bailiffs for Agatha's Escape

(v) (a) Indictment and trial in the King's Bench of Thomas de Thornhagh, bailiff of Lincoln, for the escape of Agnes Lovell, appealed and indicted for the murder of Sir William de Cantilupe; Michaelmas, 1375, at Lincoln (K. B. 27/459, Rex m.40)

[*Margin: Lincoln*]

The jurors of diverse wappentakes of the said county presented themselves at the end of the king's court at Lincoln that ... Agatha **Lovell** [sic] who was the chambermaid (*ancilla*) of Lady Maud de Cantilupe was appealed at the Lincoln court by Thomas de Kydale the sheriff of Lincoln and William Haxay the king's coroner in the parts of Kesteven in the aforesaid county concerning the death of William de Cantilupe, knight, who had been the husband of the said Maud and Agatha's lord at Scotton in Lindsey in the aforesaid county around the middle of the forty-ninth year of the reign of the king of England ... and she was suspected and imprisoned for the death of the aforesaid [knight] at Lincoln in the custody of Thomas de Thornhagh who was the bailiff of Lincoln and through the same [*per idem,* [sic]]bailiff on the Monday after the Feast of the Assumption of the Blessed Mary in the forty-ninth year of the reign of the king of England, she left the prison without permission or the due process of law and judgement [that is, she escaped].

[*There follows another indictment of Thomas de Thornhagh for escape*]
... The jurors came and swore by their sacred oath that Thomas de Thornhagh was in no way culpable of the said felony so on this occasion

it is retracted and they said that ... Agatha evaded Thomas through his negligence.

(vi) (a) Indictment and trial in the King's Bench of John Bate, bailiff of Lincoln, for the escape of Agnes Lovell; Michaelmas, 1376, at Lincoln (K. B. 27/463, Rex m. 9d.)

The jurors of diverse wappentakes of the aforesaid county [of Lincoln] came at the end of the Michaelmas term to the king's court and presented themselves... [*Thomas de Thornhagh and John Bate are indicted for various escapes*]

Item: that Augustine Morpath the servant of William de Cantilupe feloniously slew his lord ... in [Sir William's] chamber ... and that Agatha, servant of the said de Cantilupe was abetting and consented to the death of their lord, for which Agatha was in the custody of the bailiffs of Lincoln, namely John Bate and Thomas de Thornhagh for the death of the same [Sir William]...

And that Agatha **called Lovell** who was the chambermaid of the Lady Maud de Cantilupe was appealed at the court in Lincoln by Thomas de Kydale who has the sheriff of Lincolnshire and William Haxay who was the king's coroner in the parts of Kesteven in the aforesaid county, for the death of William de Cantilupe knight who was the husband of the said Maud and the lord of the said Agatha at Scotton in Lindsey... for which she was imprisoned at Lincoln in the custody of Thomas de Thornhagh and John Bate who were bailiffs of Lincoln ... on the Monday after the Feast of the Assumption of the Blessed Mary in the forty-ninth year of the reign of the king of England, she left the prison without permission or the due process of law and judgement [that is, she escaped].

[*There follows another indictment for escape*]

[The sheriff seized John Bate and he was put into the custody of the Marshal. The Marshal brought John Bate to court to answer for these felonies, and he was manumitted by John Hodelston of Lincoln, John Derfeld of Lincoln, Robert de Carlton of Lincoln, and **John de Feryby**, one of Thomas de Kydale's associates].

Robert de Cletham in Scotland

Feoffment, by Goscelin, perpetual vicar of the church of Gainsborough, John de Kilnington, and **Robert de Cletham, living in Scotland**, to John Blaunchard of Colingborn' Valence and his heirs.

Lands, tenements, rents, services, etc., in the town of Colyngborn' Valence which said Goscelin, John and Robert had of the gift of Edmund de Cornwall.

To hold to heirs and assigns of said John [Blaunchard].

Witnesses: William de Willughby, Knight, Lord of Thuneckes, **Ralph Paynell, Knight**, William Daleson of Lagthors', John Stocketes of Blyton, Nicholas Conynges.

Given at Gainsborough in the county of Lincoln, on Sunday next before the feast of the Ascension, [**29 April**] **1380**.[4]

Notes

Chapter 1
1. R.F. Hunniset, *The Medieval Coroner*, (Cambridge University Press, 1961), p. 11.
2. Ibid.
3. Gavin I. Langmuir, 'Thomas of Monmouth: Detector of Ritual Murder', *Speculum*, 59:4, (1984), p. 820.
4. Ibid.
5. Daniel Lord Smail, 'Common Violence: Vengeance and Inquisition in Fourteenth-century Marseille', *Past and Present*, 151:1, (1996), p. 28.
6. Ibid., pp. 28–59.
7. James Buchanan Given, *Society and Homicide in Thirteenth-Century England*, (Stanford, 1977), p. 1.
8. Ibid.
9. Smail, 'Common Violence', p. 28
10. L. Stone, 'Interpersonal Violence in English Society 1300–1980', *Past & Present*, 101, (1983), p. 25. According to the Historical Crime Data recorded by the Government and kept in the public domain, there was an average of 619.8 reported homicides in England and Wales per year throughout the 1980s. Stone's article was published in 1983, so he was probably thinking of the averages given for the start of the 80s or even the 1970s. The average for these years alone was 586.75 (587 rounded up), and the average for the 1970s was even lower, 511.6 or 512 murders per year. If we take a rough average of 570 murders per year across both decades, and the thirteenth century figures amount to ten to twenty times that number, then at the *lowest* the average estimate would be around 5,700 violent deaths per year, which include cases of manslaughter. At the highest, it would be an average of 11,400 murders per year. This seems astronomically high, but the majority of these deaths were among the peasants rather than the elites. If this is a fair estimate, then effectively at the lowest there were twice as many violent deaths per year than there were living knights in the whole kingdom of England. See: P.R. Coss, *The Knight in Medieval England, 1000–1400*, (Grange Books Ltd, 1993), p. 84
11. Barbara Hanawalt, *Violent Death in Fourteenth- and Fifteenth-Century England*, (Cambridge University Press, 1976), p. 305.
12. Ibid. p. 304.

13. Ibid.
14. Ibid.
15. Ibid. p. 305.
16. John Bellamy, *Crime and Public Order in England in the Later Middle Ages* (London: Routledge, 1973), pp. 6, 42.
17. Áine Foley, 'The Outlaw in Later Medieval Ireland', in *Law and Society in Medieval England and Ireland: Essays in Honour of Paul Brand*, ed. Travis R. Baker, (Routledge, 2017), p. 162.
18. J.G. Bellamy, 'The Coterel Gang: An Anatomy of a Band of Fourteenth-Century Criminals', *EHR*, 79:313, (Oct., 1964), p. 699.
19. Ibid.
20. Ibid.
21. Foley, 'The Outlaw in Later Medieval Ireland', p. 158.
22. Bellamy, *Crime and Public Order*, p. 42.
23. See Barbara A. Hanawalt, 'Fur Collar Crime: The Pattern of Crime among the Fourteenth-Century English Nobility', *Journal of Social History*, 8:4, (1975), pp. 1–17. Hanawalt notes that among the established gentry and higher nobility the crimes delineated as 'felonies' were rare, and high-profile homicides among this group were usually political in nature. 'Fur collar' crimes may involve members of this section of society instigating killings and receiving/sheltering felons, beatings and intimidation tactics, and crimes such as the extortion of fines and other payments (particularly among those holding law enforcement positions).
24. Rosamund Sillem, ed., *Some Sessions of the Peace in Lincolnshire 1360–1375*, The Lincoln Record Society, Vol. 30, (Hereford, 1936)., pp. lvii–lviii.
25. Ibid., p. lviii; *Calendar of Patent Rolls [hereafter CPR]*, Edw. III, 1374–77, (London, 1916), p. 52.
26. .Sillem, *Some Sessions of the Peace in Lincolnshire*, p. lviii; pp. 77–80.
27. Ibid.
28. William Page, 'House of Benedictine Monks of the Order of Tiron: The Abbey of Humberston', in *A History of the County of Lincoln: Volume 2*, ed. William Page (London, 1906), pp. 133–134. *British History Online* http://www.british-history.ac.uk/vch/lincs/vol2/pp133-134, accessed 19.06.2019.
29. Sillem, *Some Sessions of the Peace in Lincolnshire 1360–1375*, p. lv.
30. Ibid.
31. Ibid., p. lv.
32. Ibid., pp. liv, 21, 59, 60, 104, 105–106.
33. Ibid., p. 105.
34. Ibid.
35. Ibid. p. lvi.
36. National Archives, Kew (TNA): TNA: JUST 2/77, rot. 6

37. Possible Medieval Manor House, Scotton, Ref: MLI51282, *Lincs to the Past*, <https://www.lincstothepast.com/Possible-Medieval-Manor-House--Scotton/231605.record?pt=S>, accessed 29.09.18.
38. Site of a Medieval Manor House, Ref: MLI51281, *Lincs to the Past*, online resource, < https://www.lincstothepast.com/SITE-OF-A-MEDIEVAL-MANOR-HOUSE/231604.record?pt=S> accessed 29.09.18.
39. In English law, 'subinfeudation' is like sub-letting land to other tenants.
40. Mark Gardiner, 'Buttery and Pantry and The Antecedents: Idea and Architecture in the English Medieval House', in *Medieval Domesticity: Home, Housing and Household in Medieval England*, eds. Maryanne Kowaleski and P.J.P. Goldberg, (Cambridge University Press, 2011), p. 64.
41. Ibid., p. 54.
42. Sillem, *Some Sessions of the Peace in Lincolnshire*, p. 143, emphasis mine, translation mine.
43. Sara Butler, *The Language of Abuse: Marital Violence in Later Medieval England*, (Brill, 2007), p.185.
44. Frances E. Dolan, 'The Subordinate('s) Plot: Petty Treason and the Forms of Domestic Rebellion', *Shakespeare Quarterly*, 43, no. 3 (1992), p. 317.
45. Ibid., pp. 317–18.
46. Sillem, *Some Sessions of the Peace in Lincolnshire*, p. lxxi.
47. Ibid., p. lxx.
48. H.M. Cam, *The English Historical Review*, 54 (216), (1939), p. 722.
49. Shannon McSheffery, 'Detective Fiction in the Archives: Court Records and the Uses of Law in Late Medieval England', *History Workshop Journal*, 65, (2008), p. 65.
50. Ibid.
51. C. Rawliffe, 'Bussy, Sir John (exec. 1399), of Hougham, Lincs. and Cottesmore, Rutland', *The History of Parliament: The House of Commons 1386–1421*, eds. J.S. Roskell, L. Clark, C. Rawcliffe., (Boydell & Brewer, 1993), https://www.historyofparliamentonline.org/volume/1386-1421/member/bussy-sir-john-1399, accessed 12 September 2018.Gyse is not mentioned by name, and this can hardly apply to Kydale, whose son from his first marriage was in his twenties in 1381 and so puts Kydale himself around William's own age (30) if not older in 1375. *Calendar of Close Rolls, [hereafter CCR]*, Rich. II 1381–1385, (London, 1920), p. 272.
52. S.J. Payling, 'Murder, Motive and Punishment in Fifteenth-Century England: Two Gentry Case-Studies', *English Historical Review* 113, no. 450 (1998), p. 15.
53. Edward Powell, *Kingship, Law and Society: Criminal Justice in the Reign of Henry V*, (Oxford University Press, 1989) p. 20.
54. Payling, 'Murder, Motive and Punishment', p. 2.
55. Phillip Schofield, *Peasants and Historians: Debating the Medieval Peasantry* (Manchester, 2016), esp Ch 1.

56. Judy Giles, '"Playing Hard to Get": Working class Women, Sexuality and Respectability in Britain, 1918–40', *Women's History Review*, 1:2, (1992), p. 241.

Chapter 2
1. TNA: DL 25/2371.
2. For more on seals as representations of identity and the two Cantilupe bishops, Bishop Walter of Worcester and his more famous nephew, St Thomas of Hereford, see also, Melissa Julian-Jones, 'Sealing Episcopal Identity 1200–1300', in *Episcopal Power and Local Society in Medieval Europe, 900–1400*, eds. Peter Coss, Chris Dennis, Melissa Julian-Jones and Angelo Silvestri, Medieval Church Studies (Brepols, 2017), 239–258.
3. Surviving copies of Walter's seal are held in the National Archives, Kew (TNA): TNA: DL 25/2371. I have written more on the seals and their iconography in Melissa Julian-Jones, *The Land of the Raven and the Wolf: Family Power and Strategy in the Welsh March, 1199–c. 1300, Corbets and the Cantilupes*, (unpublished PhD Thesis, Cardiff University, 2015), pp. 297–305.
4. Walter's son, William I, had a smaller seeded fleur-de-lys design: National Library of Wales [NLW] PM_2050; the fourth William, Sir William the younger's great-grandfather, bore his coat of arms in the centre of his circular seal: TNA: E 26/A 25
5. B.W. Holden, 'Cantilupe , William (I) de (d. 1239)', *Oxford Dictionary of National Biography*, (Oxford University Press, 2004), online resource, http://www.oxforddnb.com/view/article/4572, accessed 18.09.13; B.W. Holden, 'Cantilupe [Cantelupe], William (II) de (d. 1251), baron and administrator', *Oxford Dictionary of National Biography*, online resource, http://www.oxforddnb.com/view/article/4573/4573?back=,4574, accessed 03.05.2013.
6. Julian-Jones, *Land of the Raven and the Wolf*, pp. 28–32; 53–87.
7. Julian-Jones, *Land of the Raven and the Wolf*, pp. 84–88; 162–172.
8. Matthew Paris, *Chroica. Majora* Vol. 5, ed. Henry Richards Luard, (London, 1872), p. 463; Robert Stacey, 'Cantilupe, William (III) de (d. 1254), baron', *Oxford Dictionary of National Biography*, (Oxford University Press, 2004), online resource, http://www.oxforddnb.com/view/article/4574?docPos=10 accessed 19.11.12.
9. Nicholas Vincent, 'Cantilupe, Sir George de (1251–1273)', *Oxford Dictionary of National Biography*, (Oxford University Press, 2004), online resource, http://www.oxforddnb.com/view/article/4566, accessed 03.10.2013.
10. *CIPM*, ii, Edward I, (London, 1906), pp. 17–21; T.F. Tout, 'Zouche, Alan de la (d. 1270)', rev. R.R. Davies, *Oxford Dictionary of National Biography*, (Oxford University Press, 2004), online resource, http://www.oxforddnb.

com/view/article/30300, accessed 02.11.2013; C.L. Kingsford, 'Hastings, Sir Henry (1235?–1269)', rev. H. W. Ridgeway, *Oxford Dictionary of National Biography*, (Oxford University Press, 2004), online resource, http://www.oxforddnb.com/view/article/12573, accessed 02.11.2013.
11. Barbara Ross, 'Vipers and Gardens of Balsam', in *St Thomas Cantilupe Bishop of Hereford: Essays in His Honour*, ed. Meryl Jancey, (Hereford, 1980), p. 80.
12. David Carpenter, 'St Thomas de Cantilupe: His Political Career', in *St Thomas Cantilupe Bishop of Hereford*, p. 63.
13. Nona Martin, 'The Life of St Thomas of Hereford', in *St Thomas Cantilupe Bishop of Hereford*, p. 17.
14. Ross, 'Vipers and Gardens of Balsam', p. 79.
15. Ibid.
16. '*et nomine Willelmi de Cantilupo studentis Parisivis triginta marcas.*' C.M. Woolgar (ed.), *Testamentary Records of the English and Welsh Episcopate 1200–1413: Wills, Executors' Accounts and Inventories, and the Probate Process*, (Canterbury and York Society: Boydell, 2011), p. 105. One mark was worth two-thirds of a pound, namely, 13 shillings and 4 pence (13*s* 4*d*). There were 20*s* to £1, and 12*d* in 1 shilling. This was therefore the equivalent of £20, which in 1282 had the approximate buying power equivalent of £13,881.39 in 2017's money, according to the National Archives Currency Converter, http://www.nationalarchives.gov.uk/currency-converter.
17. Enfeoffed: to be given lands and estates by someone else, freehold rather than leasehold.
18. TNA: C 143/145/17.
19. Victoria County History [hereafter VCH] Nottinghamshire, Vol. 2, pp. 105–109; VCH Lincolnshire, ii, p. 236.
20. Much has been written on the miracles of St Thomas, most recently including Ian Bass, 'Two Models of Episcopal Sanctity: Thomas Cantilupe and Thomas Becket', in *Episcopal Personalities*, eds. Peter Coss, Chris Dennis, Melissa Julian-Jones and Angelo Silvestri, Medieval Church History (Brepols, 2019).
21. Anne McGee Morganstern, *Gothic Tombs of Kinship in France, The Low Countries, and England,* (Pennsylvania State University Press, 2000), p. 223 n. 35.
22. *History of William Marshal*, ed. A.J. Holden, trans. S. Gregory, vol. I (London, 2006), line 1478.
23. Adrian Ailes, 'The Knight's Alter Ego: From Equestrian to Armorial Seals', *Good Impressions: Image and Authority in Medieval Seals*, eds. Noel Adams, John Cherry, and James Robinson, (The British Museum, 2008), p. 8.

24. David Crouch, 'The Historian, Lineage and Heraldry', *Heraldry, Pageantry and Social Display*, eds. Peter R. Coss and Maurice Keen, (Woodbridge, 2002), p. 34.
25. Ibid.
26. *CIPM*, Edw.III (1352–1360), p. 197. The currency conversion has been calculated via the National Archives Historical Currency Converter tool, which is a rough guide to put things into perspective, rather than an accurate calculation.
27. Ibid., p. 196; *CCR*, Edw. III (1369–1374) p. 252.
28. Even figuring out the actual ages of the Cantilupes involves some detective work and estimation: in 1375, Sir William the elder was said to be aged 'forty and more', when William's age was approximated at thirty (he was actually thirty-one). This is an obvious underestimation, since William was the younger son of the two. At the time of Nicholas the elder's death in 1355, Sir William the elder was said to be aged 'thirty years and more', so in the later entry 'forty' should be 'fifty'. Nevertheless, this would imply that Sir William the elder married at eighteen and had Nicholas not long afterwards, then William two years later.
29. Philippe Ariès, *Centuries of Childhood*, trans. Robert Baldick (London, 1962), p. 125. See also esp. pp. 33–49 and 128–33. For a more detailed appraisal of the historiography, see for example Barbara A. Hanawalt, 'Medievalists and the Study of Childhood', *Speculum*, 77 (2), 440–460.
30. Shulamith Shahar, *Childhood in the Middle Ages* (London, 1990).
31. Nicholas Orme, 'The Culture of Children in Medieval England', *Past and Present* 148 (Aug. 1995), p. 53.
32. Ibid.
33. Ibid., pp. 53–4, 55, 57.
34. Ibid., p. 62.
35. Ibid. p. 189.
36. Nicholas Orme, *From Childhood to Chivalry: The Education of the English Kings and Aristocracy 1066–1530*, (Routledge Revivals, 2017), p. 181.
37. Ibid.
38. See William Chester Jordan, 'The Great Famine 1315–1322 Revisited', in *Ecologies and Economies in Medieval and Early Modern Europe: Studies in Environmental History for Richard C. Hoffmann*, ed. Scott G. Bruce, (Brill, 2010), pp. 44–61.
39. Ian Kershaw, 'The Great Famine and Agrarian Crisis in England 1315–1322', *Past and Present* 59, (May, 1973), p. 3.
40. Tine Van Bortel, Anoma Basnayake, Fatou Wurie, et al., 'Psychosocial Effects of an Ebola Outbreak at Individual, Community and International Levels', *Bulletin of the World Health Organisation*, (2016), doi: http://dx.doi.org/10.2471/BLT.15.158543, accessed 10.04.2019.
41. Anthony Emery, *Discovering Medieval* Houses, (Shire Publications, 2007), p. 109.

42. This is difficult to ascertain. Joan, daughter of William de Welle (d.1349), is certainly not the correct Joan de Welle, as she was about 12 years old at the time of her father's death and so not old enough to have been married with two children by 1344. *CIPM*, Edw. III (1347–1352), pp. 322–3, nos. 423 and 424.
43. *CIPM*, Edw. III (1307–1327), pp. 200–201, no. 352.
44. *CPR*, Edw. III (1364–1367), p. 429.
45. *Calendar of Fine Rolls* [hereafter *CFR*], Edw. III 1369–1377, (London, 1924) p. 295.
46. Frederik Pedersen, 'Motives for Murder: The Role of Sor Ralph Paynell in the Murder of William Cantilupe (1375)', in *Continuity, Change and Pragmatism in the Law: Essays in Honour of Prof. Angelo Forte*, eds. Andrew R.C. Simpson, Scott Crichton Styles, Euan West and Adelyn L.M. Wilson, (Aberdeen University Press, 2016), p. 71.
47. Frederik Pedersen, *Marriage Disputes in Medieval England*, (Hambledon Continuum, 2000), p. 153.
48. Ibid., p. 153.
49. Ibid., p. 155.
50. See, Tom Johnston, 'The Preconstruction of Witness Testimony: Law and Social Discourse in England before the Reformation', *Law and History Review*, 32:1, (2014), 127–147.
51. *CPR*, Edw. III (1364–1368), p. 281.
52. Borthwick Institute, CP.E.259–9. The Strelleyes held a messuage, seven virgates of land, five acres of meadow and six acres of wood and a water mill at Shipley, which was held by Nicholas de Cantilupe by knight's service, indicating a pre-existing bond between the two families [*CIPM*, Edw. III (1352–1360), No. 84 p. 95]. Sampson also inherited directly from his grandfather, who also died in 1355 [*CCR*, Edw. III (1354–1360) p. 245]. It would appear that bypassing the married sons in favour of the unmarried grandsons was not unusual at this time, or at least it was a decision made by these two neighbours. Sampson was the sheriff of Nottingham in 1367 [*CPR*, Edward III (1364–1367) p. 429] and was commissioned to keep the peace with other nobles of the county in 1380 [*CPR*, Richard II (1377–1381), p. 513].
53. Borthwick Institute, CP.E.259–16.
54. Anna Whitelock, *Elizabeth's Bedfellows: An Intimate History of the Queen's Court* (Bloomsbury, 2013) p. 9.
55. Borthwick Institute, CP.E.259–9.
56. While Pedersen tentatively posits that this unnamed woman is a Cantilupe sister, Sampson de Strelley was married to Elizabeth, the daughter of John Hercy, according to Thoroton. This would mean Elizabeth was a cousin of some description and most likely through her mother's side, probably related in some way to Joan de Welle, Nicholas's mother. The Hercys were also distantly related to the Constables by marriage and Elizabeth's great-

grandfather had married into the de Binghams. See Robert Thoroton, 'Strelley', in *Thoroton's History of Nottinghamshire*, Vol. 2, repub. with large additions by John Throsby, ed. John Throsby, (Nottingham: J. Throsby, 1790), pp. 218–222, online resource at *British History Online*, http://www.british-history.ac.uk/thoroton-notts/vol2/pp218-222, accessed 12.06.2019.
57. *CIPM*, Edw. III (1352–1360), No. 229, p. 261.
58. Pedersen, 'Motives for Murder', p. 77. Since this is inherited, it means that other Cantilupe men must have suffered from it at some stage. If so, it might suggest an explanation for Nicholas the elder's older brother William handing over his lands and title, in which case it would have entered the family line via Eva Boltby, but this is conjecture.
59. Miri Rubin, 'The Person in the Form: Medieval Challenges to Bodily Order', in *Framing Medieval Bodies*, eds. Sarah Kay and Miri Ruben, (Manchester, 1994), p. 102.
60. Ibid.
61. Thierry Martin, *Trois Études sur la Sexualité Médiévale*, (Lille, 2001), p. 5. Martin's full transcription of the poem is as follows:

> Menton poncé, fils d'Hermaphroditus,
> Efféminé, défaute de Nature;
> Courage vain, vide de toutes virtues;
> De vice plein, qui ne tend qu'à ordure;
> Non masculine, féminine figure,
> Qui imposer seult faux norms sur autrui.
> Ains ès livres de tels gens, bien ne luy
> Quand ils ne sont en nature parfaits
> Corrupts de corps, de pensée les truys,
> Infiables, déloyaux et mauvais.

Sandra Alverez's article contains this translation:

> A soft chin, son Hermaphrodite
> Effeminate, a defect of nature,
> Faint in heart, devoid of all virtues,
> But full of vice, which tends towards nothing but filth …
> A woman out of a man, who should be bearded,
> man without hair, this is an insult to everyone.
> To meet them is nothing but misfortune,
> And their gaze can be pleasing to no one.
> They make sexual use of both kinds,
> I have known them in my time to be
> Untrustworthy, disloyal, evil.

Sandra Alvarez, 'Intersex in the Middle Ages', *Medievalists*, (2015), online resource, http://www.medievalists.net/2015/01/intersex-middle-ages/, accessed 13.06.2019.
62. Borthwick Archives, York, CP E 259.
63. Pedersen, 'Motives for Murder', p. 77.
64. Ibid., p. 78.
65. Ibid., pp. 86–87.
66. Ibid., p. 87.
67. Caroline Dunn, *Stolen Women in Medieval England: Rape, Abduction, and Adultery, 1100–1500*, (Cambridge University Press, 2013), p. 158.
68. Pedersen, 'Motives for Murder', p. 87.
69. TNA: KB 27/434, which can be viewed online at http://aalt.law.uh.edu/AALT2/E3/KB27no434/aKB27no434fronts/IMG_0117.htm, accessed 12.06.2019.
70. Pedersen, 'Motives for Murder', p. 82.
71. Ibid. The Hastings family were also distantly related to the Cantilupes by marriage via the thirteenth-century branch of the family.
72. '*mm bonis et catallis eiusdem Nich*', KB 27/434, which can be viewed online at http://aalt.law.uh.edu/AALT2/E3/KB27no434/aKB27no434fronts/IMG_0117.htm, accessed 12.06.2019. See also Pedersen, 'Motives for Murder', p. 71.
73. Janet S. Loengard, '"Which may be said to be her own": Widows and Goods in Late-Medieval England', in *Medieval Domesticity*, p. 162.
74. Ibid., p. 163.
75. Sara Butler, 'Runaway Wives: Husband Desertion in Medieval England', *Journal of Social History* 40, no. 2 (2006), p. 342.
76. Ibid.
77. For more details see Sue Sheridan Walker, 'Punishing Convicted Ravishers: Statutory Strictures and Actual Practice in Thirteenth and Fourteenth-century England', *Journal of Medieval History*, 13:3, (1987), 237–250.
78. Henrietta Leyser, *Medieval Women: Social History of Women in England, 450–1500*, (Weidenfeld & Nicholson, 2004), p. 116.
79. Ibid.
80. Frederick Devon (ed.), *Issues of the Exchequer*, (London, 1837), p. 200.
81. Ibid.
82. Pederson, 'Motives for Murder', p. 89.
83. *CCR*, Edw. III (1369–1374), p. 252.
84. *CPR*, Edw. III (1370–1374), p. 163; 'Sir John Auncell of Spalding' appears in *CCR*, Rich. II (1396–1399), p. 297.
85. *CCR*, Rich. II (1377–1381), p. 220.
86. *CPR*, Edw. III (1370–1374), p. 163.
87. The Merriam-Webster dictionary defines 'mainprise' as: 'an undertaking given to a magistrate or court that even without having an accused in

custody one will be liable for the appearance of the accused on a fixed day to defend any and all charges to be brought against him'. Similar to the modern concept of bail.
88. Louise J. Wilkinson, *Women of Thirteenth-Century Lincolnshire*, (Boydell, 2007), p. 67.
89. *CPR*, Edw. III (1367–1370), p. 39.
90. TNA: SC 8/247/12321: Joan de Cantilupe, widow of Nicholas de Cantilupe (spelt Cantalon in the petition) requests that she and Robert de Roos of Ingmanthorpe, William de Bradestoun, chaplain, and John de Felicekirk, chaplain, be granted a licence to give meadow in the vill of Leake [Old Leake, Lincolnshire] and the advowson of the church there to the dean and chapter of Our Lady of Lincoln.
91. *Calendar of Entries in the Papal Register*, Papal Letters Vol. 3, 1342–1362, (London,1897), p. 476.
92. Ibid., Papal Letters 4, (1362–1404), p. 62.
93. *CPR*, Edw. III (1367–1370), p. 72.
94. Kenneth J. Thompson, 'Chaucer's Warrior Bowman: The Roles and Equipment of the Knight's Yeoman', *The Chaucer Review*, 40:4, (2006), p. 387.
95. James Sherbourne, *War, Politics and Culture in Fourteenth-Century England*, (The Hambledon Press, 1994), p. 77.
96. Ibid., p. 80.
97. Ibid.
98. Ibid., p. 86.
99. 'Ther is ful many a man that crieth 'Werre, werre!' That woot ful litel what werre amounteth.' *The Tale of Melibee*, l. 1037, in *The Riverside Chaucer*, ed. Larry D. Benson (3rd edn., Oxford, 2008).
100. Andy King, 'What Werre Amounteth: The Military Experience of Knights of the Shire,1369–1389', *History*, 95:320, (2010), pp. 418–436.
101. Sherbourne, *War, Politics and Culture*, p. 83.
102. Ibid., pp.92–3.
103. Lucy Lynch, 'Protecting the Non-Combatant: Chivalry, Codes and the Just War Theory', *Ex Historia* (2014), 59–80, pp. 62–3.
104. Ibid.
105. A closed letter or more properly a 'letter close' was sealed so that only the recipient could read it, but with a copy enrolled in the Calendar of Close Rolls for the purposes of royal bureaucracy. This is as opposed to an open letter or 'letter patent', unsealed and meant to be read out publically.
106. *CCR*, Edw. III (1369–1374), p. 252.
107. Sillem, *Some Sessions of the Peace in Lincolnshire*, pp. 143, 147.
108. J. Albone, *Archaeological Field Evaluation Report: Land north of Laughton Road, Scotton*, (Pre-Construct Archaeology Limited, 1999), p. 4.
109. Subinfeudation was a practice where tenants of a greater lord sub-letted their lands to raise their own rents.

110. For more on medieval English Christmas traditions, see: J.A.R. Pimlott, *The Englishman's Christmas: A Social History* (Harvester Press, 1978) and Jean-Michel Mehl, 'Games in their Seasons', in *Custom, Culture and Community in the Later Middle Ages: A Symposium* (Odense University Press, 1994), pp. 71–83; Séamus Ó Cathain, 'Midwinter's Merry Dancers', *Béaloideas*, 66, (1998), pp. 163–197.
111. Sillem, *Some Sessions of the Peace in Lincolnshire*, p. lxx.
112. Mary Hamel, 'The Wife of Bath and a Contemporary Murder', *The Chaucer Review*, 14:2 (1979), p. 134.
113. TNA: JUST2/77.
114. Sillem, *Some Sessions of the Peace in Lincolnshire*, p. lxx.

Chapter 3

1. Robert Thoroton, 'Knapthorp,' in *Thoroton's History of Nottinghamshire*, vol. 3, pp. 144–147. *British History Online*, accessed April 18, 2019, http://www.british-history.ac.uk/thoroton-notts/vol3/pp144-147.
2. See R. Bevan, 'A Study of a Medieval Knightly Family: The Longfords of Derbyshire', Part 1, *Foundations*, 1:4, (July 2004), pp. 211–231; John Nichols, *The History and Antiquities of Leicestershire*, v. 4, pt. 1, (1745–1826), p.158, whom George Baker follows in Baker, *History and Antiquities of the County of Northampton*, vol. 1, p. 83 and Charles R. Young, who does not include daughters in his pedigree of the Nevilles but seems to follow Baker and Nichols in listing multiple Philips for this branch in Young, *The Making of the Neville Family 1166–1400*, (Brepols, 1996), pp. x-xi.
3. *CFR*, Edw. III (1356–1368), pp. 132, 301, 397. A William 'Dencourt' witnessed a deed of Sir Nicholas senior, as did Sir Robert Strelley, indicating close associations with both families at this time; Robert Thoroton, 'Bevall', in *Thoroton's History of Nottinghamshire*, vol. 2, pp. 242–246. *British History Online*, http://www.british-history.ac.uk/thoroton-notts/vol2/pp242-246, accessed 13.06.2019.
4. *Calendar of Inquisitions Miscellaneous (Chancery)*, [hereafter, *Cal. Inq. Misc. (Chancery)*], vol. 2 1308–1348, (London, 1916), p. 399; see also, Frederic Richard Barnes, 'The Taxation of Wool, 1327–1348', in *Finance and Trade Under Edward III the London Lay Subsidy of 1332*, ed. George Unwin (Manchester, 1918), pp. 137–177.
5. *CCR*, Edw. III (1360–1364), p. 476.
6. *CPR*, Edw. III (1343–1345), p. 491.
7. *CPR*, Edw. III (1345–1348), p. 31.
8. *CCR*, Edw. III (1337–1339), p. 633.
9. *CFR*, Edw. III (1356–1368), p. 345.
10. Nichols, *History and Antiquities of Leicestershire*, p. 158; P. McNiven, 'Neville [de Neville] family (per. c. 1267–1426), gentry', *Oxford Dictionary of National Biography* (2004), http://www.oxforddnb.com/view/10.1093/

ref:odnb/9780198614128.001.0001/odnb-9780198614128-e-54532, accessed 08.09.2018.
11. *CFR*, Edw. III (1356–1368), p. 51, 54.
12. *CIPM*, Edw. I (1272–1307), p 500, no. 819.
13. *Descriptive Catalogue of Ancient Deeds in the Public Record Office*, vol. 4, (1066–1547), no. A 8491, p. 316.
14. Sillem, *Some Sessions of the Peace in Lincolnshire*, p. 82.
15. Peter Coss, *The Lady in Medieval England, 1000–1500*, (Stroud, 1998), p. 38.
16. Ibid., p. 39.
17. Ibid., p. 46.
18. 'NEVILL (or Neville) [Scotton, Lincolnshire], gu. three fusils, in fesse, ar. a bordure, engr. or', William Berry, *Enclyclopaedia Heraldica*, vol. 2, (London, 1828), p. 643. The Cantilupe arms were also red, gold and some individuals added blue as a third colour.
19. Peter McNiven, 'Neville [de Neville] family (per. c. 1267–1426), gentry', *Oxford Dictionary of National Biography*, (2004), accessed 09.09.2018. http://www.oxforddnb.com/view/10.1093/ref:odnb/9780198614128.001.0001/odnb-9780198614128-e-54532.
20. Ibid.
21. Ibid.
22. Ibid.
23. Anthony Tuck, 'Neville, Ralph, fourth Lord Nville (c. 1291–1367), soldier and administrator', *Oxford Dictionary of National Biography*, (2008), accessed 09. 09.2018. http://www.oxforddnb.com/view/10.1093/ref:odnb/9780198614128.001.0001/odnb-9780198614128-e-19950.
24. Anthony Tuck, 'Neville, Ralph, first earl of Westmorland (c. 1364–1425), magnate', *Oxford Dictionary of National Biography* (2008), accessed 09.09.2018. http://www.oxforddnb.com/view/10.1093/ref:odnb/9780198614128.001.0001/odnb-9780198614128-e-19951.
25. Pedersen, 'Motives for Murder', p. 73.
26. Ibid.
27. Hannah Skoda, *Medieval Violence: Physical Brutality in Northern France, 1270–1330*, (Oxford University Press, 2013), p. 212.
28. M.C.B. Dawes, A.C. Wood and D.H. Gifford, "Inquisitions Post Mortem, Richard II, File 19", in *Calendar of Inquisitions Post Mortem: Volume 15, Richard II*, (London: Her Majesty's Stationery Office, 1970), pp. 202–217, no. 508. *British History Online*, accessed September 12, 2018, http://www.british-history.ac.uk/inquis-post-mortem/vol15/pp202-217.
29. J.S. Roskell, 'Parliamentary Representation of Lincolnshire During the Reigns of Richard II, Henry IV and Henry V', *Nottingham Medieval Studies*, (1993), 3, p.62.
30. J.S. Roskell, *Parliament and Politics in Late Medieval England*, (The Hambledon Press, 1981), vol. 2, p. 49.

31. *CCR*, Rich. II (1381–1385), p. 171.
32. Ibid., p. 185.
33. Rawcliffe, 'Bussy, Sir John'.
34. Ibid.
35. Mike Dash, 'Toxicology in the Middle Ages and Renaissance', *History of Toxicology and Environmental Health*, (Academic Press, 2017), 63–69.
36. Trevor Dean, 'Domestic Violence in Late-Medieval Bologna', *Renaissance Studies*, (2004) 18:4, pp. 532–3.
37. Frances E. Dolan, 'Home-Rebels and House-Traitors: Murderous Wives in Early Modern England', *Yale Journal of the Law and Humanities*, 4:1, (1992), p. 2.
38. Payling, 'Murder, Motive and Punishment', p. 15.
39. Paul Strohm, *Hochon's Arrow: The Social Imagination of Fourteenth-Century Texts*, (Princeton University Press, 1992), p. 121.
40. Ibid., p. 133.
41. Ibid., p. 128.
42. Ibid. [Strohm's translation of TNA: KB 7/54–55].
43. Ibid., pp. 128–9.
44. Ibid., p. 129, *n*.8.
45. Ibid., p. 121.
46. Hamel, 'The Wife of Bath', pp. 134–5.
47. Strohm, *Hochon's Arrow*, p. 137, *n*.13.
48. Ibid., p. 129; TNA: JUST 3/177 mem. 27a, trans. Sheila Lindenbaum.
49. Strohm, *Hochon's Arrow*, p. 129; TNA JUST 3/180 mem. 30a, trans. Sheila Lindenbaum
50. Strohm, *Hochon's Arrow*, p. 129
51. R.F. Hunnisett, *Bedfordshire Coroner's Rolls*, Befordshire Historical Society, 41 (1960), no. 342.
52. Ibid., nos. 342, 335.
53. *CPR*, Rich. II, (1377–1381), p. 557; *CCR*, Rich. II (1377–1381), pp. 492, 502.
54. *CPR*, Rich. II, (1377–1381), p. 557.
55. Pedersen, 'Motives for Murder', p. 73
56. J.S. Roskell, *Parliament and Politics* p. 49.
57. *Early Yorkshire Charters*, vol 6, eds. William Farrer and Charles Travis Clay, (Cambridge University Press, 1939) p. 13.
58. Alexander de Cantilupe and his son Ranulf appear in Somerset in 1146, Alexander having inherited this land from his father: see J. H. Round, *Calendar of Documents Preserved in France, illustrative of the History of Great Britain and Ireland*, [hereafter *Cal. Docs. France*], 918–1206, Vol. 1, (London 1899), pp. 172–3, No. 486; this was confirmed by the Bishop of Bath in the same year, p. 173, and by the Archbishop of Canterbury, Theobald, [1150–61], p. 174. Eyton has tentatively calendared the charter

under the year 1165 (Robert William Eyton, *Antiquities of Shropshire*, (London, 1856), Vol. 3, p. 85), and it appears reprinted in *Pipe Roll Society* [hereafter *PRS*] *Cartae Antiquae*, New Series 17, (1939), No. 302 pp. 142–3. This would mean that a Cantilupe would have been seized of Bruton in the late 1000s, yet, in 1086, Bruton was held by Roger de Courseulles, from Calvados, whose subtenant was simply recorded as 'Erneis'. Erneis may well be Erneis or Ernaldus/Arnold *de Cantilupe*, 'Arnold' being a name that is transmitted in the twelfth century and appears briefly in the Pipe Rolls for Surrey. See: *The Prosopography of Anglo-Saxon England Database* [PASE Database], online resource, http://domesday.pase.ac.uk/?Text_1=Bruton&qr=1&SearchField_1=Vill&col=c3&pag=0, accessed 21.10.2013; *PRS 1200*, p. 218, and Julian-Jones, *Land of the Raven and the Wolf*, pp. 51–2.
59. 'Ralph 30', *Prosopography of Anglo-Saxon England Database*, online resource, http://domesday.pase.ac.uk/Domesday?op=5&personkey=41400# summary, accessed 11.10.2018.
60. Ibid.
61. 'Roger 138', *Prosopography of Anglo-Saxon England Database*, online resource, http://domesday.pase.ac.uk/Domesday?op=5&personkey=54073, accessed 11.10.2018.
62. *Ancient Charters, Royal and Private, Prior to A.D. 1200*, ed. John Horace Round, Pipe Roll Society X, (London, 1888), pp. 47–8.
63. Ibid., p. 48.
64. Pedersen, 'Motives for Murder', p. 73.
65. *CCR*, Edw. III, (1354–1360), p. 122.
66. Pedersen, 'Motives for Murder', p. 73.
67. *CCR*, Edw. III, (1360–1364), p. 144.
68. *Calendar of Inquisitions Miscellaneous (Chancery)*, 3, (1348–1377), 188:511.
69. I am currently writing a monograph on *Inter-Marcher Conflict in the Welsh March c. 1093–1307* where this subject will be addressed more fully. See also: Melissa Julian-Jones, 'Family Strategy or Personal Principles? The Corbets in The Reign of Henry III', in *Thirteenth Century England XV: Authority and Resistance in the Age of Magna Carta. Proceedings of the Aberystwyth and Lampeter Conference, 2013*, eds. J. Burton, P. Schofield, B. Weiler, (Woodbridge: Boydell & Brewer, 2015), pp. 69–82; Edmund King, 'Dispute Settlement in Anglo-Norman England', *Anglo-Norman Studies: Proceedings of the Battle Conference*, XIV, (1991), 115–130; Brock Holden, *Lords of the Central Marches: English Aristocracy and Frontier Society 1087–1265*, (Oxford University Press, 2008).
70. *Curia Regis Rolls* [hereafter *Cur. Reg.*], vol. 11, No. 1431 p.287.
71. Ibid., No. 2392 p. 475.
72. Ibid., No. 2445 pp. 485–6; No. 2888 p. 580.
73. Thomas Duffy Hardy, ed., *Rotuli Litterarum Clausarum*, [hereafter *Rot. Litt. Claus.*] vol. 2, 1224–1227, (London, 1834), 38*b*, 44*b*, 47.

74. Henry Richard Luard, ed.,, Annales Monastici, Vol. 3, (London, 1866),p. 95; *Calendar of Charter Rolls* [hereafter *CChR*], Hen. III, 1226–1257, (London, 1903), pp. 1, 92, 180 This case is treated to a longer study in Tony Moore, 'A Medieval Murder Mystery, or the Crime of the Canteloups', *Henry III Fine Rolls Project*, Fine of the Month (April, 2006), online resource, http://www.finerollshenry3.org.uk/content/month/fm-04-2006.html, accessed 25.11.13. I have noted elsewhere that: 'Moore notes that this branch of Cantilupes 'probably shared a common twelfth-century ancestors with the main branch discussed here, probably the William de Cantilupe who was possibly the father of Walter de Cantilupe, father of William (I), since Hugh de Cantilupe also had a son named William. They may also be descended from Walter's brother (?) William, and be close cousins to the main branch. Unfortunately … as a supporter of des Roches, William I's influence at court had waned in this period, and he was unable or unwilling to support his kinsman in this case. However, William I did seem to forfeit lands in Bettingham as a result of John's murder, so it seems that the kin connection was recognized and perhaps closer than Moore believes here.' Julian-Jones, *Land of the Raven and the Wolf*, p. 236, n. 695.

75. Matthew Paris, *Chron. Maj.* iii, p. 268.

76. Moore, 'A Medieval Murder Mystery'.

77. Ibid.

78. Luttrell Psalter, British Library Add. MS 42130; see for example the images of dining in the Luttrell household, fos. 206v, 207r, 208r, 208v.

79. Richard K. Emmerson and P.J.P. Goldberg, '"The Lord Geoffrey Had Me Made": Lordship and Labour in the Luttrell Psalter', in *The Problem of Labour in Fourteenth-Century England*, eds. James Bothwell, P.J.P. Goldberg, W.M. Ormrod, (York Medieval Press, 2000), pp. 52–3.

80. *Calendar of Entries in the Papal Registers*, Papal Letters, vol. 4 (1362–1404), pp. 173, 187; *CPR*, Edw. III, (1374–1377), p. 351.

81. The western half of the old quadrangle of University College is on the site of Great University Hall. H.E. Salter, ed., *Records of Mediaeval Oxford: Coroners' Inquests, the Walls of Oxford, etc.*, (Oxford, 1912), p. 47.

82. Ibid., pp. 41–2.

83. Ibid., pp. 4–5 (two servants of Ralph de Shipton involved in an altercation that led to the death of John de Glaskow); pp. 12–13 (a servant of clerks attacked Robert Attewyndyate who was cleaning stables); 16 (Henry, servant of William de la Marche, is involved in an affray over beer); pp. 28–29 (servant of John Peggy slays a baker); 36–37 (William the cook, servant of clerks, slew Thomas Payn, a writer); p. 49 (John Grymusby was slain in bed by Henry Herdeller, but it is not clear whether John was a servant at the Hospital where he was slain or if he was one of the brothers. He has been included here just in case); p. 53 (Richard, servant of John Lally, was robbed by the scribe Henry Louche).

84. Reginald R. Sharpe, *Calendar of Coroners' Rolls for the City of London A. D. 1300–1378*, (London, 1913), where these servants are servants of the merchants and burgesses of the city as well as nobles.
See for example: pp. 10–11 (**1300**: Hervey, servant of John Wade, killed in an argument with his master's clerk); pp. 34–5 (**1321**: Thomas le Rede *garcio* of Richard de Tonge (clerk) was killed in an argument with a man called Dicoun le Clerk (given name Richard); pp. 48–9 (**1321x2**: Richard of Mountsorel, cobbler and 'servant'/employee of another cobbler, Roger of Nottingham, killed in a quarrel with Alexander le Ferrour, servant of Henry de Amondesham); pp. 96–7 (**1324**: Henry Arnald of Chesthunte, murdered in an attack upon his person by Henry de Honylane the steward of Sir Henry Beaufuitz, in Enfield, William Wygeyn of Enfield, William Cok of Enfield (skinner), Thomas le Messager of Enfield, and Richard the servant of Thomas de Norton, all at the insistence of John Cullyng, with malice aforethought); pp. 101–102 (**1324**: John de Saxton, a furbisher [restorer of old clothes] killed in a quarrel with William Campion, late the servant of Aymer de Valance, earl of Pembroke. During the quarrel, William attacked John with a drawn sword and threw him to the ground, whereupon William's friend Robert de Baldok, a fellow-servant with whom he had been in the earl's service, turned up with Cristina Galeye who encouraged them to kill John there and then. At Cristina's urging, Robert joined in the assault on John and dealt him the fatal wound);pp. 106–7 (**1324**: Robert of St Boltoph, a waterbearer, was killed in an argument with John de Paris of York, the servant of Master William de Casis de Ageneys. John stabbed Robert in the head with a knife called a 'bideu', then returned to his unsuspecting master and crossed the sea with him and thus abjured the realm); pp. 108–9 (**1324x5**: Walter the tailor of Faversham, stabbed to death in the street after a quarrel in a brew-house with John "Skut" de Caustone, late the servant of John de Caustone, [the sheriff], who chased him out of the brew-house and killed him with a knife called an 'anelaz'); pp. 109–10 (**1324x5**: John Acke, servant of Master Wybert de Littleton, killed in a quarrel with Richard the chamberlain of Sir Roger de Waltham and John le Baker, Sir Roger's cook); pp. 113–14 (**1325**: In this case, Thomas de St Alban, servant of the carpenter Richard de Rothinge, awoke in the night and realized that his master's home was being burgled by two thieves, John Futuard and his mistress Isabella. They got away with 'diverse goods' including an axe, a twybil [a sharp hand tool used for green woodworking], and linen including a blanket and sheets, among other things. Thomas raised the cry and followed the pair. Isabella ran off, leaving John and Thomas to fight – they fought for a long time, as John was unwilling to surrender. Finally, Thomas found the twybil at his feet, seized it and struck John five times in the head and throat, killing him. He then waited for the cry and waited on the spot until the coroner

arrived, when he surrendered himself into the king's peace and committed to prison by Benedict de Folsham, the sheriff. Isabella was also caught and imprisoned); pp. 118–19 (**1325**: Gilbert de Aldenham, killed by a blow to the head administered by Richard "Bukkeskyn" servant of Richard "Bukkeskyn" [sic] accidentally, when Richard was trying to hit William Wynter, with whom Gilbert was quarrelling); pp. 134–6 (**1325**: John de Glemham, apprentice of the Bench, was killed by William le Taverner, servant of William de Sandal during a tavern brawl involving many men); pp. 140–1 (**1325x6**: William Turk, fishmonger and late servant of Godewin Turk, killed Ralph of Nottingham, clerk, by hitting him across the head with a shovel); pp. 145–6 (**1325x6**: William Deveneys, skinner, was killed in a quarrel with Walter de Kirkeby, servant of Sir Walter de Bedewynde); pp. 151–2 (**1325x6**: Richard de Dancaster was killed in a quarrel with William de Tutbury, servant of "Bankin" Bromlesk); pp. 156–8 (**1326**: Servants were also careless with other's lives when civil disobedience was occurring in the city. Simon de la "Fermorye" was killed in a disturbance caused by numerous apprentices of the Bench for York and Norfolk, who were fighting amongst themselves with drawn swords, 'so that the bell was rung and crowds assembled'. The householders of Sir Nicholas de Hougate, clerk, in their master's house near St Martin le Grand, egged on one of their number, David Arpada, to fire into the crowd with his bow. David shot an arrow and it struck Simon the skinner in the stomach, of which wound he died after a few days. David allegedly fired into the crowd 'with the connivance' of his fellow-servants, John Broun, John de Cotyngham, Adam de Naffertone, Adam de Kingston, William Page of the kitchen, William de Wartre, John de Gryngele, Robert de Dryffeld, John de Thweng, Alexander de Thweng, Alexander le Keu, William de Wetewong, and Nicholas de Whitby); pp. 189–90 (**1326**: John de Wyndleshore, 'shereman', was killed in a fight with John Wymark when Wymark's son Richard, 'late the servant of Henry Monquoi, fishmonger', stabbed Wyndleshore in the back with a long knife); pp. 214–15 (**1339**: John Kyng, "currour", was killed by John le Wyse, servant of the apprentices of the Court of the King's Bench, who stabbed him in the back); p. 218 (**1339**: John de Throm was killed in a quarrel by "Paskes" of Cornwall, a groom of the kitchen, who stabbed him in the chest); pp. 226–7 (**1339**: John Grane, carpenter, was killed in a quarrel by William Malesures, servant of Ralph de Uptone, who struck him on the head with a pikestaff so that he died the next day); pp. 242–3 (**1339**: Robert Paunchard was killed in a quarrel with John Counte, cook, servant of Sir Robert de Artois); p. 252 (**1340: Middlesex:** William of Shropshire, servant of Sir John of Northampton, was found murdered by person or persons unknown); pp. 259–60 (**1340**: John, son of Richard Taillard de Hambledon, co. Rutland, was caught for the murder of William Casse, and confessed to the sheriff of the City of London that in **1332** he had also feloniously killed Geoffrey Pope, the servant of Sir Oliver de Ingham, in the vill of Burwell, Cambridgeshire, with a knife, and then had abjured the realm); pp. 264–5 (**1340**: John Gremet and Peter Tremenal, a servant in the queen of England's household, quarrelled and stabbed each other multiple times. John Gremet died, while Peter was so badly wounded that he took refuge in a church and could not be moved from there until he recovered his health. He confessed to the coroners and sheriffs and agreed to surrender himself to them once he had recovered); pp. 266–9 (**1340**: The fishmongers were at it again, but this time it was Ralph Turk, 'servant' of John Turk, who was killed in a quarrel. Ralph and other fishmongers came to the assistance of Nicholas le Leche, attacked by John of Oxford the servant of Robert de Eynsham, skinner, on account of an old quarrel between them. During this altercation, other skinners came to the aid of their fellow skinner and Ralph Turk was hit with a poleaxe. This is less to do with servants and more to do with rivalries and feuds between the different professions within the City, but since Ralph is designated as a '*serviens*', albeit more likely an apprentice or employee not a household servant, this has been included here. Three inquests were held regarding this brawl).

85. *Middle English Compendium*, Middle English Dictionary Entry 'balghstaff', online resource, https://quod.lib.umich.edu/m/middle-english-dictionary/dictionary/MED3535, accessed 26.06.2019.
86. *Calendar of Coroners' Rolls for the City of London*, pp. 149–51.
87. Peter Fleming, *Family and Household in Medieval England*, (Palgrave, 2001), pp. 74–5.
88. Dolan, 'The Subordinate('s) Plot', p. 324.
89. Scotton Medieval Settlement, Ref: MLI51283, *Lincs to the Past*, online resource, https://www.lincstothepast.com/Scotton-Medieval-Settlement/231606.record?pt=S, accessed 29.09.18.
90. Kate Mertes, *The English Noble Household 1250–1600: Good Governance and Politic Rule*, (Basil Blackwell, 1988), p. 55.
91. Kowaleski and Goldberg, *Medieval Domesticity*.
92. Mertes, *The English Noble Household*, p. 57.
93. Ibid.
94. Ibid.
95. *The Book of Margery Kempe*, Book 1 Part 1, ed. Lynn Stanley, (TEAMS Middle English Text Series, Medieval Institute Publications, 1996) lines 820–823. Rekles – reckless; swyers – squires; yemen – yeomen.
96. Thoroton, 'Parishes: Clipston', *Thoroton's History of Nottinghamshire*, vol. 1, pp. 138–40.
97. Thoroton, 'Watnow, Chaworth and Cantelup', *Thoroton's History of Nottinghamshire*, vol. 2, pp. 246–248. The Strelleys and Cantilupes went

back further: in 1304/05, Robert son of Robert de Strelley was bound to Sir William IV de Cantilupe, Richard de Willoughby and Robert Russell by a recognizance of 100 marks. This was nullified via a record of defeasance in the Michaelmas term of that regnal year (33 Edward III). [A recognizance: a legal term, a bond by which a person undertakes to observe some condition before a court or magistrate, particularly in criminal cases where the defendant promises to appear when summoned]. TNA: C 146/4422.
98. *CPR*, Edward III (1367–1370), p. 40.
99. TNA: C 241/153/54; Currency conversion calculated by the National Archives Currency Converter tool.
100. TNA: C 131/24/22; Rowena E. Archer, 'Mowbray, Thomas, second earl of Nottingham (1385–1405), magnate and rebel', *Oxford Dictionary of National Biography*, (2008), online resource, http://www.oxforddnb.com/view/10.1093/ref:odnb/9780198614128.001.0001/odnb-9780198614128-e-19460, accessed 13.11.2018.
101. TNA: C 241/174/5; this sum had the rough buying power equivalent of £77,823.57 in 2017.
102. *CPR*, Richard II (1385–1389), p. 297.
103. *CCR*, Richard II (1392–1396), p. 400.
104. *CR*, Richard II (1385–1389), p. 372.
105. R.G. Davies, 'Braybrooke [Braybroke], Robert (1336/7–1404), bishop of London', *Oxford Dictionary of National Biography*, (2004), http://www.oxforddnb.com/view/10.1093/ref:odnb/9780198614128.001.0001/odnb-9780198614128-e-3301 accessed 04.04.2019.
106. *Statutes of the Realm*, i, 307–8 (23 Edw. III).
107. Judith M. Bennet, 'Compulsory Service in Late Medieval England', *Past & Present*, 209 (Nov. 2010), 7–51, p. 9.
108. *CIPM*, Edward II (1307–1327), No. 181 p. 93.
109. Fleming, *Family and Household*, p. 73.
110. Dinah Hazell, '"Trewe Man" or "Wicked Traitour": The Steward in Late Middle English Literature', *The Medieval Forum*, 6, online resource <https://www.sfsu.edu/~medieval/Volume6/steward.html> accessed 28.09.18.
111. TNA: C 143/376/12.
112. TNA: C 143/6/7.
113. *CPR*, Hen. III, (1266–1272), p. 146.
114. *CIPM*, Edw. III (1374–1377), No. 182 p. 193.
115. Leyser, *Medieval Women*, p. 93.
116. Simon A.C. Penn, 'Female Wage-Earners in Fourteenth-Century England', *The Agricultural Review*, 35:1, (1987), pp. 4–7.
117. Cordelia Beattie, 'The Problem of Women's Work Identities in Post Black Death England', in *The Problem of Labour in Fourteenth-Century England*,

eds. James Bothwell, P.J.P. Goldberg, and W.M. Ormrod, (York Medieval Press, 2000), pp. 1–2.
118. Penn, 'Female Wage-Earners', p. 1.
119. Margaret Wade Labarge, *A Medieval Miscellany*, (McGill-Queen's Press, 1997), p. 59.
120. Margaret Shaus, *Women and Gender in Medieval Europe: An Encyclopaedia*, (Taylor & Francis, 2006), p. 742.
121. Ibid.
122. Ibid.
123. Ann J. Kettle, 'Ruined Maids: Prostitutes and Servant Girls in Later Medieval England', in *Matrons and Marginal Women in Medieval Society*, eds. Robert Edwards and Vickie L. Ziegler, (Woodbridge, 1995), p. 20.
124. Ruth Mazo Karras, *Common Women: Prostitution and Sexuality in Medieval England*, (Oxford University Press, 1996), p. 48.
125. Kettle, 'Ruined Maids', p. 21.
126. TNA: C 241/155/116
127. C.M. Woolgar, *The Great Household in Late Medieval England*, (Yale University Press, 1999), p. 20.
128. Ibid.
129. A complaint among twelfth-century chroniclers was that the kings of England were choosing 'men raised from the dust', i.e. yeomen, or those of base stock, to be ministers and officials rather than men of noble families. Terms were interchangeable but included *plebes, ignobiles, rustici,* and *servi*. On 'men raised from the dust', see, Ralph V. Turner, 'Changing Perceptions of the New Administrative Class in Anglo-Norman and Angevin England: The Curiales and Their Conservative Critics', *Journal of British Studies*, 29:2, (1990), p. 93.
130. This will be discussed further below: see, Warren C. Brown, *Violence in Medieval Europe*, (Harlow: Longman, 2011), p. 277.
131. TNA: SC 8/49/2421.
132. *CPR*, Edw. II (1313–1317), p. 545.
133. TNA: E 40/3192; TNA: SC 8/16/787.
134. TNA: E 40/3191. A final concord between John de Gyse and Hugh le Despenser, to whom Gyse released the manor of Pyrton for 100 marks.
135. TNA: C 131/2/40. According to the National Archives Historical Currency Converter, this had the buying power of around £55,000 in 2017, and was enough to pay the wages of a skilled tradesman for 12,000 days, or buy 141 horses.
136. TNA: C 131/2/19.
137. Ibid. This was roughly the buying power equivalent of £36,800 in 2017's money.
138. TNA: C 241/55/134 – 1307, Sir John de Gyse owed Oxford merchant William de Bicester 8 marks and 8 pence, an accounting denomination

equivalent to £5 7s 4d, which had roughly the equivalent buying power of £3,300 in 2017; TNA: C 241/63/80 – 1307, Sir John owed London merchant John de Raynham £23 2s 4d, roughly the buying power equivalent of £14,140 in 2017; TNA: C 241/63/82 – 1309, Sir John owed London merchant John de Raynham £16 which was roughly the equivalent buying power of just under £10,000 in 2017; TNA: C 241/74/61 – 1310, Sir John owed London merchant John de Triple £30, which was roughly the equivalent buying power of £18,350 in 2017; TNA: C 241/74/6 – 1310, Sir John also owed London merchant John de Triple £42 2s, which was roughly the equivalent buying power of around £25,750 in 2017.

139. *VCH Bedford*, Vol. 3, 'Parishes: Aspley Guise', ed. William Page (London, 1912), pp. 338–343. British History Online http://www.british-history.ac.uk/vch/beds/vol3/pp338-343, accessed 28.09.2018.
140. Geoffrey Chaucer, *The Canterbury Tales*, (Wordsworth, 2002), p. 9.
141. 'Arma Patrina', *Academic Dictionaries and Encyclopaedias: Medieval Glossary*, (2014), http://medieval_en.enacademic.com/289/Arma_Patrina, accessed 13.11.18.
142. Turner, 'Changing Perceptions of the New Administrative Class', pp. 103–104.
143. Coss, *The Knight in Medieval England*, p. 84
144. Ibid., pp. 82, 84.
145. Ibid., p. 104.
146. John Wagner, *The Encyclopaedia of the Hundred Years' War*, (Greenwood Publishing Group, 2006), p. xli.
147. Andrew Ayton, 'Edward III and the English Aristocracy at the Beginning of the Hundred Years' War', *Harlaxton Medieval Studies* 7, (1998), *n*.123.
148. Andrew Ayton, 'The Military Careerist in Fourteenth-century England', *Journal of Medieval History*, 43:1 (2017), p.5.
149. Ibid.
150. *Calendar of Entries in the Papal Registers*, p. 19.
151. Ibid, p. 20.
152. Ibid.
153. *Calendar of Coroners' Rolls for the City of London, A.D. 1300–1378*, (London, 1913), p. 254,
154. Ibid., pp. 34–5.
155. Ibid., pp. 86–7.
156. Orderic Vitalis, *Ecclesiastical History*, ed. M. Chibnall, vol. 2, (Oxford Medieval Texts, 1968), p. 30.
157. *Calender of Inq Misc, (Chancery)*, I (1219–1307), p. 589.
158. Ibid.
159. Marl or marlstone is a calcium-carbonate or lime-rich mud, used as a fertilizer. *Plea Rolls of Henry III*, in *Collections for a History of Staffordshire [William Salt Archaeological Society]*, vol. 4, (1085–1883), p. 22.

160. Brown, *Violence in Medieval Europe*, p. 277.
161. Ibid. p. 278.
162. Ibid.
163. Ibid. p. 279.
164. Ibid.
165. Ibid.
166. See the case of Aungier vs Malcake, discussed in Pedersen, *Marriage Disputes in Medieval England*, p. 153.
167. Rawcliffe, 'Bussy, Sir John'.
168. Sillem, *Some Sessions of the Peace in Lincolnshire*, p. 142, my translation, emphasis added.

Chapter 4
1. *CIPM*, Edw. III (1374–1377), No. 108, p. 105. This jury believed he died 'the Sunday before Palm Sunday last', or 8 April 1375.
2. Ibid. This jury believed he died 'on Saturday after the Annunciation, 49 Edward III', or 31 March 1375.
3. Sir Ralph Paynell served as sheriff of Yorkshire in the same decade, the holding of this office being a tradition in the Paynell family: on this, see, W. Farrer, 'The Sheriffs of Lincolnshire and Yorkshire, 1066–1130', *EHR*, 30:118 (Apr., 1915), pp. 277–285.
4. *CIPM*, Edw. III (1374–1377), No. 108, pp. 105–106. The jury also claimed that '[h]e died on 31 March last', that is, 31 March 1375, agreeing with or perhaps taking their information directly from the Buckinghamshire inquest.
5. *CPR*, Rich. II (1377–1381), pp. 309–10.
6. Ibid., p. 309.
7. Sillem, *Sessions of the Peace in Lincolnshire*, pp. 141–2.
8. *CIPM*, Edw. III (1374–1377), No. 108, p. 106. This jury also followed the death-date of the Buckingham inquest, namely, 31 March 1375.
9. Ibid. This jury also followed the death-date of the Buckingham inquest, namely, 31 March 1375. This inquest also found that he held these of his kinsman by marriage, the lord de la Zouche, by knight's service. His great-grandfather's cousin Milicent had married into the de la Zouche family and inherited a great deal of the Cantilupe lands when the last male heir, George, died in 1272.
10. Ibid., pp. 106–107. This jury also followed the death-date of the Buckingham inquest, namely, 31 March 1375.
11. TNA: C 241/134/49; TNA: C 241/131/179; £60 had the equivalent buying power to just £ 35,234.21 in 2017 while £200 had the equivalent buying power of around £117,447.36 in 2017 according to http://www.nationalarchives.gov.uk/currency-converter, accessed 04/04/19.

12. TNA: C 241/131/185; £400 had the buying power equivalent of around £234,894.72 in 2017 according to the National Archives Currency Converter, http://www.nationalarchives.gov.uk/currency-converter, accessed 04/04/19.
13. TNA: C 241/133/191; £1000 had the buying power equivalent of £587,236.80 in 2017, according to http://www.nationalarchives.gov.uk/currency-converter, accessed 04/04/19.
14. National Archives Currency Converter, http://www.nationalarchives.gov.uk/currency-converter, accessed 04/04/19.
15. TNA: C 241/153/131.
16. TNA: C 241/131/185.
17. See Margaret E. McKenzie, *Filicide in Medieval Narrative*, (unpublished PhD Dissertation for the Catholic University of America, 2012).
18. Sara M. Butler, 'A Case of Indifference? Child Murder in Later Medieval England', *Journal of Women's History*, 19:4 (Winter, 2007), p. 76.
19. McKenzie, *Filicide in Medieval Narrative*, p. 20.
20. Ibid. p. 27.
21. Marilyn Sandidge, 'Changing Contexts of Infanticide in Medieval English Texts', in Albrecht Classen ed., *Childhood in the Middle Ages and the Renaissance: The Results of a Pardigm Shift in the History of Mentality*, (De Gruyter, 2005), p. 299.
22. Butler, 'A Case of Indifference?', p. 76.
23. Ibid. p. 73.
24. Ibid. pp. 71–2.
25. *Calender of Inq Misc, (Chancery)*, I (1219–1307), p. 589.
26. Ibid.
27. *CCR*, Edw. I (1272–1279), p. 364.
28. Ibid. Richard's mainperners were Richard de Wytacre, Henry de Scheldon, William Fundu, Anketil de Insula, Simon de Blagrave, Thomas Otheyn, William de Sydenhale, Ralph de Cully, Roger de Buryate, Norman le Venur of Middleton, Robert de Longasse and Nicholas Nichtegale of Wyshawe, county Warwick.
29. The 'insanity' (*fatuitatis*) of Richard de Arden is referred to in the Patent Rolls: *CPR*, Edw. I (1272–1281), p. 328. This is translated as 'idiot' in *CPR*, Edw. I (1272–1281), p. 361.

Chapter 5

1. Susan Mosher Stuard, 'Burdens of Matrimony: Husbanding and Gender in Medieval Italy', in *Medieval Masculinities: Regarding Men in the Middle Ages*, eds. Clare A. Lees, Thelma S. Fenster and Jo Ann McNamara, Medieval Cultures 7, (University of Minnesota Press, 1994), pp. 61–2.
2. Jan Rüdiger, 'Married Couples in the Middle Ages? A Case of Devil's Advocate', in *Law and Marriage in Medieval and Early Modern Times*,

eds. Per Andersen, Kirsi Salonen, Helle Møller Sigh and Helle Vogt, (Denmark, 2012), p. 87.
3. David Crouch, *William Marshal: Knighthood, War and Chivalry, 1147–1219*, 2nd edn, (Routledge, 2002), p. 69; Rüdiger, 'Married Couples in the Middle Ages?', p. 87.
4. Stuard, 'Burdens of Matrimony', p. 62.
5. Roughly 1500–1750/1800.
6. Mark Breitenberg, 'Anxious Masculinity: Sexual Jealousy in Early Modern England', *Feminist Studies*, 19:2 (1993), p. 377.
7. Bronach Christine Kane, *Impotence and Virginity in the Late Medieval Ecclesiastical Court of York*, (Borthwick Paper No. 114, 2008), p. 6.
8. *CPR*, Rich. II (1377–1381), p. 395.
9. Phillipp R. Schofield, 'Peasants and the Manor Court: Gossip and Litigation in a Suffolk Village at the Close of the Thirteenth Century', *Past and Present*, 159 (May, 1998), pp. 3–7.
10. Rüdiger, 'Married Couples in the Middle Ages?', pp. 83–4.
11. Butler, 'Runaway Wives, p. 342.
12. Lindsay Bryan, 'Marriage and Morals in the Fourteenth Century: The Evidence of Bishop Hamo's Register', *The English Historical Review*,121:491, (2006), p. 485; http://www.jstor.org/stable/3806139.
13. Ibid.
14. Ibid.
15. A. Fletcher, *Gender, Sex and Subordination in England 1500 –1800* (New Haven and London, 1995), pp. 192–203.
16. Dean, 'Domestic Violence in Late-medieval Bologna', p. 527.
17. Ibid.
18. Ibid., *n*. 2.
19. Sara Butler, *The Language of Abuse*, p.185.
20. Ibid., p. 192.
21. Ibid.
22. Sara Butler, 'The Law as a Weapon in Marital Disputes: Evidence from the Late Medieval Court of Chancery, 1424–1529', *Journal of British Studies*, vol. 43, no. 3 (2004), pp. 291–316.
23. Butler, 'Runaway Wives', p. 340.

Chapter 6
1. Kate Mertes, *The English Noble Household 1250–1600: Good Governance and Politic Rule*, (Basil Blackwell, 1988), p. 2.
2. Ibid., p. 52.
3. Ibid., p. 17.
4. Ibid.
5. Phillipp R. Schofield, 'Peasants and the Manorial Court', *Past and Present*, 159 (May, 1998), p. 7.

6. Ibid., p. 8.
7. J.S. Beckerman, 'Toward a Theory of Medieval Manorial Adjudication: The Nature of Communal Judgements in a System of Customary Law', *Law and History Review*, 13:1 (1995), p. 21.
8. Buchanan Given, *Society and Homicide*, p. 52.
9. Ibid, pp. 53–4.
10. *Calendar of Coroners' Rolls for the City of London, A. D. 1300–1378*, (London, 1913), pp. 78–80.
11. Smail, 'Common Violence', p. 36.
12. Jonathan Rose, *Maintenance in Medieval England*, (Cambridge University Press, 2017), p. 214.
13. Ibid., pp. 317–8.
14. Ibid., p. 182.
15. See Appendix for the full record of Richard Cantilupe's excesses. See also: *Calendar of the Justiciary Rolls or Proceedings in the Court of the Justiciar of Ireland*, Edw. I, vol. 1 (1295–1303), pp. 25–6.
16. *Select Bills in Eyre, 1292–1333*, Selden Society 30 (1914), p. 10.
17. *CCR*, Edw. III, (1374–1377), p. 470. The thirty-five 'great and powerful men' were named as: Hugh de Riston; John de Beverle; John de Reppes; William Redberd; Thomas Redberd ; Richard Elys; Thomas Elys; John Elys; Richard Tate; Henry Beneyt; Thomas de Stalham; Richard de Beverle; Thomas Box; John Rodynhale; Richard Spicer; William Welbourne; John atte Gappe; Edmund Sylke; Roger Adams; William atte Gappe the younger; William Rokhaghe; John Herward; Thomas Ailsham; Peter Vesselier; Nicholas Wildegos; William Worstede; Robert Howelyn; John Rollesby; Hugh Fastolf; Geoffrey de Fordele and Geoffrey his son; John atte Fenne; Ralph Pampyng; Thomas Drax and Robert de Beverlee [sic].
18. Henry Swinden, *A History and Antiquities of the Ancient Burgh of Great Yarmouth in the County of Norfolk: Collected from the Corporation Charters, Records, and Evidences; and Other the Most Authentic Materials*, (Great Yarmouth, 1773), pp. 926–7.
19. Stephen Alsford, *The Men Behind the Masque: Office-holding in East Anglian boroughs, 1272–1460*, <http://users.trytel.com/~tristan/towns/mcontent.html>(1998), Ch. 7.
20. Hanawalt, 'Fur-Collar Crime', p. 5.
21. Ibid.
22. Ibid.; Hunnisett, *Bedfordshire Coroner's Rolls*, p. 82.

Chapter 7
1. *English Historical Documents 1327–1485*, ed. A.R. Myers, (Eyre & Spottiswoode, 1969), p. 541 no. 345.
2. Definition of *oyer and terminer:* Anglo-Norman French, *to hear and determine*, a commission issued to judges on a circuit to hold courts.

3. *English Historical Documents*, p. 541 no. 345.
4. Scott L. Waugh, *England in the Reign of Edward III*, (Cambridge University Press, 1991), p. 153.
5. Ibid.
6. Bernard Knight, 'Crowner: The Origins of the Office of Coroner', *Britannia History*, http://www.britannia.com/history/coroner1.html, accessed 06.11.18.
7. Hunniset, *The Medieval Coroner*, p. 118.
8. Ibid.
9. TNA: C 131/17/10 – their ship, the Katherine of London, was seized in Bristol along with their goods and chattals, in order to pay off their debt.
10. The National Archives, Kew, *Currency Converter*, http://www.nationalarchives.gov.uk/currency-converter/#currency-result accessed 06.11.18.
11. Hunniset, *The Medieval Coroner*, p. 123.
12. W. Stubbs, *The Constitutional History of England in its Origin and Development*, vol. 2, (Oxford, 1880 edn), p. 225; F.W. Maitland, *The Constitutional History of England*, (Cambridge, 1908), p. 234.
13. William II Cantilupe was sheriff of Warwickshire and Leicestershire for a few terms in the thirteenth century. See Julian-Jones, *Land of the Raven and the Wolf*, p. 66 and especially Ch 1 and Ch 2.
14. Richard C. Gorski, *The Fourteenth-Century Sheriff: English Local Administration in the Late Middle Ages*, (PhD Thesis, University of Hull, 1999), p. 11.
15. Waugh, *England in the Reign of Edward III*, p. 129.
16. Ibid., p. 129.
17. G.A. Holmes, *The Estates of the Higher Nobility in Fourteenth Century England*, (Cambridge University Press, 1957), p. 80.
18. Ibid.
19. C. Rawcliffe, 'Thorley, John, of Lincoln', *The History of Parliament: the House of Commons 1386–1421*, eds. J.S. Roskell, L. Clark and C. Rawcliffe, (Boydell and Brewer, 1993), https://www.historyofparliamentonline.org/volume/1386-1421/member/thorley-john, accessed 18.11.2018.
20. *CCR*, Edw.d III (1369–1374), pp. 591–2. As John de Thorle was mainperned by John de Burton of London, *tapicer* (weaver of worsted cloth); William de Stanley of London (dyer); Ralph de Billingeye of London (cordwainer) and Godfrey de Barton of London (corwainer).
21. Sillem, *Some Sessions of the Peace in Lincolnshire*, pp. 13–14.
22. Ibid p. 14.
23. Rawcliffe, 'Thorley, John'.
24. Ibid.
25. *CCR*, Edw. III, 8 (1369–1377), p. 592. According to the National Archives Currency Converter, £20 had an approximate purchasing power equivalent of £14,600 (rounded up).

26. Ibid., p. 272.
27. *Cal. Just. Ire.*, Edw. I, vol. 1, (1295–1303), pp. 23–6. The full record is reproduced in the appendix below. Richard son of William de Cantilupe, the king's serjeant and deputy sheriff, is one example of Richard the sheriff's nepotism. This other Richard was also brought before the justices accused of the murder of William FitzHugh and Richard de Hereford, receiving felons [one of them being his own son Patrick, a robber], indicting those he knew weren't guilty to extort money from them, and keeping his own household costs down by living off poor people of the county for a week or more with his wife and two sons. He even allowed a child 'imputed to be his son' to be eaten by pigs, and kept the pigs instead of delivering them to the coroner.
28. Carpenter, 'St Thomas Cantilupe', p. 59.
29. For more on the Second Barons' War, see John Sadler, *The Second Barons' War*, (Pen and Sword Books, 2008). See also Sophie Ambler, *Bishops in the Political Community of England 1213–1272*, (Oxford University Press, 2017).
30. *Register of Thomas Cantilupe*, vol. 1, p. 67.
31. '*Et dic quatuor militibus ex illis qui visui illi interfuerint, quod sint coram Justiciariis nostris apud Westmonasterium, a die Sancti Martini in xv dies, ad testificandum visum illum.*' Ibid., p. 68.
32. Lancashire Record Office: DDBL 55/4.
33. A.E. Corbet, *The Family Corbet: Its Life and Times*, Vol. 2, (London: The St Catherine's Press, 1914), p. 174. Peter Corbet's brother-in-law Brian de Brompton and his son are both referred to as '*nepotes* of the Lord Peter' in the *Register of Thomas de Cantilupe*, p. 71.
34. Lancashire Record Office: DDBL 55/4.
35. This is the first entry where Asterton is identified as being unambiguously the Bishop's land (*terram Thome, Episcopi Herefordensis, in Esthamptone*), and is said to border the Corbet manor of Wentnor (*terram Petri Corbet in Wentnoure*). *Register of Thomas Cantilupe*, vol. 1, p. 68.
36. Ibid., p. 69.
37. Ibid., p. 70.
38. '*ad terram Thome, Episcopi Herefordensis, in Ledebury North, et terram Petri Corebet in Cauz*'. Ibid., 70–71.
39. '*tum quod non habebant certum numerum xij militum gladio cinctorum, tum quod predictus Petrus in predictos tres liberos et legales homines de predictis xij tunc noluit consentire, licet alias coram me in ipsos consensisset*'. Ibid., pp. 71–2.
40. '*Et scias quod graviter amerciatus es, eo quod preceptum nostrum inde tibi directum non es executus sicut tibi preceptum fuit; et gravius amerciaberis nisi hoc preceptum nostrum plenius exequaris*'. Ibid., p. 72
41. Ibid., p. 72.
42. *Register of Thomas Cantilupe*, p. 73; compare with p. 63 – the first jury list includes 'Johannem fitz Aere and 'Johannem Picheford', as knights

(*milites*), and has four freemen, one of whom is 'Johannem de Esthope'. The later jury list excludes these two knights and replaces them with 'Adam de Mungomery' and 'Rogerum Pichard'. The remaining jury members are the three freemen (*liberos et legales homines*) listed in the original jury, 'Robertum de Bullers, Lucam de Rutone, et Ricardum de Dodemanestone', and it is the presence of these three men which provokes Corbet's challenge.
43. TNA: SC 8/192/9571.
44. *Register of Thomas Cantilupe*, p. 73.
45. Shakespeare Birthplace Trust Library and Archives : DR10/1341.
46. '*Et sciatur quod maximus defectus est militum gladio cinctorum in Comitatu Salopie*', *Register of Thomas de Cantilupe*, i., p. 72.
47. Namely, John of Easthope, Robert de Bullers, Richard of 'Dodemanestone', and Lucas de Rutone. Turner argues from plea roll evidence that 'lawful knights' were men of substance and, most importantly, landowners. Ibid., p. 104.
48. There were only eight knights on this original list: Walter of Bokenhull, William of Hungerford, John fitz Aere, John of Ercalewe, Roger Springhose, Thomas Boterel, John of Picheford and Walter of Bredwardin. Ibid., p. 69. It can be inferred that the first perambulation was void since although boundary details were ascertained in March 1278, a writ was issued to the sheriff that June directing him to appear at Westminster to answer for his neglect. This implies that the first perambulation was unsatisfactory. The sheriff had explained, '*tum quod predictus Petrus in predictos tres liberos et legales homines de predictis xij tunc noluit consentire*'. Peter did not consent to the presence of three freemen on the jury, despite the lack of belted knights.
49. The freemen are the same as before but without John of Easthope; the knights, however, *had* changed, swapping John fitz Aere and John of Picheford for Adam of Montgomery and Roger Pichard. *Register of Thomas Cantilupe*, p. 71.
50. Ibid.
51. For a fuller exploration of the jurors and how they were connected (or not) to the Corbets, see Julian-Jones, *The Land of the Raven and the Wolf*, pp. 133–136.
52. *CPR*, Rich. II (1381–1385), p. 351. The men named with Sir Ralph are: William Gascrick; the clerk John de Middleton; John Welford; Henry Bayons; Walter Boteller; William Smyth 'forster'; Roger Barbour of 'Glaunfordbrigge', and Ralph Kaynill of Goushull.
53. Ibid.
54. C. Rawcliffe, 'Hawley, Sir Thomas (d.1419/20), of Grisby and Utterby, Lincs.', *The History of Parliament: the House of Commons 1386–1421*, eds. J.S. Roskell, L. Clark, and C. Rawcliffe, (Boydell and Brewer,

1993), online resource, < https://www.historyofparliamentonline.org/volume/1386-1421/member/hawley-sir-thomas-141920>, accessed 29.09.2018
55. TNA: C 241/139/120
56. TNA: C 241/135/138; TNA: C 241/138/106; TNA: C 241/138/169; TNA: C 241/139/31; TNA: C 241/138/176
57. TNA: E 358/5
58. TNA: E 101/176/1
59. TNA: E 156/28/53
60. TNA: C 241/150/129. According to the National Archives' Currency Converter tool, £40 c. 1370 was the equivalent of around £19,600 in 2017. It had the buying power of about 57 horses, or 2000 days' wages for skilled tradesmen: see online resource, http://www.nationalarchives.gov.uk/currency-converter, accessed 29.09.2018.
61. TNA: C 241/71/120. According to the National Archives Currency Converter tool, this was the equivalent to around £9,175 in 2017, and had the equivalent buying power of 17 horses, or 1500 days' wages for skilled tradesmen. Wages rose after the Great Famine of 1315–1322 which killed an estimated 10–15% of the population.
62. TNA: C 131/209/35. According to the National Archives Currency Converter tool, this was worth the equivalent of around £16,500 in 2017.
63. TNA: C 241/181/8. The National Archives' Currency Converter tool estimates that this was worth around £43,368.93 in 2017.
64. Manchester University: Manchester University Library CRU/209
65. Derbyshire Record Office: D5236/9/13
66. TNA: SC 8/83/4126; TNA: C 241/108/265; TNA: C 143/61/9; TNA: C 241/80/249.
67. C. Rawcliffe, 'Sothill, Gerard (d.1410), of Redbourne, Lincs.', *The History of Parliament: the House of Commons 1386–1421*, eds. J.S. Roskell, L. Clark, C. Rawcliffe, (Boydell and Brewer, 1993), online resource, https://www.historyofparliamentonline.org/volume/1386-1421/member/sothill-gerard-1410, accessed 30.09.2018.
68. Ibid.
69. *CPR*, Rich. II (1377–1381), p. 346.
70. Ibid., p. 299. The list of men in the order they appear are: William de Skipworth, Roger de Kirkton, Ralph Paynell, Thomas de Kydale, John Poucher, John de Boys, Thomas Pynchebek, Robert de Cumberworth, Nicholas de Hattecliff and Roger Toupe.
71. Ibid, p. 302.
72. C. Rawcliffe, 'Rochford, John (d.1410), of Fenn of Boston, Lincs.', *The History of Parliament: the House of Commons 1386–1421*, eds. J.S. Roskell, L. Clark, and C. Rawcliffe, (Boydell and Brewer, 1993), online resource <https://www.historyofparliamentonline.org/volume/1386-1421/member/rochford-john-1410> accessed 29.09.2018.

73. Kingsford, 'Hastings, Sir Henry'.
74. L.S. Woodger, 'Braybrooke, Sir Gerard I (c. 1332–1403), of Colmworth, Beds. and Horsenden, Bucks.', in *The History of Parliament: the House of Commons 1386–1421*, eds. J.S. Roskell, L. Clark, and C. Rawcliffe, (Boydell and Brewer, 1993), online resource, <https://www.historyofparliamentonline.org/volume/1386-1421/member/braybrooke-sir-gerard-i-1332-1403>, accessed 29.09.2018.

Chapter 8

1. Charles Duff, *A Handbook on Hanging*, (The History Press, 2011).
2. Sillem, *Some Sessions of the Peace in Lincolnshire*, pp. 143–47.
3. *CCR*, Rich. II (1377–1381), p. 269. Widows had to take an oath that they would not marry without the king's permission, as a fine was charged for the licence itself and was a form of revenue for the Crown.
4. Sillem, *Some Sessions of the Peace in Lincolnshire*, p. 151.
5. Ibid. pp. 147–49.
6. Wiltshire and Swindon History Centre: Savernake Estate Title Deeds, 9/12/4.
7. Sillem, *Some Sessions of the Peace in Lincolnshire*, p.
8. Drawn and hanged: drawn by a horse to the site of execution, then hanged by the neck until dead.
9. Sillem, *Some Sessions of the Peasce in Lincolnshire*, pp. 150–52.
10. Ibid., pp. 151–2.
11. My translation.
12. For a readable and well-researched book dealing with this subject see Kate Summerscale, *The Suspicions of Mr Whicher, or the Murder at Road Hill House* (Bloomsbury, 2009).
13. My emphasis. Feet of Fines: TNA: CP 25/1/142/141, No. 44, trans. in 'Feet of Fines Abstracts', *Medieval Genealogy*, http://www.medievalgenealogy.org.uk/fines/abstracts/CP_25_1_142_141.shtml accessed 18.04.19.
14. TNA: 9/12/4.
15. *CPR*, Rich. II (1385–1389), p. 368.

Appendix

1. (oner.atur - load, burden; oppress)
2. Women were 'waived' rather than 'outlawed' although the practical outcome was the same.
3. *Nisi Prius:* Refers to the court of original jurisdiction in a given matter.
4. Wiltshire and Swindon History Centre: Savernake Estate Title Deeds, 9/12/4.